York St John
Library and Information Services
Normal Loan

Please see self service receipt for return date.
If recalled the loan is reduced to 10 days

RETURNED 1 8 DEC 2008		
17/1/14.		1 5 MAR 2024
		WITHDRAWN

Fines are payable for late return

Technology as Experience

Technology as Experience

John McCarthy and Peter Wright

The MIT Press
Cambridge, Massachusetts
London, England

Set in Stone serif and Stone sans by The MIT Press. Printed and bound in the United States of America.

Library of Congress Cataloging-in-Publication Data

McCarthy, John.
Technology as experience / John McCarthy and Peter Wright.
p. cm.
Includes bibliographical references and index.
ISBN 0-262-13447-0 (alk. paper)
1. Technology—Social aspects. 2. Interactive multimedia. I. Wright, Peter. II. Title.
T14.5.M4   2004
303.48'3—dc22   2004049934

10 9 8 7 6 5 4 3 2 1

to Mary, Janet, Megan, and Maddie

Contents

Preface

We don't just use technology; we live with it. Much more deeply than ever before, we are aware that interacting with technology involves us emotionally, intellectually, and sensually. For this reason, those who design, use, and evaluate interactive systems need to be able to understand and analyze people's felt experience with technology. While there is a great deal of concern with *user experience* in Human-Computer Interaction and related fields, both in practice and comment, it is often unclear what is meant by the idea. In this book, we provide foundations for a clearer analysis of user experience by developing a way of looking at technology as experience.

Taking as our starting point the pragmatism of philosophers of experience, especially John Dewey and Mikhail Bakhtin, we explore people's interactions with technology in terms of aesthetic engagement, situated creativity, centers of value, and sense making. For example, Dewey, in *Art as Experience* (1934), argued against museum conceptions of art that separate it from most people's experience. Instead, in a move that we also make with respect to technology, Dewey argued that we should approach art as part of ordinary, everyday lived experience, thus restoring the continuity between aesthetic and prosaic experience. Bakhtin's contribution in this regard was to emphasize the particularity and feltness of experience, which is also central to our view of technology as experience.

Following Dewey and Bakhtin, we show technology to be deeply embedded in everyday experience, in ways that are aesthetic and ethical as well as functional. As an expression of this continuity, we hold up the zestful integration that marks aesthetic experience as paradigmatic of what human experience with technology might become. This aesthetic turn gives our contribution to Human-Computer Interaction a critical edge.

What we offer in this book, then, is a new way of seeing experience with technology: as creative, open, and relational, and as participating in felt experience. There is always room for surprise when action is seen as situated creativity and when each moment has potential. This is not meant to be a utopian statement—experience with technology is as often frustrating as it is fulfilling. However, the new way of seeing technology that we offer suggests that we have a hand in giving shape to a world that is always open and unfinished. Moreover, it is only by seeing technology as participating in felt experience that we understand the fullness of its potential.

Acknowledgments

We would like to thank University College Cork and the University of York for permitting us to take study leave to complete this book. During his sabbatical, Peter was hosted, with grace and generosity, by Antonio Rizzo and Patrizia Marti at the University of Siena's Department of Communication Science. Many thanks to them. John spent parts of his sabbatical at the University of York, supported by EPSRC Visiting Fellowship 006R02641. Thanks to York and EPSRC for making such a happy return possible.

We are both fortunate to have colleagues in York and Cork, whose general encouragement and support has been invaluable, especially Michael Harrison, Andrew Monk, and Elizabeth Dunne. A number of people have influenced the shape of the book by discussing ideas with us—too many to name them all here. However, we had particularly detailed and clarifying comments from Liam Bannon, Mark Blythe, Andy Dearden, Alan Dix, Darren Reed, Paul Sullivan, and Davina Swan. We were also fortunate in the quality of the comments we received from a number of anonymous reviewers on early drafts of various chapters. We received good support from The MIT Press, especially from Doug Sery and Paul Bethge.

Our families suffered while we were working on this book. Thanks to Janet, Megan, Maddie, and Mary for their patience and support.

1 | Living with Technology

As social scientists we have long given too much weight to verbalizations at the expense of images. Lived experience, then, as thought and desire, as word and image, is the primary reality.

—E. M. Bruner (1986, p. 5)

A man who works in a library is having a normal working day: checking books in and out, helping people find the author they were looking for, organizing inter-library loans, and so on. Then he receives a mobile phone text message from a friend who is visiting New Zealand. It is a short message, no more than 160 characters, yet it feels like a very personal, intimate contact—a hug or an affectionate touch. He is moved to send a reply. It is even shorter than the message he had received, and it is in a personal, intimate style not typical of him. For a moment, the two friends, though a world apart, feel intensely present to each other.

A nurse has just spent an hour caring for an extremely ill patient. Having ministered to the patient's medical needs, she sat with him for a time, encouraged him to eat some yogurt, talked to him about his family, and helped him to get more comfortable in the bed. As she walks back to her station she feels sad for the patient, who has by now become something of a friend. Still involved with that patient, she starts to write up her notes from her morning rounds, recording carefully any changes in condition and any medication that she has administered. She is comfortable doing that. It feels like a few moments quiet time reflecting on her patients, how they are, what she is doing, and what more she can do for them. But now she must enter the relevant patient movement and bed management data on the hospital's information system. Which patients are moving to another ward in the hospital? Are any patients due to move into this ward?

Who is due to be discharged? Who is due for a procedure in the next 24 hours? Bed vacancies? What drugs have been administered, and to whom? It takes only 10 minutes twice a day, but this really frustrates her. She feels she is being taken away from her patients. This is time she could be spending with them. She feels this information system has nothing to do with her work.

A father comes home from work. As he rushes into the hall, he keys in the password to disable his house alarm. His daughter comes in behind him. He needs to get the dinner prepared, so he switches on the computer in the study for his daughter and sets up her favorite game for her. Once she is settled in, he goes to the kitchen, prepares the food, and places it in the oven. He listens to his phone messages while doing this. Eventually he sets the temperature and timer and leaves the food to cook. As he passes down the hallway to the sitting room, he pops his head into the study. His daughter asks him to play with her. "Back in two minutes love." In the sitting room, he programs the VCR to record a drama that he and his wife want to watch later. Now he is heading for the study to play his daughter's computer game with her.

The Experience of Living with Technology

We don't just use or admire technology; we live with it. Whether we are charmed by it or indifferent, technology is deeply embedded in our ordinary everyday experience. Arnold Pacey noted in his 1999 book *Meaning in Technology* that academic and professional comment on technology resists discussion of personal experience. It seems too subjective. But as we have seen in the vignettes above, our interactions with technology can involve emotions, values, ideals, intentions, and strong feelings. According to Pacey, much academic framing of technology plays down this side of the relationship between people and technology in favor of something more objective, on the basis that objective analysis is required to advance theory and change practice.

Although there is an overlap, our interests in technology are narrower than Pacey's. Whereas Pacey ranges from industrial and scientific to military technologies and from architecture to civil engineering, our interest is in relationships between people and interactive technologies or information and communication technologies. Aspects of these relationships have been addressed by research and practice in areas such as Human-Computer Interaction (HCI) and Computer-Supported Cooperative Work (CSCW) since the late 1960s and the mid 1980s respectively. In recent years there has been a perceptible shift in nomenclature toward Interaction Design or User Experience Design when referring to relationships between people and interactive technologies. This reflects a broadening of focus from computers to a wide range of interactive technologies and from work-related tasks to lived experience. At least in some quarters, then, academic and professional comment on relationships between people and interactive technologies is open to discussion of experience. The web sites of many computer and mobile phone manufacturers promote their attachment to ensuring that their technologies enrich user experience. Books about the Internet are as likely to consider how people have appropriated it and made it part of their relationships and activities as they are to consider the technical accomplishment that it is. Indeed, in HCI, the profile of experience seems constantly on the rise. For example, Ben Shneiderman (2002, p. 2) has recently argued that we are entering an era of "new computing": "The old computing was about what computers could do; the new computing is about what users can do. Successful technologies are those that are in harmony with users' needs. They must support relationships and activities that enrich the users' experiences."

The vignettes at the beginning of this chapter speak to the ways in which interactive technologies have become part of our ordinary everyday experiences at work and home. We recognize them and identify with them. We know those moments in our own interactions with technology. The vignettes draw attention to the importance of experience in each person's interactions with technology and raise the question of whether the technology supports relationships and activities that enrich experience.

The hospital information system does not enrich the nurse's experience. In fact, it takes her away from what she finds meaningful and rewarding in her work. The problem is not so much the time involved in recording data on the information system, as it is the experience of being pulled out of the world of relationships and activities that is nursing for her. Her commitment to nursing centers on the experience of nurturing and caring relationships with patients. She may well put up with inadequate pay and difficult working conditions as long as *they* leave her to get on with what she got into nursing for, caring for patients. For her, caring for patients involves really getting to know them, spending time with them, and looking after them as people. By focusing on management and on the financial aspects of ward activities, the hospital information system requires her to treat the people for whom she cares as bits of information. This fractures her experience of nursing.

The father returning home from work interacts with a variety of technologies that are part of the prosaic experience of home life for many in the Western world today. People are used to videos and remote controls and have become blasé about bar-code programming of their VCRs and rewinding precisely to the start of a TV program. Security alarms have become incidental to the owners. Timers in cookers, caller ID on telephone displays, electronic maps and navigation systems in cars, digital cameras—all enchanting when new, all ordinary and invisible now. Unlike the hospital information system for the nurse, these technologies do not take the father out of the relationship with his daughter and the household activities that are most important to him at that time.

The computer is probably still the most obvious expression of the increasingly pervasive nature of technology for those of us who can remember how difficult it was to get our hands on a computer in a university in the 1980s. However, as desktop computers have become commonplace in many homes, the initial excitement and playfulness that we experienced with computers is reserved for particularly enchanting applications or product designs.

Shneiderman and other commentators point to mobile phone text messaging, electronic mail, and Internet chat as technologies that succeed in supporting relationships and activities that enrich the users' experiences. Shneiderman argues that they have been as successful as they have because they provide people with alternative ways of doing what they already love doing: communicating. They augment people's ability to communicate and fit in with a value system that treats communication and relationships as important. This may not sound like a convincing argument to readers who see teenagers absorbed in text messaging and assume that they are wasting their time or (worse) actually diminishing their ability to "really" communicate. But studies that look closely at the teenage experience of text messaging do not support such skepticism.

Many studies of mobile phone use and text messaging describe the teenage experience with these media as expressive and creative (see Katz and Aakhus 2002, for example). Teenagers put a lot of effort into composing short messages that convey precisely what they feel and what they think will be understood by the recipient. They seem to evoke the other person, how that person thinks and feels, while composing a message. The constraints of the medium and teenagers' desire to express themselves clearly make text messaging very personal for them. They collect personally significant messages to evoke the moment they were received, to recall, and to reminisce. Some are reluctant to give up their old mobiles for a newer model because the old model holds messages that are dear to them. A downloaded or handwritten version would not do. The phone, display, and format of the text and the sensory activity of holding the phone and calling up a particular message all help to evoke the original moment. They are like the wrapping and the card signifying that an object is a special gift—put away in a drawer, come upon every now and again, always evoking that moment. The enchantment of technology. And yet a prosaic experience for many teenagers and adults.

We live with technology and, as commentators and practitioners, we must consider the implications for theory and practice. We see some of the implications at least being tabled in the emergence of a marketing concern for "user experience" among manufacturers and distributors of interactive technologies. We also see it in research attempts to define and measure user experience. However, as there is little history of interest in experience in HCI and related research areas, we suggest that a pause for reflection is needed lest we all jump on a marketing bandwagon without knowing what we are getting into. Although HCI research and practice is already moving toward experience as a response to the need to deal with technologies that we live with, there is now more than ever, a need for clarification on what we mean when we talk about experience of technology.

HCI and the User Experience

It is no longer considered sufficient to produce a computer system that is effective, flexible, learnable, and satisfying to use—the characteristics of usability according to Shackel (1990)—it must now also be useful in the lives of those using it. The hospital information system mentioned above may have been technically state-of-the-art and may have been highly usable, but it was not experienced as useful by a nurse who wanted to get on with caring for her patients. In contrast, the tools for text messaging in many mobile phones would win no prizes for usability, yet text messaging is experienced by many adults and teenagers as instrumentally and expressively useful (Katz and Aakhus 2002). It augments people's ability to organize complex and busy work, family, and social lives. For many it also provides an opportunity to express themselves, their feelings and emotions, in ways not previously available to them.

Experience of technology refers to something larger than usability or one of its dimensions such as satisfaction or attitude. However, HCI and related disciplines are not used to dealing with experience. HCI grew out of collaboration between the disciplines of computer science and psychology, the academic aspects of both of which are more comfortable with the laboratory than the outside world, and directed more toward functional accounts of computers and human activity than toward experience. Against this background, it might be worth looking briefly at the emergence of interest in experience with technology and how HCI currently understands user experience. Kuutti (2001) characterizes the history of "the user" in HCI. The user started out in the 1970s as a cog in a rational machine, became a source of error in the 1980s and then a social actor in the 1990s, and is now a consumer.

The User as a Cog in a Virtual Machine

During the 1970s and the 1980s the dominant approach to understanding relationships between people and technology assumed a single user sitting in front of a computer screen and keyboard performing a fairly well prescribed task. In terms of attempting to develop a science of human-computer interaction this could be seen as a sensible place to start. It contained within it the scientific virtues of reduction and generalization, assuming that this human-computer system captured the essence of what it was like for any person to interact with any computer. Its simplicity also made it a good model for engineering HCI systems. It also had face validity in the business context, as the single-user approach matched the management style in many offices and factories where workers were assumed to use computers to execute their individual part of the work of the office. In this context, the computer was seen as a tool through which set work was accomplished. Underlying the scientific and organizational reduction was a model of the structure of action that was a deliberate simplification of action.

Instantiations of this class of cognitive model of action can be found in Card, Moran, and Newell's (1983) GOMS model and in Norman's (1988) seven stages of action. Norman's seven stages included one for goals, three for execution, and three for evaluation.

Donald Norman was very careful to describe his model as approximate. It was a useful model for answering the kinds of questions that Norman thought were central to understanding how people interacted with the objects of the world, including interactive technologies. For him, what was central was what makes something—e.g., threading a film projector, sending a text message, or editing a spreadsheet—difficult to do. Norman was well aware of the limitations of the model. In hindsight we can now read his critical evaluation of the model against the character of everyday activity as prescient of where the study of human-computer interaction would go after it appropriated the relevant aspects of the cognitive science that informed Norman's model. In his critique, he pointed to the opportunistic aspects of everyday activity:

> For many everyday tasks, goals and intentions are not well specified: they are opportunistic rather than planned. Opportunistic actions are those in which the behavior takes advantage of the circumstances. Rather than engage in extensive planning and analysis, the person goes about the day's activities and performs the intended actions if the relevant opportunity arises. (Norman 1988, pp. 48-49)

As long as we stay with performance criteria and the planned actions of individuals, Norman's model of action is a very useful resource in specifying what makes something difficult to do or error prone. However, if our interests include how people feel about sending a text message, what participating in text-messaging culture does for their sense of self, and what values are implicated in texting, then Norman's model is seen to be lacking.

The User as a Social Actor

During the late 1980s and the 1990s the opportunistic or contingent aspects of everyday activity became the central focus of challenges to the dominance of information-processing psychology. These challenges came mainly from the disciplines of sociology and anthropology and were geared toward asserting the salience of the social context of activity in discourse about people and technology. One way to see this is in terms of their claims that the contingent character of everyday activity is at least as important as mental structures in shaping human-computer interaction. By moving everyday activity to center stage, and by insisting that all action is richly con-textualized, this approach began the process of promoting experience over abstraction. It fits comfortably with our vignettes of text messaging and domestic technology, and it helps explain the sense the nurse has of the technology interfering with her primary preoccupation of patient care.

Lucy Suchman and Jean Lave have been two of the most influential fig-ures in helping to contextualize action in human-computer interaction. Their emphasis on the situatedness of action offers a radical alternative to the task-based, information-processing accounts of action characteristic of the single-user approach. For example, Suchman (1987, p. 186) argued that, in contrast with task-based frameworks where the situation is characterized as an aspect of the means to achieve ends or part of the conditions for accomplishing a goal, situations and actions are intimately linked: ". . . the detail of intent and action must be contingent on the circumstantial and interactional particulars of actual situations." For Suchman, the inherent openness of situations defies carefully planned responses, and any regular-ity emerges not as a result of plan-based action but as a result of local responses to contingencies.

Lave (1993, p. 7) also offered an explicitly relational account of socially situated practice insisting that people acting and the social world of activity cannot be separated: "Theories of situated activity do not separate action, thought, feeling, and value and their collective cultural historical forms of located, interested, conflictual, meaningful activity." Moreover, Lave pro-poses that the character of situated practice is heterogeneous and multi-focal. She points to the ways in which people who constitute "a situation" know different things and speak with different interests and experience. For Lave, the unit of analysis is the person-acting-in-setting through culturally constituted resources for learning and sense making.

Although our work has benefited greatly from the way in which approaches such as Lave's and Suchman's have opened up human-computer interaction to the contingencies of ordinary everyday life, and our interest in experience has in part been primed by their work, we shall argue in chap-ter 2 that their approaches miss some of what we want to insert into dis-course on experience of technology. While fully accepting the contingency of action, we are keen to develop a stronger sense of the felt life and the emotional quality of activity in our approach to experience. We are also keen to embed these dimensions in the sense-making aspects of experience.

Specifically, we are referring to the affection, hopes, and imagination of text-messaging teenagers and the fears, frustrations, and anxieties of the nurse obliged to use a hospital information system that cuts against her sense of who she is as a nurse. These emotional, sense-making aspects of experience seem underplayed in situated accounts of action.

Consumers and the User Experience

The 1990s saw the development of the dotcom companies and a multi-million-dollar games industry; strong penetration of computers into the home; the confluence of computer and communications technologies; and the beginnings of wireless, mobile, and ubiquitous computing. The industry vision now is not of desktop computers or even laptop computers but of information appliances and interactive consumer products that will penetrate many aspects of our lives.

Interaction with technology is now as much about what people feel as it is about what people do. It is as much about children playing with GameBoys, teenagers gender swapping, and elderly people socializing on the Internet as it is about middle-aged executives managing knowledge assets, office workers making photocopies, or ambulance controllers dispatching ambulances. The emergence of the computer as a consumer product has been accompanied by very explicit attention to user experience. For example, a leading textbook presents user-experience goals as one of the sets of goals of interaction design, related to but not subsumed by the more readily recognized usability goals:

. . . user experience goals differ from the more objective usability goals in that they are concerned with how users experience an interactive product from their perspective rather than assessing how useful or productive a system is from its own perspective. (Preece et al. 2002, p. 19)

Though any attempt to move the industry's attention toward experience is to be welcomed, we have reservations about some of what is being offered in the name of user experience. In this area, it seems that technological development and business momentum may have outstripped reflective commentary and analysis.

Computer manufacturers aspire to designing computers as full-fledged consumer products and as part of that process they are concerned with creating the total user experience. Employing the phrase "user-experience design" as a reminder or motivator to designers to pay attention to people's experience of technology is one thing. Employing the phrase to indicate that a particular user experience can be designed is another thing altogether. The latter suggests a return to the simplicity of a technologically determinist position on what experience is. This neglects the agency of people interacting with technology, a focus that has been hard won by the likes of Lave and Suchman. While giving those who use "experience design" and similar phrases the benefit of the doubt, it is part of the job of a book that claims to examine experience of technology to take the language of user experience seriously. For example, the Apple Macintosh Developer page defines "User Experience" as "a term that encompasses the visual appearance, interactive behavior, and assistive capabilities of software." The orientation to user experience here is technology driven. Although the authors are interested in enriching user experience, they have a technological vision of how this can be achieved. Their approach is similar to the approach described in many books on designing web site user experiences. For example, although Garrett (2002) attends to both business and user needs in his book directed at improving user experience of web sites, his attempt to resolve them depends on a conceptual integration of information design, information architecture, and interface design. Two quotations from the book illustrate his conviction that experience can be shaped or controlled by good design:

The user experience development process is all about ensuring that no aspect of the user's experience with your site happens without your conscious, explicit intent. This means taking into account every possibility of every action the user is likely to take and understanding the user's expectations at every step of the way through that process. (ibid., p. 21)

That neat, tidy experience actually results from a whole set of decisions—some small, some large—about how the site looks, how it behaves, and what it allows you to do. (ibid., p. 22)

IBM's web site contains a richer, more transactional approach to user-experience design:

User Experience Design fully encompasses traditional Human-Computer Interaction (HCI) design and extends it by addressing all aspects of a product or service as perceived by users. HCI design addresses the *interaction* between a human and a computer. In addition, User Experience Design addresses the user's initial awareness, discovery, ordering, fulfillment, installation, service, support, upgrades, and end-of-life activities.

It is not our aim to dismiss the phenomenon of user-experience design or the approach to user-experience design outlined on the web sites of some of the major manufacturers. Indeed, as will be evident in the following chapters, our own description of experience is quite compatible with the view of user-experience design proposed on the IBM web site. And we are heartened by the fact that the consumer metaphor underlying notions of user experience treats activity as emotionally laden. Klein (2000) demonstrates that consumer product branding is concerned with establishing and maintaining emotional ties, the sense of belonging or feeling of warmth that differentiates one product from another. If the HCI construal of users as consumers is taken seriously, the relationship between person and computer cannot be construed as mechanistic or as shaped by relationships with social structure alone. The consumer metaphor implies an emotional-volitional component, which is currently underdeveloped.

Our concern with the consumer metaphor and user experience in HCI is that business momentum may take a potentially rich idea and reduce it to design implications, methods, or features. There are literatures on consumer activity and experience that seem to have been missed by those who imagine that they can design a user experience. DeCerteau (1984), for example, has a framework for analyzing how consumers make use of producers and distributors. People develop their own paths around supermarkets, tactically resisting the architecture and advertisements designed to shape their shopping behavior. Consumers appropriate the physical and conceptual space created by producers for their own interests and needs; they are not just passive consumers. Klein (2000) similarly describes the potential for immunity to advertising and the anti-advertisement culture that suggests healthy resistance, and even activism, in the face of global consumer capitalism. The general point that we must remember when thinking about interactive technologies as consumer products and people who buy and use them as consumers is that consumers are not passive; they actively complete the experience for themselves.

This brief review of the history of perspectives on people and computers in HCI suggests that although interactive technology designers and manufacturers have taken a shine to the idea of user experience and consumer products, their understanding or use of experience is limited. For some of them, experience is a fuzzy concept—you know when you have had an experience. For others, it is inherent in interface and information design and architecture, as if consumers will not make of the interface and architecture what they need and desire. The lesson of the mobile phone and particularly of text messaging that seems not to have been learned yet is that the quality of experience is as much about the imagination of the consumers as it is about the product they are using. It is our aim to fill some of these lacunae by developing an account of experience of technology that mines the rich conceptual resources already available to complement the technological and business momentum toward experience.

Toward a Deeper Understanding of Technology as Experience

Perhaps it would be useful to view interactive technology in general as an experience, even if it is sometimes an experience of indifference or resistance. This is the position that this book sets out to explore. Given the lacunae in our treatment of experience in HCI to date, a central part of our exploration is a critical discussion of the approaches to experience that are current in HCI and a characterization of experience that enables us to interpret the influence of technology in our lives. Although the detail of our position is developed through the rest of the book, we will briefly describe it here to provide an overview against which the detail can be read. The overview can be seen as a series of six propositions.

- *Our first proposition is that, in order to do justice to the wide range of influences that technology has in our lives, we should try to interpret the relationship between people and technology in terms of the felt life and the felt or emotional quality of action and interaction.*

Klein (2000) reminds us that, in a world of signs and meanings, a Starbucks coffee is not just a coffee; it is an experience of warmth and homeliness that provides a space of belonging. Likewise, a car is not just a car, and a mobile phone is not just a mobile phone. In both cases, the color, the shape, and the manufacturer's name convey something of our selves to ourselves and to others. Apple knows that image matters to most people in some circumstances. The Powerbook G4's large screen, its lightness, and its titanium casing evoked the mobility and robustness people had always expected from a portable computer but never quite had.

On a long train journey, some people would feel lost without their mobile phones; they so need to feel connected. Others on the train become annoyed and irritated by the constant noise of phones ringing and people talking aloud to absent others. For those who get irritated, it is not the idea of people talking on their phones in a public space that is annoying. It is the sensory or physical quality of the intrusion. The noise seems to permeate a boundary. The noisier it is or the more grating the ring or the voice, the more violent the intrusion. Curiously, the emotionally and sensually absent other is also a source of trouble. People generally enjoy overhearing others' conversations, but not one side of a conversation.

As we indicated earlier when discussing the popularity of mobile phones and texting, those who love their mobiles very often do so because of their expressive quality. They keep messages sent by friends and prefer to keep an old phone rather than swap it in order to have those messages in their original state. There seems to be something about the felt and sensual quality of the phone, the snug fit, the sound of a friend's voice, the ring tone associated with a particular caller, the shape of a text message, and the pleasure of scrolling through it. For those who engage with these practices, the sensory and emotional qualities of phone and text message constitute the felt experience of calling and texting. Again it is not the abstract idea of communicating, perhaps not even the social practice, but the felt and sensual quality of the particular communication that gives it an expressive quality.

Returning to the vignettes at the beginning of this chapter, we are arguing that in order to understand the relationship between the friends texting each other across the world and their mobiles, or between the nurse and the hospital information system, we must understand what the experiences of texting and using the information system feel like for those people. We must understand the emotional response and the sensual quality of the interaction.

Because the word 'experience' already expresses the *feltness* of life for us, when we write about experience of technology we have this felt quality very much in mind. We have become used to interpretations that emphasize the *livedness* of experience in HCI, especially with the significant contribution of practice and activity theories since the mid 1980s. In this book, we prioritize feltness to emphasize the personal and particular character of experience with technology. For us, *felt* experience points to the emotional and sensual quality of experience. Our first proposition is that these qualities should be central to our understanding of experience of living with technology.

■ *Our second proposition is that social-practice accounts of interactive technologies at work, at home, in education, and in leisure understate the felt life in their accounts of experience.*

Suchman, Lave, Susan Leigh Star, and others have convinced us that cognitive models of action are not the most appropriate models of human action for human-computer interaction. Instead of looking for an account of coherence of action in psychological processes in the head, they have convinced us to look to the particular social and physical circumstances of action and interaction for interpretations that are more relevant to understanding, designing, and evaluating interaction. Suchman's (1987) implication that the significance of artifacts and actions is intimately related to their particular circumstances has influenced design discourse since the mid 1980s. And Bowker and Star (1999) have shown how artifacts in particular situations create classifications and boundaries that raise moral and political issues. Lave's (1993) orientation toward a broad social and community context elicits questions about people's concerns, values, and identity. Lave also explicitly addresses experience and how it relates to action or practice.

Our aim is not to put ourselves in some fruitless competition with practice-based approaches. Rather, we would like to build on what those approaches have already contributed to HCI by giving a more prominent position to feltness in an account of people's experience with technology than they do. In this regard, we part company with practice-based approaches and theories when they play down the emotional and sensual quality of experience. For example, despite developing a very rich account of concerned action, it seems to us that Lave's commitment to dialectical theorizing leads her to treat experience as belonging to an analytical order different from the sociocultural order. Likewise, theoretical commitment to the primacy of circumstances and methodological commitment to *in situ* observation seem to constrain the treatment of individual differences in situated-practice accounts. We argue that this simplifies the concepts of self, person, and subject that are crucial to the reflexivity of felt experience. It may be that in order to interpret felt experience we have to inquire from the subject what the activity felt like as felt experience entails reflection, after the event, on the personal meaning of the experience.

Diane Hodges's (1998) account of how she felt as a trainee teacher, which attempts to give due weight to both circumstances and feelings, is an example of what we aim for in this regard. It seems to us that discourse on individual differences will have to be enriched if we are to have an account of experience of technology that satisfactorily addresses questions around the presentation of self and the construction and management of identity. The starting point of Sherry Turkle's analysis of life on the Internet is that people differ in many ways, including how they integrate computers into their lives. In Turkle's research, "experiences on the Internet figure prominently"; she argues, however, that "these experiences can only be understood as part of a larger cultural context" (1995, p. 10). From our perspective, Turkle's approach is complementary to the situated action approach, its methodology focusing on the personal or felt experience in context.

It would be easy to reduce felt experience to the subjective dimension of experience. This is not our intention at all. Like Hodges and Turkle, we guard against it by seeing every situation as emotional or felt but not treating those emotions or feelings as separate from the situation. The possibility of doing this in a coherent and sustained manner is created by a pragmatist philosophical stance, about which we shall say more later.

■ *Our third proposition is that it is difficult to develop an account of felt experience with technology.*

Developing an account of felt experience with technology is difficult partly because the word 'experience' is simultaneously rich and elusive. It is also difficult because we can never step out of experience and look at it in a detached way. Experience is difficult to define because it is reflexive and as ever-present as swimming in water is to a fish. However, we argue that useful clarifications can be garnered from sources as diverse as philosophy, psychology, literature, drama, and filmmaking. Some examples of what is available should suffice to make this point.

Brenda Laurel set out to interpret experience of computers by analogy with experience of theatre, suggesting that "both have the capacity to represent actions and situations . . . in ways that invite us to extend our minds, feelings, and sensations" (1991, p. 32). Her interest in the senses relates to her concern for action, engagement, and agency in the context of people interacting with computers. As a consequence, engagement is at the heart of user experience for Laurel. She holds it up as "a desirable—even essential—human response to computer-mediated activities" (ibid., p. 112).

In another context, we explored a filmmaker's analysis of people's experience of film in an effort to start thinking about the possibility of enchantment with technology (McCarthy and Wright 2003). In an analysis of what makes a film "grab, and hold, and move an audience," Jon Boorstin, a writer and producer of Hollywood films, suggests that the key is to understand that we don't watch movies in one way, we watch them in three ways. Each way of seeing has a distinct pleasure and magic associated with it: the pleasure of something new and wonderful, the pleasure of emotional engagement, the thrill of a visceral response (Boorstin 1990, p. 8). The point is not to try and import this analysis into human-computer interaction but to learn about the complexity of technologically mediated experience from it.

Other approaches highlight a specific quality as central to experience. For example, Ciarán Benson (1993) sees absorption as one of the pivotal characteristics of an aesthetic experience. He describes being aesthetically absorbed as a breaking down of barriers between self and object, as an outpouring of self into the object. Absorption is associated with being completely attentive, engrossed, intensely concentrated, and immersed or lost in an activity. Benson also uses the words 'entrancement', 'enchantment', and 'bewitchment' when describing absorption. He associates such words with connotations of pleasure, wonder, and delight.

As we mentioned, Shneiderman highlights human needs and social relations in his view of HCI and argues that technologies must support relationships and activities in ways that enrich people's experiences and their sense of togetherness. Norman (2002) places enjoyment at the center of his new analysis of design. His three-level model of enjoyment concerned with relating people's visceral, behavioral, and reflective responses to an object or product has similarities to our own analysis (presented in chapter 5) and to Boorstin's (presented above). Norman also analyses the everyday and mundane activities of customization, personalization, and personification to make the case that we are all designers and that we make products our own and come to love them or hate them.

Paul Dourish (2001) presents a close reading of philosophical ideas on embodiment in order to develop foundations for approaches to the design of human-computer interaction that emphasize tangibility and sociality. He argues that Husserl's phenomenology has had considerable influence in turning attention to everyday experience rather than formalized knowledge, and to that experience as a phenomenon to be studied in its own right. For Dourish, embodied phenomena occur in real time and in real space, are concrete and particular, and gain their meaning through participative status as objects in felt experience.

■ *Our fourth proposition is that pragmatist philosophy of experience is particularly clarifying with respect to experience, and that the models of action and meaning making they encompass express something of felt life and the emotional and sensual character of action and interaction.*

Pragmatism also sees knowledge as participative. According to this view, any knowledge we have is dependent on the technology, circumstances, situations, and actions from which it was constructed. It is knowledge in a community of engaged people, in a situation, from a perspective, felt, and sensed. For pragmatists, therefore, knowing, doing, feeling, and making sense are inseparable. Pragmatism is a practical, consequential philosophy, a practice that is concerned with imagining and enriching as much as understanding. The test it sets itself is to improve things.

Richard Coyne (1995) argued that pragmatism is the operative philosophy of the computer world, and that designers and developers are more likely to be influenced by Marshall McLuhan and John Dewey than by Bertrand Russell and A. J. Ayer. They are more likely to talk about freedom, community, and engagement (the language of pragmatism) than about formality, hierarchy, and rule (the language of analytic philosophy). We have found the ideas of one mainstream pragmatist (John Dewey) and those of another whom we position as a pragmatist though he would not be universally considered so (Mikhail Bakhtin) to be particularly clarifying in our attempts to conceptualize felt experience.

For Dewey, experience is constituted by the relationship between self and object, where the self is always already engaged and comes to every situation with personal interests and ideologies. Dewey's perspective on human action—the key to understanding felt experience—is that action is situated and creative. There can be no separation of means and ends in a world where people are always already engaged, rather people create goals and the means to achieve those goals in the midst of their engagement with the world. Dewey's model of action is not unlike the way we think of children at play, free to define and redefine ends and means, even to redefine the situations in which they find themselves. For him, action is emotional, volitional, and imaginative, and experience is a process of sense making.

Bakhtin, a philosopher with a more literary bent than Dewey, emphasizes the emotional-volitional quality of experience and relates it to an account of everyday meaning making that is aesthetic and ethical. In this context he highlights the particularity of everyday experience, the way in which the emotional-volitional quality of a particular activity in a particular context shoots through felt experience. For Bakhtin, the unity of felt experience and the meaning made of it are never available *a priori* but must always be accomplished dialogically. It always occurs in the tension between self and other. I make sense of my self only in terms of how I relate to others and to my own history of selves—the way I was and the way I would like to be. Collapsing the traditional distinctions between speaker and listener, between reader and writer, and between tools and results, a dialogical perspective on sense making orients us to the idea that meaning is a process of bringing together different perspectives and, in this creative bringing together, forging understanding. Bakhtin refers to this as *creative understanding*.

■ *Our fifth proposition is that the importance given to the emotional-volitional and creative aspects of experience in pragmatism prioritizes the aesthetic in understanding our lived experience of technology.*

According to Dewey, aesthetic experiences are refined forms of everyday, prosaic experience in which the relationship between the person (or people) and the object of experience is particularly satisfying and creative. Note that, in contrast with analytical aesthetics, the emphasis is on the experience, not on the formal properties of the object of experience.

Richard Shusterman (2000) has written an interpretation of pragmatist aesthetics in which he describes aesthetic experience as above all an immediate and directly fulfilling experience. He develops his argument by deliberately drawing on forms of music, such as funk and rap, that would never be considered aesthetic by those who define 'aesthetic' in terms of the formal properties of the art object. In taking this approach, he continues Dewey's project of seeing aesthetics in experience or in the particular relationship between self and object. The pragmatist approach to aesthetics opens up for us the possibility of aesthetic experience in work, in education, and in interaction with technology, not just in interaction with high' art objects. This brings us back to Shneiderman's description of New Computing as supporting "relationships and activities that enrich the users' experiences." In Dewey's terms, this is an aesthetic aspiration for computing. For Shusterman (ibid., pp. 55–56), an aesthetic experience (or perhaps an enriched user experience) is "an experience of satisfying form, where means and ends, subject and object, doing and undergoing, are integrated into a unity."

Pragmatism provides tools for analyzing the aesthetic quality of felt experience in the form of, for example, Dewey's characterization of *an* experience and the internal dynamics of experience. We shall describe and use these later in the book. They are complemented by Bakhtin's aesthetics, which focuses on the struggle to achieve the sense of fulfillment that can be seen as characterized in Dewey's characteristics of *an* experience. For Bakhtin, this becomes a study of consummation of experience, the archetype of which is consummation of self in other.

■ *Our sixth and final proposition is that the revisionary theorizing of pragmatism is particularly valuable for understanding technology and design.*

Dewey criticized scientific theorizing as backward looking. By this he meant that it seeks to describe and explain the world as it is; unlike design, it does not concern itself with how the world might have been or might become. In his theorizing, Dewey was concerned to change, not to represent. When he practiced philosophy of education, he was concerned to improve educational practice. When he practiced philosophy of art, he was concerned to inquire into how prosaic experience could become as satisfying, fulfilling, and creative as possible. When we attempt to pragmatically conceptualize people's experience of technology, we are concerned with inquiring into what pragmatism has to offer toward enriching those experiences, even to the point of imagining what a rich experience of technology could be.

A revisionary theory is valued not so much for whether it provides a true or false representation of the world as for whether it helps us think through relationships between for example, people, technology, and design. It is less concerned with representing existing relationships than with imagining new relationships and experiences. When later in this book we describe Dewey's model of action as being something like children at play, we are not suggesting that this represents human action as we have observed and known it. Rather, in the spirit of pragmatism, we are attempting to reorient the way we think about action to take account of the potential for playfulness and creativity in action. When we conceptualize technologies as experience, we are attempting to re-view technology by making visible aspects of experience of technology that would otherwise remain invisible. For pragmatists, theorizing is a practical, consequential activity geared toward change, not representation.

Some might argue that revisionary theorizing may not be as well suited to inquiry about technology as it is to inquiry about topics that are more obviously in the domain of the humanities, such as education, art, politics, and literature. However, it could also be argued that the very proposition we are testing in this book is that reflective practice on experience of technology could be well served by a humanist cast, the test of which is whether it changes readers' thinking about technology to the point where questions about the expressiveness, feelings, values, and sense of self evoked by interactions with particular technologies are as natural as questions about form and function. Moreover, it is worth recalling that both Dewey and Bakhtin were concerned with the production and consumption of artifacts. Dewey was concerned with the production and consumption of works of art, Bakhtin with the production and consumption of novels. Many of their ideas about the relationships of producer, consumer, artist, appreciator, author, reader, and character, and about the process of creative understanding, can be usefully employed in conceptualizing the relationship of designer, technology, and user.

Representational or reflective theorizing makes sense only when the "world" being explored is considered to be relatively stable. If it is considered stable, then what is important will always be important. A representation or categorization of technology, once achieved, remains valid. In contrast, when the world being explored is constantly changing, and in fact has become a byword for change (as technology has), representational theories are always chasing to catch up with the latest manifestation but one. Moreover, an important constructive dimension of theorizing is missed with the reflective stance. As technology is ever changing, it is not only reflected;

it can also be made. Cognizant of this potential, people who create new technologies adopt a revisionary or forward-looking orientation that can also be adopted by theorists whose theories are geared toward developing new ways of looking at technologies rather than reflecting past practice. In this context, theorizing becomes active intervention in which we provide a conceptual elaboration of technology that facilitates a re-orientation among designers, users, and observers. Not just any re-imagination, but one that is practically, experientially, and ethically rewarding, and that is oriented toward how technologically mediated action is lived and felt.

Plan of the Book

So far, we have sketched the position we intend to develop in this book. The remaining chapters will be used to provide more detail and to discuss in depth the issues that have been raised. Chapters 2–5 provide a detailed explanation of our conceptualization of technology as experience. In chapter 2, we clear the ground by reviewing relevant developments in HCI and CSCW since the 1980s. In so doing, we review what we have termed the turn to practice and argue that the feltness of experience has been underplayed in practice theories.

In chapter 3, we clarify what we mean by experience, outlining the pragmatist approach to experience that we employ and describing the particular contributions of John Dewey and Mikhail Bakhtin, the writers on experience who have most influenced our own thinking. In setting out the pragmatist approach to experience, we describe three defining commitments of pragmatism: the primacy of prosaic action (and, in particular with respect to Dewey and Bakhtin, the continuity between aesthetic and prosaic experience), the situated creativity of action, and the relationality or dialogicality of understanding.

In chapter 4 we ask what a pragmatist account of people's experience with technology might look like. We describe the threads of experience and then use these threads to analyze some examples of people's experience with technologies, starting with film and moving on to more interactive technologies. Whether we are watching a film, playing a computer game, or using a spreadsheet, pragmatism tells us that our experiences do not come to us ready made. Rather, as meaning-making creatures, we bring as much to the experience as the filmmaker or designer puts into it.

In chapter 5, we provide an account of the variety of ways in which people make sense of their experience, an important analytical resource in exploring relationships between people and technology.

Chapters 6–8 are in the form of short case studies about technology use that illustrate some of the ideas developed in chapters 3–5. Chapter 6 presents a personal experience of Internet shopping. Chapter 7 is based on a pilot's reflections about his experiences of procedure following. Chapter 8 is an attempt to characterize the experience of ambulance control in two different settings, one of which involves a high-tech system.

Chapter 9 pulls together some of the major strands and considers how they relate to emerging trends in HCI and interaction design.

2 | Going on from Practice

If there has to be anything "behind the utterance of the formula" it is *particular circumstances*, which justify me in saying I can go on—when the formula occurs to me. Try not to think of understanding as a "mental process" at all—For, *that* is the expression which confuses you. But ask yourself: in what sort of case, in what kind of circumstances do we say, "Now I know how to go on," when, that is, the formula has occurred to me?
—L. Wittgenstein (1953, p. 61, no. 154)

Questioning concerning technology, to borrow a phrase from Heidegger, is an important and incurably complex activity. It touches on many areas of our lives: what work is and what it is likely to be; our orientation to fun and leisure; possible futures for education; boundaries between private and public, between home and work, and between knowledge and information; and even our own sense of what it is to be ourselves, people situated in an increasingly strange relationship with time, place, and other people. In this chapter we argue that in order to do justice to this wide range of influences of technology in our lives we have to understand it in terms of our lived and felt experience with technology. We argue that, despite the growing interest in the place of technology in practices such as work, leisure, and education, an experiential account of technology that addresses itself to felt life is still lacking.

In order to make this argument, we review what has been called "the turn to practice" in HCI. However, it is apparent that there are a variety of versions of the turn depending on the conceptual and methodological commitments of the people involved. A helpful approach is to view each approach, the turn to phenomenology, the turn to ethnography, and so on as inscriptions in a tradition, in much the same way as Silverman (2000) sees the post-modern inscribed on the modern. Such a perspective would not reject technical rationalism but rather inscribe practice on it. Berg's (1997) treatment of the use of formalism and technical tools in medical practice is a good example. He analyses the experience of hospital workers who adapt their practice to the use of formal tools. He notes that, although formal tools influence practical reasoning and decision making, personal and social history and preferences shape tool use.

Although the various approaches that make up the turn to practice represent an impressive attempt to embed discussions of technology in concern for people's ordinary everyday activities, they fall short of providing the experiential account of technology that is required. Describing what is lacking in each of these approaches begins the task of clarifying what we think is required of a theory of human activity that gives priority to experience with technology.

In this context, our agenda is to clear a space for explication of felt experience in our questioning concerning technology, to attend explicitly to the experiential connectedness of self and object, action and material, thought and feeling, individual and community, technical and practical. We view the turn not as an object separate from traditional concerns in relations between technology and people, such as cognition, knowing, and learning, but as a process of inscribing the experiential onto them as a way of going on. In chapters 3–5 we do the more constructive work of describing the conceptual building blocks of such a theory.

The Turn from Rationalism to Practice

Turning toward practice involves developing a sensibility to a plurality of perspectives on sociocultural practices, of which technologies such as mobile phones, automatic teller machines, and the Internet are a part. It is also a turn away from the hegemonic discursive practices of rationalism, which dominated the study of technology up to the mid 1980s and which still dominate much educational practice in schools of computer science, information technology, and design. 'Rationalism' refers to discursive practices that promote the notion of separation of mind, mental processes, and ideas from any material manifestation or embeddedness; the inherent purposefulness and intentionality of action where action is seen as the execution of a well-formed plan; and reification of cognition or knowing above being and participating.

It is not our aim in this book to advance a critique of rationalist approaches to technology. Many such critiques are now widely available (see, for example, Winograd and Flores 1986; Coyne 1995; Agre 1997a). Although it is our impression that rationalism still dominates academic and pedagogical practices around technology, computers, and design in many countries, and that the turn to practice is not complete, we feel that the groundwork has already been very well laid by the aforementioned authors. Our aim then is to advance a critique of the way in which the turn to practice is playing out in the study of technology, to argue that it is still in many cases incurably and sometimes paradoxically "cognitive" treating the people who use technology as unlikely to experience technology, resistance, doubt, ambiguity, or suffering. Therefore, we introduce the main features and examples of a rationalist approach to technology here only to point to the context out of which the turn to practice emerged and to point to some of the important sources of that turn.

According to Coyne (1995), the rationalistic orientation can be seen most clearly in four approaches to computer systems: cognitive modeling and artificial intelligence, formal theory, methodology, and empirical studies. Coyne argues that artificial intelligence brings the main tenets of rationalism into sharp relief: the separation of the inside world of the thinking subject and the outside world of the object; the essence of thought described in terms of formulas, production rules, and axioms, processed through context-independent reason; communication seen as passing information from one subject to another through the medium of the external world; the priority of goal-driven, plan-directed human action that uses internally represented knowledge in plan execution. Rationalism is also apparent in formal approaches to design. Design methods attempt to capture and represent design expertise, making the process objective and explicit. As with artificial intelligence, design methods work from the idea that design proceeds from a problem statement to a solution, with well-articulated methods as the means for reaching the desired end. The methods approach is rationalistic insofar as it treats a problem statement as objective; sees means as separable from ends; assumes that understanding can be articulated in formulas, diagrams, and charts; and assumes a privileged relationship between these representations of knowledge and thinking. Finally, empirical studies that treat complex behavior as reducible to measurable variables, means as separate from ends, and experimenters' values as irrelevant are also rationalistic.

The turn to practice came about because rationalism had created an obstacle to thinking about technology by reifying technological artifacts as objects of study apart from their making and use. The sharp focus provided by this methodology became an obstacle to understanding the very technology that was picked out. Separated from the materiality of practice and experience, the study of technology became the study of idealizations of technology. Computers became the idealized computer, a black box transforming inputs to outputs systematically, or an information transmission, storage, and accumulation machine. Computer users, somewhat recursively, also became information-processing devices. Designing computers became a process of transforming formal representations from a statement of a problem or requirements through design specification to artifact, equally idealized. Although these idealizations may not be obstacles in themselves, when they over-determine our thinking about and our practices around technology they are stultifying. The turn to practice can be seen as an attempt to restore the continuity between technological artifacts and the prosaic experience of making and using them that had previously been sundered by rationalism.

Sensitivity to the particular circumstances of use invokes a qualitative shift in thinking about the design and use of technology. Simple observation demonstrates that technology gets a mixed reception in people's lives. Different individuals, or even the same individual at different times, may experience technology in quite different ways, and that is not easy to capture in rationalist models. Rationalist models abstract in a way that excludes particular circumstances, perhaps the very circumstances that turn out in practice to be most salient. The rationalist separation of reason from the material, contingent, and particular requires that model makers make an *a priori* decision about what is interesting or relevant about the technology under consideration—in short, what the technology *is* in the world of the model. For example, a mobile phone may be modeled as a device for transmitting and receiving information or as a medium for communication, though the distinction between information exchange and communication will not always be made. As hypotheses or imaginative "what ifs" about the technology, these models may open up previously unconsidered possibilities and thereby enrich experience with the technology. As commitments to what the technology *is*, they close off discourse and limit imagination. And very often that is how rationalist models are used in technology design. Sensibility to practice tells us that closing off is not always a bad thing. Local, tactical closing off might even be practically necessary (Bowker and Star 1999). However, rationalism stultifies when a discursive strategy becomes transformed into an ontological commitment. In contrast with rationalism, practice leans toward the material, practical, particular circumstances for its discourses about technology, creating potential for surprise and imagination and opening up aspects of experience not even imagined *a priori* and which would be excluded by an *a priori* model such as an information-processing model.

It could be argued that practice theorists set up a straw man and perhaps even a straw knight to knock him over. But the variety of experiences with any particular technology tends to indicate otherwise. For example, as we pointed out in chapter 1, many have received mobile phones enthusiastically even though there are nagging doubts about the social and intellectual consequences of the widespread use of some features such as text messaging. For the enthusiastic owner, they are a practical tool, a source of fun, and a badge or fashion statement. They both do and say something. Look at the advertising and design effort made to render a telephone "cool" for teenagers or chic for their parents: the lines, the colors, the shape, the diminishing size. And look at the success of that effort on the streets, in trains, and in homes where everybody has to have his or her own mobile phone. Most important of all, look at how they are used differently by different individuals and groups, from the individuals who use mobile phones only for security as they drive late at night, to the groups of teenagers who use them to say "Hi," to connect with each other, either by means of a quick call or increasingly a short text message with graphics. Mobile phone use can also create magical moments that would not have been possible without them, like the call I (Peter) received from my young daughter while I was at work in York and she on top of the London Eye. For a moment, the world seemed smaller and more intimately connected due to this unexpected use of a mobile. However, for many of the uninitiated obliged to listen to phones ringing in the cinema or even on the street, or to one side of many simultaneous conversations on a train, the experience is quite different and mobile phones are a pestilence.

Phones are not the only example of a technology for which people have found a variety of uses or some would say misuses. ATMs provide a welcome 24-hour service, but they are also a ready-made opportunity for mugging, and the technology that supports them is used to argue for reduced staffing and closing bank branches. In a small village near the University of York, local residents have successfully campaigned for closure of ATMs between midnight and 6 A.M. because of the nuisance of late-night revelers seeking top-ups of cash for trips to clubs and restaurants in the city. The Internet can be a boon for education, a source of entertainment, a medium of expression and social interaction, a worry to parents concerned about their children getting access to materials they would prefer them not to have, or simply frustrating because of the huge amounts of useless information that must be waded through before finding the nugget. Process automation can reduce the requirement for physical labor (good and bad depending on your perspective), and can enhance precision, but can make reliability an even more complex issue as can be seen when a minor software bug renders Air Traffic Control ineffective for a couple of days. A computerized information system can be novel and exciting, feared, or part of the infrastructure of work, like a road almost unnoticed until it goes wrong.

Turning to practice offered alternatives that lightened technological being. Unlike Kundera's ironic "unbearable lightness of being," the lightness of practice was fresh, airy, and playful; at the same time, it was geared toward serious purposes in design, evaluation, and theory. The focus shifted away from developing and evaluating ways of thinking about and representing technological artifacts and their behavior toward a concern for the particular circumstances of their design and use, away from argument about the merits of particular specification languages to the detailed particulars of use. Once the case for "meaning in use" was made, idealizations of technology in formal models, users in cognitive models, and human-computer interaction in formal specifications could no longer be the heights of our aspirations in studying the design and use of technology. The context had changed. The contingency, plurality, and historicity of sociocultural practices created a metacontext within which the values and limitations of abstract models had to be seen. The playfulness of working with ideas, prototypes, and particularities of use was inscribed on processes of developing and using abstractions, creating circumstances that justify going on.

The Turn to Phenomenology: A New Foundation for Design

The turn to phenomenology as a new foundation for design was perhaps the first turn to practice visible in the HCI community. Indeed, Winograd and Flores (1986) are often cited as providing a seminal critique of rationalism that made a significant contribution to bringing about the turn to practice in understanding technology use and design (see, for example, Coyne 1995; Bannon and Bodker 1991; Dourish 2001). Broadly speaking, they questioned the viability of separating subjective knowing from objective knowing, mental processes from the material conditions and cultural-historical traditions that produce them, thought from situated practice, information or knowledge from context, and action from setting or situation. Put more positively, these challenges argue that technology should be seen as something inherently social and practical, situated in ordinary, everyday activity.

Winograd and Flores used their reading of hermeneutic and phenomenological philosophy to develop an alternative to the rationalist orientation to technology. Their alternative sees technology as a transformation of tradition:

> . . . we can let our awareness of the potentials for transformation guide our actions in creating and applying technology. In ontological designing, we are doing more than asking what can be built. We are engaging in a philosophical discourse about the self—about what we can do and what we can be. (Winograd and Flores 1986, p. 179)

For Winograd and Flores, ontological design is necessarily both reflective and political. It is an interaction of understanding and creativity that looks back to the traditions that form us, our heritage and existing ways of being, and also looks forward to transformations of our living together that have not yet been created. Understanding technology and understanding design go hand in hand for Winograd and Flores:

> In order to understand the phenomena surrounding a new technology, we must open the question of design—the interaction between understanding and creation. In speaking here of design, we are not restricting our concern to the conscious methodology of design. We address the broader question of how a society engenders inventions whose existence in turn alters that society. We need to establish a theoretical basis for looking at what the devices do, not just how they operate. (ibid., pp. 4–5)

Winograd and Flores's argument suggests that as designers and users of technology, indeed as participants in society, we are all already engaged in transformation. This renders notions of design as consciously controlled activity unviable. In creating and using new technologies, we can attempt to anticipate breakdowns in our everyday practices and tool use. But we do this knowing that, although we may specify the particular perturbation by introducing a new artifact or by changing a structure, we cannot predict the response to that perturbation. Following Maturana and Varela's (1980) conceptualization of living systems as self-regulating, Winograd and Flores argue that we cannot impose any structure on another person, people adapt to perturbation in their own way. Moreover, as inevitable participants in the transformation of a tradition, we cannot predict the course of that transformation. Yet, as we will see later, Winograd and Flores have been criticized for developing a design philosophy and a technology for coordination that are rationalistic and prescriptive.

Winograd and Flores use ideas from philosophy, linguistics, and biology to develop an understanding of technology, its design and use, which they maintain is not rationalistic. Indeed they argue that the importance of introducing the work of Heidegger, Gadamer, Maturana, and Austin to students of technology is in its potential for unconcealing the rationalist tradition in which we are all already immersed. Winograd and Flores go beyond critique of rationalism by pointing to "a new orientation" which is developed out of the unconcealing of rationalism. They argue that in their new orientation action is given primacy over cognition, that is, that cognition is viewed as an engaged activity within a situation. With "throwness" as a condition for being-in-the-world, we are always already acting, engaged in acting within a situation without the opportunity to disengage and become detached observers. According to Winograd and Flores (1986, p. 31), we are always already experiencing and understanding without reflection. This has obvious implications for the rationalist notion of goal-directed, plan-controlled action. With respect to the design and use of technology, it suggests a move away from understanding technology as cognitive, for example as augmenting knowledge and supporting decision making, and toward technology as participating in the kinds of actions that make up our lives. Moreover, when action is given primacy over cognition, knowing is always engaged activity. There can be no detached understanding. Rather, understanding depends on pre-understanding, which is the result of an individual's experience within a tradition. In this regard, Winograd and Flores lean on Gadamer's contention (1976, p. 9) that prejudices or pre-understandings "constitute the initial directedness of our whole ability to experience. . . . They are simply conditions whereby we experience something—whereby what we encounter says something to us."

Winograd and Flores facilitated the turn to practice in understanding the design and use of computer technology by unconcealing the pervasiveness of rationalist assumptions. This unconcealing is what was seminal in their work. But the project of Winograd and Flores (1986) should be seen as two projects: unconcealing rationalism and building a new foundation for design. When they moved from unconcealing to making a foundation, Suchman (1993) and Bowers (1992) argue, Winograd and Flores fell foul of precisely the pervasive rationalism they aimed to challenge. Despite these criticisms, Winograd and Flores's work still bears close reading as an introduction to the movements toward practice in technology use and design and to the debates still ongoing as part of that movement.

Winograd and Flores draw on speech-act theory as the foundation for their language/action perspective on design and for the design of their particular technological intervention in the organization of work called The Coordinator. Speech-act theory is a theory of language as meaningful action initiated by Austin (1962) and formalized by Searle (1969). Austin developed his account of language as social action out of a conviction that language could not be theorized apart from use, that is, that language had to be understood as action, as something people do. However, as Suchman (1993) notes, subsequent theorists have paradoxically taken this to mean that a theory of language constitutes a theory of action. They draw more on Searle's formalization and categorization of speech acts than on the impetus for Austin's initial formulation. In this light, Winograd and Flores's use of speech-act theory could be characterized as an attempt to theorize the coordination of cooperative activity as a formal linguistic system.

Winograd and Flores (1986, p. 156) describe organizational life as comprised of speech acts combined into "recurrent patterns of communication in which language provides the coordination between actions." This idea is most clearly articulated in their state-transition diagram of a "conversation for action" in which the interplay of speech acts, such as requests and commissives, are directed toward cooperative action. According to Winograd and Flores, their interest in developing the conversation for action is to demonstrate the possibility of formally modeling the basic structure of language use. Winograd and Flores are concerned with "the basic structure, not the details of content" (ibid., p. 66). Moreover, they acknowledge that participants in a conversation are aware of the structure of conversation only when there is a conversational breakdown. Therefore, as analysts, Winograd and Flores occupy a position in the domain of observers, explicitly detached from the domain of participants.

In the domain of observers, Winograd and Flores separate form and content in a way that may not be viable in actual communicative practice. They pull out the structure of a conversation for action from an *a priori* categorization of utterances as types of speech acts and recurrence in language in terms of types of conversations. They articulate their own categorization of conversational events in the form of a diagram and rules. By formally separating the domains of participation and observation, they also privilege these representations of knowledge and thinking and point to a kind of understanding not available to people in the throes of communicative practice.

In the theorizing of Winograd and Flores, language as a system of recurring conversational patterns becomes a reduced representation of cooperative or joint activity or, in their words, organizational life. As such it becomes a means of universal description or at least tradition-wide description of cooperative activity. Leaning toward such generalization inevitably leads to leaning away from the particulars of practice. As well as becoming the representation of action, language as system also becomes the means to achieving the end of cooperative activity. Means and ends are separated such that neither language nor activity can be both means and ends in this framework. As we will argue later, this takes them out of the realms of engaged, experienced participation in activity.

Another feature of Winograd and Flores's approach to design, highlighted in Suchman's critique, is the failure to treat the political aspects of *a priori* categorization *per se*. Suchman (1993, p. 2) develops a critique of a "class of technologies that seeks to develop canonical frameworks for the representation and control of everyday communicative practices." Control is at the heart of this political critique. Suchman argues that "the adoption of speech act theory as a foundation for system design, with its emphasis on the encoding of speakers' intentions into explicit categories, carries with it an agenda of discipline and control over organization members' actions" (ibid., p. 2). The conversation for action describes a conversational structure that, at least in observing communicative practices, gives logical priority to the rules that pattern conversation over the contingent, circumstantial elements used to make conversation *in situ*. Critiquing just such structuralist moves, Rabinow and Sullivan (1987, p. 12) argue that "the conditions which make the enterprise possible—the establishment of operations and elements, and an algebra of their combinations—assure from the beginning and by definition that one is working on a body of material which is pre-constituted, stopped, closed, and in a certain sense, dead."

The argument has been made that representations such as the conversation for action mobilize and authorize a certain impression of rationality. Suchman (1993, p. 9) put it this way:

The picture of the basic conversation for action unifies and mathematizes the phenomena it represents. It works by transforming a set of colloquial expressions into a formal system of categorization that relies upon organization members' willingness to reformulate their actions in its (now technical) vocabulary.

Moreover, members' willingness to reformulate their actions is not solely a theoretical issue. Winograd and Flores's structuring included a technological representation of conversation, The Coordinator. Using The Coordinator to coordinate cooperative activity requires users to follow a menu-driven process for encoding their communicative intentions and making visible their commitments. This allows managers to keep track of commitments made by members of a team. It allows them to rationalize and formalize what would otherwise be a complex texture of indeterminate human activity. As Rabinow and Sullivan (1987) warn, this rationalization is achieved through limiting what is possible by pre-constituting the communicative practices of this organizational life. It is worth noting the ingenuity and adaptivity of many workers faced with the constraints of The Coordinator selectively using and ignoring aspects of it in an *ad hoc* fashion (see, for example, Bullen and Bennett 1990). By creating a technological representation of their understanding of conversation and inserting it into practices where it is used to prescribe action possibilities, Winograd and Flores not only pre-constitute categories for discussing organizational life, they also impose those categories as ontological reality on practice.

Bowker and Star (1999, p. 320) have argued that, when pre-constituted categories become part of the information and organizational infrastructure, action is displaced into representation and the politics of conflict to the invisible politics of form and bureaucracy. Through these displacements, information technology and the information infrastructure generate layers of complexity and interdependency constraining human action. As

Bowker and Star put it, several dances between classifier and classified are observable. Bullen and Bennett's observation of people working around the constraints of The Coordinator can be seen as an apparently harmless case of dancing around constraints. However, it exemplifies Bowker and Star's clarification about classification, which is that, in making distinctions between what is the same and what is different, classification creates the space for the classifier and the classified to come into conflict on moral, political, practical, or aesthetic grounds. Even the most apparently rationalist of human activities, classification, turns out in practice to be contingent, messy, ethical, and political. Though they would not necessarily put it this way, Bowker and Star's work suggests that the turn to practice leads not to further rationalization through the imposition of rules and categories but to a rethinking of technology as experience.

Though Winograd and Flores can be credited for contributing to unconcealing rationalism in thinking and design through their readings of Heidegger, Austin, and Maturana, they can also be charged with having failed to make a radical turn to practice—despite the claims of Coyne and others. Turning to practice requires a more radical move than they were prepared to make. It requires descriptions and explanations of technology use to be based on an understanding of the prosaic activities of users as experienced by themselves. In short, it requires an ethnographic turn.

An Ethnographic Turn

One of the limitations of Winograd and Flores's foundation for design of technology is that it views organizational life, communicative practices, and working relationships from the outside. Pre-constituting their categories of interest ensures that. In contrast, ethnography tries to understand practices, relationships, and cultures from the inside. There are many descriptions and varieties of ethnography, and, as in many disciplines, the arguments within ethnography about what ethnography is and what ethnographers do are legion. However, the subtle distinctions that would be grist for the ethnographer's and the methodologist's mills need not concern us here; our main purpose is to describe the place of ethnography in the turn to practice. For that, a reasonable working definition will suffice.

Geertz (1973) suggests that we think of ethnography as thick description which is interpretive of social discourse where the interpretation consists in trying to rescue the "said" of such discourse from the perishing occasion of its saying. As the occasion passes, the ethnographer attempts to inscribe the sense or meaning of the occasion into an account that persists and can be consulted again. As Anderson (1994), Blomberg (1995), Button (2000), and others interested in explicating a role for ethnography in systems design have pointed out, it is more than scenic description, fieldwork, or requirements capture. It involves an analytic mentality that is geared toward providing interpretations of or explanatory frameworks for whatever is observed. More specifically, those interpretations tend to be in terms of social theory, what Geertz referred to as "the interpretation to which persons of a particular denomination subject their experience" (1973, p. 15)— in this case the anthropological denomination. Ethnography involves participating in and conversing with subjects about their experiences and participating in and conversing with colleagues and peers about (anthropological) interpretations of those experiences. The double task of interpretive ethnography, according to Geertz, is "to uncover the conceptual structures that inform our subjects' acts, the 'said' of social discourse, and to construct a system of analysis in whose terms what is generic to those structures, what belongs to them because they are what they are, will stand out against other determinants of human behavior. In ethnography, the office of theory is to provide a vocabulary in which what symbolic action has to say about itself—that is about the role of culture in human life—can be expressed." (ibid., p. 27)

Writing ethnography is a process of displaying other people's sense making in a language that we understand. Moreover, ethnographic inscription is always open to contest and debate; it is never finalized. Geertz suggests that, looked at in this way, the aim of ethnography and anthropology is "the enlargement of the universe of human discourse" (ibid., p. 14). Put another way, ethnography makes available community sensibilities that might not otherwise be encountered. For example, an ethnography of art should make available the sensibilities of artists to modes of thinking and meaning making that might have more to do with color, line, and movement than most non-artists would be used to in their own ways of making meaning. With respect to technology, Anderson (1994) has suggested that ethnography of design should make available the sensibilities of designers that legitimate particular approaches to design problems and solutions. When we display the logic of other people's ways of doing, we inscribe other sensibilities into a culture to show that the dominant sensibilities of that culture are not the only ways of making meaning—to open up options and to critique monologue.

One of the major contributions of ethnography to the turn to practice in understanding technology can be seen in ethnographies of work. Many of these ethnographies aim to inform design by analyzing relations between particular technologies and the organization of work: for example, the use of shared artifacts in structuring communication and coordination practices in control rooms (Heath and Luff 1992) and the use of standardized forms to aid classification in nursing practice (Bowker and Star 1999). Others characterize aspects of work as organized from within in a generative, metaphorical language: for example, Lave and Wenger's (1991) analysis of the social character of learning in terms of participation in communities of practice and Star's analyses of information infrastructure (Star and Ruhleder 1996; Bowker and Star 1999) and institutional ecology (Star and Griesemer 1989; Star and Strauss 1999).

The ethnographic turn is generally seen as a turn away from the possibility of neutral description. There can be no literal interpretation of the logic of other people's sense making, and certainly there can be no transliteration from their way of making sense to ours. Moreover, there is no way of writing the preceding sentence without opening up for consideration the categories "ours" and "theirs," or, as Suchman (1995) put it, "we" and "other." "We" can be a community of observers, an academic or practitioner community, making use of the experiences of "others" for our purposes, where "others" are those being observed and playing only a passive role in the ethnography. This is reminiscent of Winograd and Flores's Domain of Participation and Domain of Observation. Alternatively, ethnography can be relational, reflexive, and perspectival, and "we" and "other" engage in a human dialogue open to the hazards and uncertainties of any genuine relationship. Suchman (1995, p. 63) put it as follows:

. . . recent anthropology proposes a view of ethnography as an encounter between actors differently embedded within particular social/cultural milieus. On this view culture is always relational. Rather than describing attributes of a population from some neutral position outside the field of view, accounts of cultural meanings and practices are inevitably created from particular standpoints that set up lines of comparison and contrast between the speaker/writer and the persons and practices described.

As we shall see in chapter 3, the ethnographic stance on the interpretation of cultures—engaged, relational, perspectival, and plural—is close to our own position on interpreting felt experience.

A Political Stance

Among those interested in relationships between technology and work, some have taken an explicitly political stance. A perspective that explicitly prioritizes workers' concerns has been championed by what has become known as the Scandinavian approach to human-computer interaction. Though this idealization suggests a homogeneous Scandinavian worldview on relations between work and technology, it does not exist. The label is also misleading in suggesting that only Scandinavian researchers are interested in workers' concerns. Nonetheless, it would be fair to say that researchers based in or connected with Scandinavian schools of computer science and informatics (e.g. Bodker 1991, 1998; Bjerknes, Ehn, and Kyng 1987) lead the unconcealment of the political in technology. In fact they lay their cards on the table twice with respect to perspective. First, they accept that researchers or observers of work practices inevitably observe and report from their own perspective; their observation is inevitably reflexive. They cannot help but be engaged with the situation they observe as we are all always engaged and there is no detached observation and thinking. They inevitably participate in what is observed. Second, they turn what could be a purely academic, methodological issue into a practical one by arguing for a particular politically committed perspective. Inescapable engagement and participation having been accepted, the decision then becomes one of what form this participation takes. It is not simply a matter of being stuck with reflexivity, engagement, and perspective as humans. Rather, we can make choices and commitments in how we engage and participate. Specifically, these researchers characterize traditional design as management-centered and propose an alternative design philosophy based on favoring the tacit knowledge and skills of users and on supporting their interests, an alternative worldview in which the observer inevitably participates in what is observed. A stance is taken in these Scandinavian studies of work and design that explicitly favors workers' interests, and a so-called objective stance is not allowed to detract from that engagement. This position is intentionally reflexive, explicitly acknowledging observers' engagement in their observations, interpreters' engagement in their interpretations, and theorists' engagement in their theories.

The implications of such an explicitly political stance can be seen in at least three developments. First, there is a broad concern for the political impacts of technology. This can be as broad as a reading of Heideggerian enframing into discussions of information technology design, posing questions about the extent to which people are dominated by technology as a category or mode of thought (e.g. Coyne 1995). A less philosophical version of this development involves critical analysis of technology implementation and design methods in the light of their impact on workers and on democracy in the workplace and in society (Bjerknes et al. 1987; Star 1995; Nardi and O'Day 1999). Second, there is a development of this critique of traditional design methodologies in the form of participatory design (Schuler and Namioka 1993)—an approach that involves users in every stage of system design. Third, the emergence of a political sensibility motivated particular design projects. For example, UTOPIA (Bodker et al. 1987) was a trade-union-based development of and training in computer technology, the goal of which was to develop skill-enhancing tools for graphics workers. In this project, technology development was seen in the context of workers' skills, qualifications, and education. Very often the major criteria for design decisions are the standard and relatively narrowly defined engineering and management criteria of efficiency and effectiveness. UTOPIA drew attention to the implications of decisions, based on such criteria, to transfer skilled graphics work from people to technology. While these decisions may result in short term efficiencies, they can also diminish the skills and qualifications of workers in an industry. In the longer term this can result in problems for the workers and for the industry, which finds itself short of skilled labor. The UTOPIA challenge is to see design in the broader political context and a longer developmental time frame and therefore to design tools that enhance skills as well as increasing efficiency.

In terms of tracing the turn to practice in technology design and use, the most important result of the development of a political sensibility may be the emergence of critical questioning concerning technology design and use. Political questions about particular projects or methods can be applied recursively to the higher-order categories of design and use themselves. Is it sensible to think of intervention *per se* as a political or moral act? Is the relationship between observer and observed, designer and user, political? Who is in control, how, and why? A small but important development in theorizing design that argues for an explicitly critical design is an approach to design that prioritizes control relations in considering the implications of any design decision. Much of the design discourse that comes from software engineering, for example, assumes that all design serves either the management paying for the design or the broader technical-rationalist goals of more efficient and more effective working. Critical design asks us to question all these assumptions. It raises questions about ownership of skill and knowledge in an organization, and, as we have seen in UTOPIA, it raises questions about the meaning of efficiency and effectiveness for an organization in the longer term.

An Ethnomethodological Turn: Constituting Categories from Within

As we draw this review of the turn to practice in technology design and use to a close, one major issue remains outstanding. So far, we have discussed the seminal contributions to unconcealing rationalism, the ethnographic turn to prosaic practice (which adds a commitment to empirical observation, interpretation, and inscription), and the emergence of an explicit politics of technology. However, the issue of pre-constitution of categories is not satisfactorily resolved by any of the foregoing. As long as there is pre-understanding and an interest in theoretical articulation of observation, the researcher plays a significant role in constituting the categories.

As Button (2000, p. 322) has pointed out, the observation and interpretation of ethnography is not a two-step process, the ethnographer first describing and then explaining. The explanatory framework informs the observation and description; it gives a cast to observation. The object of the exercise—to produce a sociological or anthropological account—interpenetrates observation and interpretation. In this sense, Button argues, the ethnographic account of particular work practices in terms of social solidarity or power relations is a professional account, not a lay account. It depends on lay description of the activities but does not make the lay description visible. In this sense, it is a secondary account, one step removed from the lay description. Therefore, Button argues, although ethnography appears to articulate social organization from the inside, in fact it demotes such primary description in favor of secondary description. Button argues that an alternative approach developed by Garfinkel and

Sacks—that is, ethnomethodology—offers a radical respecification of the human sciences by focusing on investigating how primary descriptions are assembled and deployed in local circumstances. This "shifts the emphasis away from the production of sociological accounts and theories of social doings to an emphasis upon the description of the accountable practices involved in the production of naturally organized phenomena" (Button 2000, p. 325). So ethnomethodology deals with the pre-constitution of categories problem in social theorizing by attending precisely to the production and use of categories in social practice.

The ethnomethodological stance has been quite important in effecting the turn to practice in some specialized areas of the study of technology, particularly CSCW (Computer-Supported Cooperative Work). CSCW reacted against the dominance of cognitive science in studies of human-computer interaction by emphasizing how to support collaborative work over designing interfaces for single-user systems. This required an understanding of the nature and organization of the work to be supported by the system. We have already mentioned that one way of accomplishing this understanding is to involve users in the design process (e.g. participatory design). Another approach, which draws on the ethnomethodological sensibility to the situated production of work, involves observing people at work, more specifically people interacting with technology, to describe how they do their work *in situ*. At around the same time as Winograd and Flores were beginning to excite new thinking on technology design and use, Suchman (1987) made a seminal contribution of this type.

Taking an ethnomethodological tack, Suchman developed a provocative critique of theories of human action which assume that plans determine action and which ignore or seriously underplay the situatedness of action. In contrast with the rationalist position on action founded on plans, Suchman argued that action is founded on local interactions with our environment informed by reference to abstract representations of situations and actions. The function of these abstract representations is not to specify local interactions, but to exploit some contingencies of our environment and to avoid others. Plans elaborate actions just to the level that elaboration is useful and are vague with respect to the details of action just at the level at which it makes sense to forgo abstract representation and to rely on particular embodied responses. In this sense, Suchman argues that plans are resources for actions, like maps. Maps don't control action but can be viewed as a useful resource for travel. She argues that understanding action *in situ* requires accounts of the productive interaction between symbolic representations and the unique unrepresented circumstances in which action occurs.

Suchman developed her argument around a detailed analysis of interaction between novice users and an "intelligent" photocopying machine. Her claim was that "the organization of situated action is an emergent property of moment-by-moment interactions between actors, and between actors and the environment of their action" (1987, p. 179). This conceptual commitment to the emergence of organization from interaction implies a methodological commitment to building generalization inductively from records of particular, naturally occurring activity. Any theory that emerges must be accountable to that evidence.

The ethnomethodological stance has added to the study of technology a critical sensibility not only to the situated production of organization but also to the meaning of work. Together with ethnography, it highlights the importance of a resolutely empirical practice for the study of technology. However, it takes a more radical stance than ethnography on the need to study the production of social practices and relations from within, and, at least as articulated by Button, it displays skepticism about the place of social theory (or sociological accounts) in understanding practice. We read this as skepticism of a particular approach to theorizing that builds an account of social structure as the foundation of human action and uses observation to refine and improve the initial account, all the while developing closer approximations of the culture or society being studied.

The ethnomethodological position is that categories are constituted in interaction and that the analyst's job is to describe the accountable practices involved in producing these categories. In ethnomethodology, generalization is accomplished inductively from descriptions of particular practices. Clearly, this process leans heavily on primary description. However, we need to be aware that the possibility of primary description of experience is problematic and is a source of debate in philosophy and social theory. For example, Ricoeur's (1971) writings on interpretation suggest that there is no primary description. Even as we describe a simple event, we are interpreting, and this interpretation is laden with theory. While we may be able to escape particular theories, we cannot escape the kinds of theories we might call beliefs and ideology. Whether primary description is possible or not comes back to the issue raised earlier of whether an objectivist, detached stance is available. Could ethnomethodologists so resolutely defend the possibility of primary description if they accepted that even "primary description" is engaged? Wetherell (1998) takes up this issue in a dialogue with Schegloff about the value of making explicit the ideological standpoint informing one's observations. Wetherell argues for an analytic stance that is both top down and bottom up. For example, she argues that one's beliefs about identity are as much part of an account of people constructing their identity in practice as the talk and text of the situated interaction. Ethnomethodological resistance to beliefs and ideologies seems to display an attachment to realism and objectivism not always shared with ethnography.

Even if it could be established that the ethnomethodological stance on observation and theory was viable (that is, if it was possible to analyze practice without using theory analytically, and without the cast of ideology or interest), would it be useful, particularly in studies of technology? One of the accomplishments of ethnography is its willingness to play with ideas and descriptions in an attempt to enlarge discourse, serve imagination, and heighten particular sensibilities. One could argue that the ethnographic stance on theory is revisionary. In its attempts to enlarge discourse and heighten particular sensibilities, it aims to reorient and change things, not just describe them. This is surely particularly salient to those of us interested in technology use and design, which is always already an intervention in the world, which revises toward some end. Shapiro (1994) suggests that ethnomethodology on its own, despite the obvious merits of its methodology, may not provide the best way forward for design. Though it makes space for experience, its objectivist leaning with respect to lay accounts inhibits its potential for contributing to imagined futures.

Evaluating the Turn to Practice: Self, Identity, and Diversity

The turn to practice in understanding technology, specifically the turn from technicist cognitive science and software engineering, benefits the study of people's transactions with technology by enlarging and enriching the universe of discourses about technology, drawing attention to everyday activities and challenging the traditional boundaries drawn between people and technology. However, the turn to practice itself may now be becoming an obstacle to going on. It has become heavily laden with theoretical and methodological encumbrances and disciplinary dispute. The purity and the zeal of the ethnomethodologist are used to beat off any ideological interventions. The primacy and the reification of the social are used against invaders bearing concerns about individuality or individual subjectivity. The weight of social systems and systematic theorizing oppresses playfulness with particular events and experiences—and perhaps paradoxically also denies them the weight of their moment. The very continuity that practice was intended to restore is thus sundered by it. Our case is that this is due to a tendency in many practice approaches to simplify the individual by presenting an underdeveloped account of self, identity, and individual diversity. Wenger (1998), for example, reduces individual diversity to four categories of participants: insider, outsider, peripheral participant, and marginal participant.

In their attempts to radically undo Cartesian dualism, practice and activity theories have replaced a solely individualistic concept of self, always separate from the material world, with a communitarian conception of self that is predominantly external and has only impoverished access to its own mental states. Bakhurst (1997), in a philosophical defense of a communitarian approach to consciousness, accepts that externalizing thought poses problems for questions concerning people's access to their own mental states, feelings, and values. With respect to people's relationships with technology, we want to be able to reflect on the particular experiences that people have, the moral and political weight of a moment, the fun people have with their cyber-pet or mobile phone, the irritation and offense they feel when forced by circumstances into using a system that cuts against their values. It is difficult to reflect on these issues within a communitarian framework, which treats the social context as a given. Moreover, once the external or the social is encapsulated in system-oriented design representations, the felt life of individuals' experiences of that system is lost.

Some theorists try to do justice to both social practice and the individuals involved. For example, in their analysis of infrastructures of classification, Bowker and Star (1999) show an interest in the consequences of classification for those people who are affected by it. Their analysis is suggestive of what it feels like to be a nurse working with a disease-classification system or a child living under apartheid classification. However, their primary interest is in classification as a social and societal process, and their analysis always comes back to a center that contains infrastructures of classification. The metaphors they provide—for example, monsters, boundary objects, brokers, and borderlands—are certainly evocative, but the voices of individuals are lost in them.

Among practice theorists, Lave (1988) comes closest to providing an account of the individual in practice. She acknowledges that the possibility of conceptually elaborating both sociocultural order and individual experience is inhibited by cognitivist tendencies to conflate culture, knowledge, and society to mental representations and anthropological tendencies to conflate them into a superorganic system of meaning. In place of these reductive options, she attempts to accommodate the social and the individual by positing a dialectical relationship between them, and she commends "person acting in setting" as a unit of analysis that allows conceptual elaboration of both sociocultural order and individual experience of it. This allows Lave (ibid., p. 98) to illustrate the conceptual underpinnings of a theory of practice, including "the notion of multiple ongoing activities, the concept of structuring resources, their proportional articulation, and the ways in which they shape processes that generate and resolve arithmetic dilemmas."

Lave's conceptualization of structuring resources depends on an intimate relationship between social practice and individual experience. She sees activities such as mathematics and grocery shopping and their interrelations as providing structure for quantitative relations in the supermarket and the classroom. Glossing a mathematics problem in a classroom setting as a shopping problem is likely to be seen for what it is, a disguised mathematics problem. However, in practice, supermarket shopping is seen to generate its own mathematical dilemmas, which shoppers are likely to organize to fit the concerns of buying food. But Lave (1988, p. 124) also points out that situated activity is not the only source of structuring resources; social relationships and people's subjective experience of problems also contribute to structuring or organizing resources: "Math and standard crystallized forms of quantity such as those to be considered here—the system of currency and systems of measurement as well as algorithmic arithmetic—carry meaning and values *as such*, and these too are subjectively experienced." Lave also characterizes practice theorists as claiming that "cultural systems and their structural entailments, *as aspects of a particular constitutive order*, motivate experience and are resources drawn upon in the fashioning of intentional activity in the lived-in world" (ibid., p. 178).

According to Lave, people experience mathematics problems subjectively as dilemmas to be resolved. Somehow the problem and the system of measurement *as such* in Lave's conceptualization of activity can be separated from experience. Thus, Lave posits social interactionism as overcoming, on the one hand, some of the shortcomings of a functional approach to activity that has system without experience, and, on the other hand, a phenomenological approach that has experience but no system.

While Lave's position comes close to our own, we find her separation of experience from activity and social relations, and her subjectivization of experience unnecessary and unhelpful moves. It may be that the dilemma that we see in Lave's analysis is created by her construction of experience as essentially subjective in a dialectical theory. Dewey and Bakhtin offer ways of resolving this dilemma by viewing experience relationally. For both of them, subjective-objective dualism is the result of an illusion of perspective outside perspective, and system or structure are occasionally useful concepts but not ontologically necessary bases for making sense of social life.

The Problem of Watered-Down Concepts in Service of Design

Three offerings of the turn to practice to the study of technology design and use are *a resolute commitment to empirical practice, an entry into the difficult world of social practice and theory*, and *a reflexive turn*.

There can be little argument now with the position that technology (like language for Wittgenstein) is best understood in use, in specific social practices (or language games). Moreover, the problematic positioning of researcher, designer, and user are widely acknowledged. However, we need to be a little concerned that the three offerings can become reduced in technology research and design practice. The commitment to empirical practice can, as Button (2000) notes, become a tendency toward scenic description of settings. This is related to tourist theorizing, a tendency to adopt weak versions of the social-theoretical positions employed. In a review of "activity" as an explanatory principle, Tulviste (1999) regrets the popularity of the "weak" version, which studies mental processes such as learning, thinking, and classifying in an activity context. The strong version involves explaining processes "through activity" rather than describing them in an activity context. And reflexivity becomes a fashionable accessory rather than a thoroughgoing commitment to engagement and participation.

As an example of the way in which these offerings can become watered down when they migrate in service of design, consider the construct "community of practice." This is a case in which a rich, complex, dialectical account of concerned people acting has sometimes become a simple, unproblematic emblem for social perspectives and against individual perspectives on work and technology. Following Tulviste and Button, the weak version, popularly used in studies of technology, involves describing work in a "community" context rather than analyzing and explaining work through the dialectical relations that constitute communities of practice. The strong version is always already circumstantial, contingent, problematic.

The "community of practice" account exemplifies some of the benefits and limitations of the turn to practice with respect to technology. It can be seen as an ethnography of situated learning which provides the kind of secondary description that creates a space for the imagination. For a time, it revised and reoriented discourses on technology and work, opening up a deeply contextual discourse in which the meaningfulness of technology lay in its relation to social practices. But it could be argued that "community of practice" has already become a fad. The rich, complex discourse of the original is in danger of becoming an emblem and losing its substance: a substance that depends on not reducing the conceptual and practical tension between individual and community. As it is used in research concerned with technology and education (Brown and Duguid 1991; Rogoff, Matusov, and White 1996), the individual experiencing subject has largely been lost. As a consequence, the dialectical tension is minimized and the social reified to the point where individual experience is rendered irrelevant. As we argued earlier in this chapter, in traditional theorizing about practice the richness and messiness of experience becomes subordinated to the technical in both technology and theory. From our perspective, what appears to be lost when this happens is the connectedness of experience, which binds the concepts together in practice and without which the concepts can float free and meaningless.

The practical and theoretical importance of employing the strong version can be seen in Hodges's (1998) account of her own difficulties participating in a particular community of practice. Hodges develops her account of her own experience by "bringing a language of identity and difference into a sociocultural analysis [which] makes more apparent the intersections of normative practice with difference" (ibid., p. 272). Hodges attempts to elaborate the "community of practice" model, in this case based on her attempts to understand her inability to identify herself as a "teacher" having participated in an apprenticeship for early childhood educators. Her theoretical contribution is to enrich the conceptual base of community of practice by bringing identity and practice together, resulting in a conceptualization of participation which includes non-participation, multiple identificatory possibilities, lags in participation, and conflictual moments of identification. Her practical contribution is to highlight the possibility for feelings of "agonized compromise" in becoming a member of any community.

By drawing our attention to the discursive production of identities in practices and particularly to the emotional investment of the individual in this production, Hodges points to the individual dimension and ultimately to individual sufferings, which are almost inevitably overlooked by weak versions of the "community of practice" model geared toward describing social structure. She opens up layers of complexity in the relationship between individual and community and orients us toward experience as something felt. The detailed focus on the discursive and the interactive in Hodges's empirical work allows for the emergence of emotional response and personal compromise in a way that does not seem possible in the empirical work reported even by Lave and Wenger, which was mainly observation of adults in largely solitary, self-regulated activity (see Agre 1997b).

If community of practice is to develop as an account of technologically mediated work, it seems to us that it must elaborate its account of the conjunction of practice and identity, specifically how particular identities are produced in community practices. Walkerdine (1997) has argued that community-based models that appeal to the reasonableness and rationality of participants produce covert controlling or regulating relationships, which center on ideas of what is normal. As long as the processes of regulation in the community, the control relations, are left unexplored, the community of practice has what Walkerdine calls an illusory quality.

The various approaches that constitute the turn to practice make a very useful contribution to understanding people's relations with technology by shifting the empirical focus from laboratory to the worlds in which we live with technology, heightening the sensibility to the social, and drawing attention to the reflexive. However, for the most part, they leave us with a sense of something's having been lost or played down. In shifting discourses on technology toward social practice, they have left us with little sense of what it feels like to participate in these social practices.

From Practice to Felt Life

As it stands, then, the lacuna in the turn to practice in studying technology and work is felt experience. As we have already indicated, this may have more to do with the sometimes schematic presentation and use of ethnography in studies of work and technology. It could be argued that experience is absent altogether from the technical description of the sequential organization of interaction—perhaps appropriately so, in view of the narrow focus of describing a systematics of interaction. However, it is implicit in much of the ethnographic work that has been influential in CSCW. Concealing experience in theories of practice or activity partly explains the ease with which the turn to practice can result in weak versions, where richer, more complex versions are available. Without experience, it is easy to read weak versions as descriptions of behaviors, states, or processes that can be modeled and implemented.

One of our main goals in writing this book is to create a space for the individual and felt experience, as something lived through, in the turn to practice in studies of technology. It seems to us that without explicit reference to felt experience, without a discourse on practice that includes what it feels like, communities of practice will develop the illusory quality referred to by Walkerdine and will become a simplified representation of what Lave and Wenger treated as a complex, problematic process.

The same could be said for many of the other potentially generative approaches to practice in studies of technology. We have already alluded to the limitations of weak versions of activity theory and scenic description passing for ethnography. Context of use, including individuals' "concerns," has equally been reduced to a set of models by Beyer and Holzblatt (1997). Our argument is that what is missing in each case is a sensitivity to practical, felt experience. We are sure that in most cases the turn to practice was intended to be a turn to practical experience but the contingencies of research and design meant that those communities preferred simplified formulas—and the zeitgeist in those communities was from individual to social. Practice was recruited to serve that agenda. In the next three chapters, we describe our approach to experience, which seeks to reassert felt life and the individual as central to our understanding of practice and of technology in use.

3 | A Pragmatist Approach to Technology as Experience

Meaning arises when we try to put what culture and language have crystallized from the past, together with what we feel, wish and think about our present point in life.
—V. Turner (1986, p. 33)

Clifford Geertz (1986, p. 374) wrote that without experience, or something like it, "cultural analyses seem to float several feet above their human ground." If culture is not to be used in a meaningless manner, separate from people fearing, hoping, imagining, revolting, and consoling, "it must engage some sort of felt life, which might as well be called experience" (ibid.). The turn to practice from cognitive science and software engineering has certainly renewed our understanding of people's relationships with technology. However, when the social becomes reified in our considerations of people and technology, practice theories also float several feet above their human ground. By excluding or separating off people's felt experiences with technology in order to concentrate on the logic of practice, people's concerns, enthusiasms, and ambivalence about participation are abstracted away or averaged out. Hodges's articulation of the "agonized compromise" of participation in community, where her participation is like complying or taking part despite feelings to the contrary, is simply not expressed. The "felt life" is not engaged in many socially oriented or culturally oriented explanations of people's participation in community, including technologically mediated community. If we are not to hover above the human ground, we must engage with the felt life, "which might as well be called experience."

'Experience' is the word that is most likely to express something of the felt life. It is a very rich word, discursively open and complex, and redolent of life as lived, not just as theorized. Without wanting to foreclose on experience, we should clarify how we are going to use the term in reflecting on technology. The openness of 'experience' is likely to become confusing unless we do some ground clearing, and that is quite hard to do for a couple of reasons. One is that experience is ever present. We are always engaged in experience even when we are trying to stand back from it to describe it. For example, I (John) can describe my experience of walking the Samarian Gorge in terms of the length and narrowness of the gorge, at points almost being able to touch both sides and not see the top, the tremendous heat and the concomitant pleasure in a drink of water, thoughts of the valley flooded in the winter, goats standing on tiny ledges high up the sides of the gorge, wonder at how they got there, the tiredness and parched thirstiness of ten miles of hot walking shockingly and giddily relieved by a black beach and the cooling Mediterranean at the end. Any description of an experience like this is constituted of things and events, what they did to those involved, and how they responded. Standing back from the experience of walking the gorge to describe it to a friend is, of course, living the experience of describing not the experience being described. But it is nevertheless an experience. Because we are always involved in experience, there is no God's-eye view or privileged position of neutrality or authority. Whatever we say about experience must therefore be provisional, a consequence of the reflexivity of seeing described in chapter 2.

A second difficulty is that we tend to believe that we already know what experience is. As a consequence, it may be difficult to even convince readers that there is a need for further discussion in order to clarify how the word is being used. A gentle reminder of how inconsistently we use the word in everyday discourse might help shake our certainties about what we mean by experience. We make distinctions between learning something and having a learning experience, as if learning something is not an experience. We separate what we have learned from education and from our own experience, as if we were not involved in our own education. We distinguish between relationships we have over the Internet and relationships that we experience directly. Again, who exactly was experiencing the Internet relationship? We can also make distinctions between doing something like reading and having the real experience. Of course there is nothing silly about any of these uses of 'experience'. One of the beauties of our use of language is the flexibility with which we use words and phrases without losing our interlocutors. It is not that people see reading as something other than experience, but perhaps that they see a difference worth making between reading about somebody else's experience and having that experience themselves. It may not be that people see school learning as something other than experience but that they see the passivity of much school learning as far from an ideal that involves agency and engagement. In everyday discourse, we can handle layers of meaning when we talk about experience. However, in this context we need to attempt some clarification of how we are going to use the term experience.

The good news, of course, is that we are not the first to try to make sense of experience or use experience to make sense of something like people's transactions with technology. Philosophers, psychologists, and anthropologists have tangled with the term for a long time and those who describe their work as pragmatist or phenomenological have made it a central focus. Bruner and Turner's 1986 book *The Anthropology of Experience* collects together a range of anthropological contributions that try to describe experience and the variety of ways it is expressed in a range of cultures. The philosophical writings of John Dewey and Wilhelm Dilthey from the early decades of the twentieth century make their presence felt in that collection, and continue to stimulate, inform, and perplex anybody interested in understanding experience today. William James's 1902 book *The Varieties of Religious Experience: A Study in Human Nature* is a classic psychological investigation of people's relationships with religion as a particular striving for meaning that gives people a hold on reality. Academics are not the only ones to try to develop a systematic account of experience. Many writers and filmmakers practice their craft under the influence of a practical understanding of experience and how they might influence or help create experience. For example, Boorstin (1990) argues that the Hollywood moviemaker must be able to experience the movie in the way the public will but also must know what it takes on a technical level to help the public construct just that experience. In attempting to clarify our own use of experience, we have been particularly influenced by pragmatist approaches to experience.

Background to Pragmatism and Experience

Pragmatism's practical focus and the richness of its explorations of experience give it a modernity and a freshness that serve well our inquiries into technology as experience. Coyne (1995, p. 17), writing about technology, lists the following features of a pragmatist approach: "[It] embraces the primacy of human action, the practicalities of human involvement, the materiality of the world, the interaction of the senses, and the formative power of technology." Although this is a very useful starting point, it does not express the vitality of a pragmatist approach to experience—the livedness and feltness of it, the ordinariness and enchantment, the organic rhythms and personal engagement. For this, and to really appreciate the potential in a pragmatist approach to experience, we need to look much more closely at how pragmatists think of action and involvement. Behind the basic commitments lie aspects of action that are lacking in the practice-oriented and activity-oriented approaches discussed in chapter 2. Our approach to getting behind those words is to look closely at what two pragmatists, John Dewey and Mikhail Bakhtin, have to offer.

Although Dewey's and Bakhtin's working lives overlapped and they had a common interest in developing accounts of activity and experience that were not constrained by the demands of analytic philosophy or positivist science, there is no sign that they influenced each other in any way, or even that they read each other's work. And although they were both committed to shaping a philosophical approach that would contribute to enriching the ordinary everyday experience of life, they approach the task in quite different ways. Nonetheless, we find in their interests and approaches the potential for a synthesis that helps us to clarify what we mean by experience and that could contribute to enriching our lives with technology. Most particularly, we find the emphasis both men placed on aesthetic experience and its continuity with everyday experience an enlivening antidote to the means-to-ends instrumentalism that marks much discussion of people and technology and that is often used as a criticism of pragmatism itself. The criticism goes like this: If it is concerned with practice and with the consequences of action—rather than with high ideas—pragmatism must be instrumentalist, concerned with means apart from ends. As we shall see later, nothing could be further from the truth. Indeed, the pragmatist aesthetics of Dewey and Bakhtin requires us to inquire creatively about ends as well as means and about the relationship between means and ends.

John Dewey

John Dewey (1859–1952) was one of the first and most influential exponents of pragmatism. Along with Charles Sanders Peirce, William James, and George Herbert Mead, Dewey contributed to the development of a radical, and some suggest distinctly American, response to the social, political, and intellectual developments—slavery and abolitionism, the American Civil War, industrial unrest, probability theory and relativity theory, challenges to religious faith, and philosophical questioning of what it is to know by Kant and Hegel—that brought an end to metaphysical certainties (see for example Joas 1993; Menand 2002). Dewey and his fellow pragmatists worked at a time when foundational questions were being asked about science and knowledge and about the relationship between scientific representation and the world being represented. Although each of them developed a distinctive response, they shared an approach that marked an important beginning for pragmatism. Rather than attempting to replace the old metaphysical certainties with new certainties based on another philosophy or theory, "their endeavor under these conditions was geared to inquiring after the possibilities of science and of democracy and to finding a meaningful life for the individual" (Joas 1993, p. 1). They drew attention to the gap that had developed between science and the ordinary everyday experience of being and acting in the world and responded in a practical revisionary way by inquiring into what science might be and how it might be used to make life more meaningful for people.

Dewey was equally concerned about the relationship between philosophy and life as lived. As far as he was concerned, a philosophy that is not critically relevant to life and its living should be changed or abandoned. He argued that, because ideas survive only while they help us to make sense of and deal with our situation, we should never feel trapped by outdated theories or worldviews. Dewey's commitment to relevance was made in the context of a view of the world as marked by change. As Stuhr (1998) put it, Dewey's "pragmatic philosophy emphasized precariousness, disturbance and instability, sweeping social change and technological transformation, genuine novelty and real beginnings and endings." Stuhr argued that against this background Dewey constructed a philosophy that was always at bottom a social and political philosophy, concerned with creating a democratic culture.

Our interest is in using Dewey to help clarify aspects of experience in the context of people's changing relationships with technology. Stuhr's point is that all of Dewey's writings on education, work, art, technology, morality, and religion, his discussion of inquiry and logic, and also his comprehensive account of experience is social and political philosophy. Moreover,

Stuhr argues that it is through this lens—philosophy as criticism, discriminating judgment, and appraisal of value—that Dewey and pragmatism retain their relevance today. It is in response to his social and political concerns, his concern for a philosophy that helps us to think critically and make value judgments, that Dewey makes experience the heart of his work. If a pragmatist focus on experience does nothing else, then, it reminds us that philosophy must deal with life as lived and felt. Furthermore, if positioning experience in the context of the work to be done to develop a democratic culture does nothing else, it takes it out of the slippery world of packaged and marketed experiences and places it firmly in the ordinary, everyday worlds of people working at life.

In contrast with other philosophical approaches whose starting point is a theory of knowledge or subjective states, pragmatism starts with experience and, by committing to a holistic, relational worldview, tries to ensure that experience is never reduced to categories such as knowledge, behavior, or feelings. For pragmatists such as Dewey, experience is more personal than behavior; it involves an active self who not only engages in but also creatively shapes action. It is more inclusive than knowledge because it tries to encapsulate a person's full relationship—sensory, emotional, and intellectual—with his or her physical and social environment. And, embedded as it is in what people do in the world and what is done to them, it is more than feelings. If these reductions are rejected, experience can be seen as the irreducible totality of people acting, sensing, thinking, feeling, and making meaning in a setting, including their perception and sensation of their own actions. Dewey offered a useful definition along these lines. Experience, he wrote, "includes what men do and suffer, what they strive for, love, believe and endure, and also how men act and are acted upon, the ways in which they do and suffer, desire and enjoy, see, believe, imagine—in short, processes of experiencing. . . . It is "double barreled" in that it recognizes in its primary integrity no division between act and material, subject and object, but contains them both in an unanalyzed totality." (1929a, pp. 10–11)

According to Dewey, therefore, experience is constituted by the relationship between self and object—by concerned, feeling people acting and the materials and tools they use. The concerned person is always already engaged and comes to every situation with personal interests and ideologies. Moreover, as we shall argue in detail later, Dewey's model of action was designed to restore the continuity between refined and intensified forms of experience—the paradigm of which is aesthetic experience—and the everyday events, doings, and sufferings that constitute ordinary experience. He argued that all experience can be rich and fulfilling, and that creative democracy can thrive only when we value rich experience in all aspects of our lives and are prepared to work toward fulfilling the potential in human life.

Mikhail Bakhtin

Whereas Dewey was clearly in the vanguard of American pragmatism, the Russian Mikhail Bakhtin (1895–1975) would be unlikely to appear in any history of pragmatism. Although many commentators treat his work as phenomenological, others such as Holquist and Emerson have pointed to the pragmatic character of some of his work, especially his approach to knowing. For us, a pragmatist reading of his work is warranted by his commitment to knowing as a practical process, a plurality of perspectives, and historicity in thinking. In the social sciences, a revival of interest in pragmatism has coincided with the emergence of Bakhtin and this has generated some interest in juxtapositions between Bakhtin and pragmatism. For example, Francisco Loriggio (1990) has teased out the similarities and differences between the Bakhtin Circle and Pragmatist Psychology in their conceptualizations of mind. Caryl Emerson, an eminent Bakhtin scholar, has argued that the "three founders of American pragmatism—James, Dewey, and Mead—can be usefully juxtaposed to Bakhtin" (1993, p. 2). Michael Holquist, another major Bakhtin scholar, describes Bakhtin's earliest philosophical interests as including "the status of the knowing subject, the relation of art to lived experience, the existence of other persons, and the complexities of responsibility in the area of discourse as well as in the area of ethics" (1990, p. 2). Perhaps not surprisingly in view of the interests just listed, Holquist refers to Bakhtin's philosophy as "a pragmatically-oriented theory of knowledge" (ibid., p. 15).

The context for Bakhtin's work is similar in some respects to the social, political, and intellectual context of the development of American pragmatism. The Russian Revolution, the First World War, Marxism-Leninism, neo-Kantianism, and the new physics provide an active background of change, uncertainty, and violence. However, Bakhtin did not have a university career, and he was in exile in Kazakhstan while other founders of pragmatism were advocating for academic freedom in the United States. Bakhtin lived in a world of suspicion and hardship where he became politically suspect for participating in discussion groups and where some of his manuscripts were damaged for want of decent living conditions. So while the American pragmatists and Bakhtin shared a world of change and uncertainty, their experiences of it could hardly have been more different.

It is hardly surprising that political readings of Bakhtin's work abound. Hirschkop (1986), for example, sees a number of Bakhtin's ideas, including novelistic discourse, carnival, and dialogue, as attempts to confront Stalinism and its culture by using concepts of a popular subversive tradition. Though the specifics of particular political readings of Bakhtin are hotly debated, most commentators agree that Bakhtin's work on experience and discourse is a response against the totalizing tendencies of movements as diverse as totalitarian governments and scientific rationalism, indeed any movement that forecloses on individuality and personhood. Specifically, his response is an attempt to carve out a niche for the humanities in discourse on personal and social life. For Bakhtin, the humanities highlight the weight of each particular moment and encounter, the proper corrective to totalizing tendencies.

Bakhtin's resistance to totalizing systems and their associated morality—like Dewey's social and political philosophy—strongly influenced the ways in which he conceptualized experience and the commitment he made to felt life. He thought that totalizing systems worked by alienating people from the most meaningful quality of everyday experience, the particular response formed in relation to and with others from which a sense of self emerges. This analysis led Bakhtin, especially in his early essays, to focus on developing a clear sense of individuality. For example, in *Towards a Philosophy of the Act* his concern was with how a sense of self emerges in everyday activities. In contrast with those approaches described in chapter 2, his approach to activity is to focus on how individuals intone acts of living and knowing. By 'intone' he means how individuals make acts their own, how they make them unique, personal experiences through the particularities of interpreting, feeling, and making value judgments and distinctions that are ethically worthwhile. Thus, although experience always occurs in cultural, historical, and material contexts, meaningful engagement depends on the event or action being felt, known, and valued in unique ways. This is also the kind of meaningful engagement that transforms people and systems.

If Dewey gets us some of the way from social practice to meaningful experience, Bakhtin takes us the rest of the way to the primacy of felt life. Perhaps his suspicion of system would not allow him to settle on and idealize community as the American pragmatists, including Dewey, did. His resistance to reifying any social structures takes him to the point where one of the central focuses of his work is the way in which individuals continuously reinforce and de-stabilize each other, and in the process create selfhood. As we will see later, this is the kind of nonconformism that leads him to propose that all unity is relational or dialogical, a claim that is central to his radically processual view of human experience. His suspicion of system also pushed his conceptualization of the particular moment and intoning of experience to a methodological focus on small personal lives. For him the formation of subjectivity and intersubjectivity occurs in a world of "proper names" (Bakhtin 1993, p. 53) in relationships between particular people who cannot be abstracted to systems.

Enriching Activity through Aesthetic Experience

In contrast with the approaches to action and practice described in chapter 2, both Dewey and Bakhtin present a view of activity as simultaneously sensual, emotional, and intellectual. And although it is more explicit and more radically personal in Bakhtin, both also describe individuals making their acts unique experiences through their own particular interpretations, feelings, and value judgments. It is all well and good to make such claims for experience; it is another matter to make them convincingly, to bring readers along and to leave them feeling that this view of activity is both viable and valuable. Both Dewey and Bakhtin try to do this by holding up aesthetic experience as the paradigm for all experience.

For both Dewey and Bakhtin aesthetic experience is the key to understanding how rich all experience can be. They argue that it is in aesthetic experience that our need for a sense of the meaningfulness and wholeness of our action is fulfilled. One of the most important points that Dewey and Bakhtin make about aesthetic experience is that it should be seen as continuous with ordinary experience. Their aim is to demonstrate just how rich experience can be and to inquire into the nature of aesthetic experience so that we can see its character and conditions well enough to use them in other areas of our lives.

Although the word 'aesthetic' is normally used to refer to fine art, Dewey's and Bakhtin's use of aesthetic experience is not reserved for art or what we normally think of as art. In *Art as Experience*, Dewey argued directly against a museum conception of art and an identification of aesthetic experience with art objects. Recently, Shusterman (2000) updated this argument by providing a rigorous defense of the aesthetic merits of rap music. Moving outside of the realms of art altogether, Dewey made links between the aesthetic experience of looking at paintings or listening to music and everyday raw aesthetic experiences that demand our attention and make us come *alive*. Here Dewey had in mind both dramatic events, such as a fire brigade speeding by, the controlled implosion of a tower block, or a particularly spectacular goal in a game of football, and more sedate activities, such as gardening and mindfully caring for a child. Making a similar move, Bakhtin drew attention to the aesthetic qualities of loving relationships in which one person values another as a separate center of value. What holds all these examples together is that they describe the kinds of moments and activities in which we live fully, activities filled with meaning and value that are also often primarily sensuous.

If aesthetic experience is not to refer exclusively to art objects, what is it that marks out aesthetic experience and gives it its value? For Dewey, aesthetic experience is paradigmatic of the potential richness of all experience not because of any single quality it possesses but because of its "more consummate and zestful integration of all the elements of ordinary experience," which gives "the experiencer a still larger feeling of wholeness and order in the world" (Shusterman 2000, p. 15). According to Dewey (1934, p. 40), the enemies of the aesthetic are "the humdrum; slackness of loose ends; submission to convention in practice and intellectual procedure."

In aesthetic experience, the lively integration of means and ends, meaning and movement, involving all our sensory and intellectual faculties is emotionally satisfying and fulfilling. Each act relates meaningfully to the total action and is felt by the experiencer to have a unity or a wholeness that is fulfilling. Not fulfilling in a shallow, self-satisfying sense, but in the sense that in connecting fully with the precariousness of living, in the suffering and undergoing, the expressiveness of experience is revealed to us. Connecting fully produces enduring changes. The world is changed by the outcome on the world of the total action and also by the changes brought about in the experiencer, whose sense of self may be transformed, and whose perspective and attitudes are likely to have changed.

An Example of Aesthetic Experience: Jazz with Courtney Pine

The first example that comes to mind of a personal experience that fits with this description of aesthetic experience involves a jazz session that I (John) attended years ago. I enjoyed jazz and I particularly liked going to sessions at the Cork Jazz Festival because there was also something about the festival experience that I enjoyed, not just this festival, I had the same feeling for the Cork Film Festival. Perhaps it was the intense concentration on something I already liked. Or perhaps it was the feeling that a fairly tame interest—listening to jazz records occasionally or going to a film every couple of weeks—became something vibrant and important for a while. Of course, the crowds of people going from one film to another for a week or one jazz session to another for a long weekend clearly demonstrated that others shared these interests with me. And in socializing with these people, what started out as simple enjoyment threatened over time to become a passion.

The general interest and involvement notwithstanding, one jazz session still stands out. Twenty years later, I would still identify it as the one that opened me up to a musical world that went beyond the immediate pleasure of listening. This was the first time I heard Courtney Pine play. He was young and relatively unknown, and I was fairly uninitiated into jazz. It was an afternoon session at the Cork Jazz Festival, not one of the major names. Somehow though word had got around that this was going to be a good session and it turned out to be a crowded house. The introduction. The expectation. The curtain. What an amazing look. The band, immaculately dressed in suits with a slight African edge. Courtney Pine holding the saxophone with love and respect. The sound. The band started to play, and from the first saxophone solo I was carried away. In hindsight it seems apposite that Pine was playing numbers from *Journey to the Urge Within*, because whatever he did that day got me in the gut. The sounds Pine made with a saxophone seemed to control my bodily response—in turn tightening and opening up my chest. But they also controlled what I was feeling and thinking. I was caught up and carried away. Why? How?

Although I could not play any instrument, I was mesmerized by what Courtney Pine did with individual notes. He seemed to go as low as any instrument would allow, and as high, and sometimes both together. When he went low, I felt low, but a low that was full of life. It really did touch an urge within. And when he seemed to play two notes at once, I felt torn. When he went high, I could feel the whole crowd around me getting up with him. And he held notes for so long that they seemed to teeter on the brink and we worried about whether they would fall off or not. That tension was only released when he released it by taking a breath and moving on. The experience was full of sensual and emotional complexity. A very respectful pose paid tribute to the genre and the instrument while the playing seemed to stretch both to the point where they might break. Other jazz that weekend got me tapping, but nothing else moved me—sensually, emotionally, and intellectually—the way this concert did. It had layers and layers of sound, feeling, and meaning. Placed alongside many other jazz performances at the festival, it made statements about what was possible with jazz but what was not always happening. The performance seemed to make a young, rebellious statement about jazz and life that I identified with. And it did so beautifully, respecting tradition, recognizing the pain of change, but changing everything in the act. It also seemed to say something about being black and having African roots, that I could not understand, but with which I felt raw sympathy. So it was not just sensually complex but also complex in emotional and intellectual terms, taking us on a journey through our values and thoughts. Values and thoughts about jazz itself, what we expected from it and were prepared to give, about tradition and change, about race and culture, and about ourselves. And it did all this with music, very few words. In going with the precariousness of this performance, experience expressed itself.

Examples of Technology as Aesthetic Experience

The suggestion that we think of technology in the way I have just been describing my experience of jazz is not new but it is not commonplace either. So there is merit, in terms of the plausibility and clarity of the suggestion, in providing some brief examples from the literature of technology being treated as aesthetic experience.

Brenda Laurel's aesthetic account of interacting with computers argues that engagement is "a desirable—even essential—human response to computer-mediated activities" (1991, p. 112). Laurel draws parallels between the experience of theatre and the experience of computers suggesting that

"both have the capacity to represent actions and situations . . . in ways that invite us to extend our minds, feelings, and sensations" (ibid., p. 32) but that in order to do so they must first engage us. By that, Laurel meant that they must draw us into a first-person experience of the action, akin to the personal, self-reflexive model of action described by pragmatists. She also describes a number of qualities of engagement or first-person experience that characterize a good experience at a play or with a computer, including playfulness, agency, and the integration of a variety of sensory modalities in the action.

Janet Murray (1997), in her book *Hamlet on the Holodeck*, explores the aesthetic properties and pleasures of digital environments that are connected with the traditional satisfactions of narrative. She interprets experience in a number of narrative microworlds, from cyber-literature and cyber-drama to virtual-reality-mediated story telling. She is concerned with the kinds of stories they make available, the power of imagination they support, and the worthiness or otherwise of the rapture they sometimes evoke. For example, VR story telling raises issues concerning the power of sensory presence and sense of participation, meeting characters who sense our presence and respond to us, provoking plot changes by our actions while still sustaining the power to surprise and delight. In her analysis she identifies three characteristic pleasures of digital environments: immersion, agency, and transformation. She is very careful not to paint a utopian (or dystopian) picture, making it clear that digital media can be used to create trashy narratives—that are intrinsically degrading, fragmented, and destructive of meaning as well as the opposite.

Sherry Turkle, who may be best known for her analysis of identity in the Internet age, also provided an interesting cultural analysis of our relations with computers themselves. Turkle (1995) identified three distinct subcultures—hackers, hobbyists, and users—based on the variety of ways in which people make sense of computers and allow computers to make sense of them. Hackers and hobbyists are part of a modernist, technological aesthetic characterized by reduction and control. They get a feel for their computers by interacting with them as machines. The hacker's pleasure is in the thrill and danger of pushing large, complex systems to their limit in almost out of control projects. The opportunity to exercise their virtuosity in risky situations is a key part of their aesthetic. In contrast, hobbyists enjoy controlling small machines such as personal computers. Their pleasure is in neatness and control. For a user, the computer is only of interest to the extent that it supports an application. In this context, the myth of the IBM is that it is like a car you could control. The myth of the Macintosh is that it is like a friend you could talk to. In much the same way as we get things done socially by negotiating with people, the Macintosh design entices us to get things done on our computers by negotiating rather than analyzing. The interface is a space for exploring, negotiating, and tinkering. The aesthetic is one of simulation, playing, and surface manipulation in blissful ignorance of underlying mechanism.

So if ours is not the first attempt to describe technology as aesthetic experience, what does it offer that is new? First, it suggests a clear continuity between aesthetic and prosaic experience that is not always evident when the focus is on computer games and cyber-drama. For our approach to work, we need to be able to make an aesthetic contribution to discussions of nurses using patient care record forms, people shopping on the Internet, and pilots using their procedure manuals. Second, in keeping with the spirit of pragmatism, we try to develop tools to be used in analyzing aesthetic experience with technology. Third, although our analysis, like some of those outlined above, does provide a means for discussing individual experiences, it also attempts to go beyond them to look at connections between individual experiences and their history and circumstances.

The Rhythmic Dance of Aesthetic Experience

In turning to aesthetic experience, Dewey brings to the fore the rhythms of life, the tension and release of engagement, and feelings of vulnerability in the face of our own needs and desires. Thomas Alexander's reading of Dewey's aesthetics suggests that "the rhythmic flow of life is the basis for our experience of meaning and value in the world" (1998, p. 11) and that it is in the rhythmic dance of resistance and release that "both self and world become imbued with felt, emotionalized, or expressive significance" (ibid., p. 10). The rhythmic dance of aesthetic experience has an internal, dynamic structure. Dewey identified closely related processes such as cumulation, conservation, tension, and anticipation to refer to the internal dynamics of experience.

Cumulation refers to the build-up that attends the temporal unfolding of an experience. As we saw above, when listening to jazz, emotionally this can be felt as tension or anticipation, intellectually as an increase in the internal complexity of the work or as deepening of meaning. Without such a build-up there is no fulfillment, and without fulfillment there is no aesthetic experience. The experience of shopping for books over the Internet seems designed to be cumulative. Browsing, searching, putting goods into a shopping basket, going to a checkout, receiving an email confirming the order and further emails notifying of progress, and finally the box. The box has the supplier's name on the side and an amount of padding inside. Getting at the books, opening them, feeling and smelling them, ensuring that they are as ordered is slightly delayed by the sturdy packaging. It seems to both protect the books and build up the tension one last time before the experience is complete.

Conservation refers to the tendency to hold onto some of what has gone before, be it energy or meaning. For Dewey, oppositional forces—energies resisting each other—required to hold a physical entity together are also required to constitute a whole experience. Listening to jazz, movement in one direction is followed by movement in the other, and any resistance in this rhythmical pattern of movements conserves energy until it is released and expanded. Meaning can also be conserved as the meaning of a Journey to the Urge Within was conserved from number to number in that session. The character of Courtney Pine as visually and musically presented ensured that. It is similar to reading a book or watching a film; what happened in the past is carried in the present. We rarely need to go back over what went before in order to make sense of the present. The past is somehow embedded in the present, and Dewey argues that, by virtue of its compression in the present, it forces the mind to stretch forward to what is coming.

Tension refers to both the opposition of energies within the experience and between people involved in the experience. With respect to energies within the experience, Dewey is concerned with the rhythmic interplay of compression and release that gives life to experience. "Resistance prevents immediate discharge and accumulates tension that renders energy intense. Its release from this state of detention takes necessarily the form of sequential spreading out." (Dewey 1934, p. 179) Tension results from a compression of energy seeking release. As one form of energy seeks release another blocks it. The struggle between them is the source of tension. Clearly, for Dewey tension itself can be energizing. Freedom to act and constraints upon action need to be in balance to create tension, and therefore energy. Too much freedom or constraint, and by implication too little of both, decreases the energy available for an activity. In aesthetic experiences, the tensions undergone and problems encountered deal with the reciprocal relationship between parts of the experience. They are concerned with the integrity of the experience itself.

Stores selling books on the Internet can take advantage of the energy entailed in tension. For somebody who is very interested in books, an Internet bookstore can be a potential Aladdin's Cave, full of unimaginable treasures. But most people can only afford to buy a limited number of books on each visit. The tension between desire and capacity is played out through personal recommendations and reviews that draw the buyer in. Putting books in your shopping basket but delaying the decision to buy, or which to buy, adds to the tension.

Anticipation can be seen as occurring in two temporal phases. The first occurs before the aesthetic experience as such has properly begun: the buzz going around a jazz festival that this newcomer is something special. The second relates to what happens during the aesthetic experience. Anticipation is strongly related to the continuity of experience discussed earlier. When an expectation is met, the past is conserved as if the antici-pation is folded naturally into the experience itself. When experience does not come up to our anticipation, it is as if conservation is breached. This brings us up short and we find ourselves intellectually reflecting on the experience, teasing out failures of means as if they were separate from ends. Of course experience can exceed anticipation, in which case we find our-selves pleasantly surprised or even overwhelmed by the richness of the experience.

Cumulation, conservation, tension, and anticipation describe the inter-nal dynamics of any integrated experience. While experience cannot be aesthetic without being integrated into a rhythmic dance of resistance and release, not all integrated experiences are aesthetic. What makes them aesthetic is the dynamic, always moving toward fulfillment:

That which distinguishes an experience as aesthetic is conversion of resistances and tensions, of excitations that in themselves are temptations to diversion, into a move-ment toward an inclusive and fulfilling close. (Dewey 1934, p. 56)

This close should not be confused with an end point, some kind of fracture in the seam of experience. It speaks more to the quality of each moment of aesthetic experience than to a place in time, to the sense of unity in each moment and between that moment and all the others:

The form of the whole is therefore present in every member. Fulfilling, consummating, are continuous functions, not mere ends located at one place only. An engraver, painter, or writer is in process of completing at every stage of his work. He must at each point retain and sum up what has gone before as a whole and with reference to the whole to come. (ibid., p. 56)

Although analysis of the internal dynamics of aesthetic experience points up qualities that help me to describe and make sense of aspects of that jazz session with Courtney Pine or the experience of buying books on the Internet, there are limits to the perspective on experience that it offers. This analysis can be a useful tool for trying to understand why a particular experience is not as rich or fulfilling as it might be. It can also help us to answer questions about why a person would find a particular technology boring or the experience of interacting with the technology fragmented. However, as a description of the internal dynamics, its usefulness begins with the onset of an experience and ends with its conclusion, and there is more to experience than that. For example, for Dewey the rhythmic dance also connects aesthetic experience to its history and circumstances. The dance involves a continuous interplay between past, present, and future, each shaping and renewing the others:

. . . the principle of continuity of experience means that every experience takes up something from those which have gone before and modifies in some way the quality of those which come after. (Dewey 1938, p. 35)

At its best, continuity becomes growth or an unfolding of potentiality. We see this when continuity between experiences increases a person's power to perceive differences and to engage effectively with his or her environment. Certainly my engagement with jazz, which has developed over time into interest in the history, characters, traditions, philosophy, and form, has enhanced my critical perception of music. Realizing what can be done has made me more discriminating and less tolerant of what I see as mediocre music, by which I mean jazz that does not have an edge. More than that my experience of jazz demonstrated for me the potential for emotion and intelligence in music, in other arts, and in other activities. I feel dissatisfied if I am not passionately—emotionally and intellectually—engaged with whatever I am working on. It also showed me how it is possible to be respectful to tradition and passionate about pushing to the edge at the same time. In terms of unfolding perceptual powers, this results in impatience with fusions that are not respectful of the soul of jazz.

Are rhythmic dance and the unfolding of potentiality relevant only to experiences with art and music, or does it make sense to talk about technology in this way? For example, would these concepts help us to understand Murray's experience with digital literature, Laurel's with computer games, or a nurse's with an electronic patient record? When we turn to specific technologies, we could start by inquiring into the quality of engagement.

- Do the technologies connect or fragment experience and life?
- Do the technologies help to enrich our experience of what we already value, or do they impoverish it?
- Do the technologies facilitate unfolding potential, critical perception, and engagement?
- Specifically, does the Internet increase the potential for new relationships and new forms of communicating, or does it inhibit relating?

We can also explore the aesthetic implications of introducing new technologies into an organization:

- Does bringing technology into the organization help to connect values, emotions, and physical activities, or does it fragment them?
- Is it respectful to tradition—the meanings already given to activities and artifacts by workers in the organization—while at the same time offering the kind of edginess that can release potential?
- Does the introduction of new technologies respect the stories we tell ourselves about what is important while also allowing us to create new stories?

The last point, which emphasizes the relationship between tradition and innovation, can involve a delicate balance. For example, in my (John's) long experience as somebody committed to Macintosh computers, the introduction of colored casing for Macs did not respect the Mac tradition and the Mac values I cared for—it made them too much like children's toys—but the Titanium G4 Powerbook did, and it also expanded the universe of stories available to me as a Mac user. Its lightness and sleekness and its titanium casing fused adventures on a human-computer interface with adventures in space in an enchanting way. It made sensuous, emotional, and intellectual sense of the edgy Mac aesthetic that I had bought into over the years. It is worth noting that an aesthetic approach to technology is not against function in any way, just against an exclusively functional approach to understanding relations between people and technology. The Mac must work and the software must function properly. The point is that the analysis should not stop there.

Experience as Simultaneously Aesthetic and Ethical

Deborah Hicks (2000, pp. 231–232) draws attention to the closeness of aesthetic and ethical experience in Bakhtin's work, both leaning on a rich, engaged responsivity to the other:

> Responding, in Bakhtin's early essays, entails richly seeing. Bakhtin contrasted the kind of seeing that might be characteristic of scientific inquiry with artistic or aesthetic contemplation. In the special case of aesthetic seeing the artist forms a felt and valuational relationship to the object of her activity. . . . Aesthetic contemplation entails seeing this separate center of value as unique and then forming a response to it from the special value position that is one's own. This kind of seeing can entail strong feelings; minimally, it requires more than an instrumental or objective response.

The close proximity of aesthetic and ethical aspects of experience should not be too surprising. From a pragmatic perspective, both aesthetic and ethical experience derives from the feelings, emotions, and values that populate responsive relations with others. Aesthetic and ethical experiences are both aspects of the consummation of self in an other. With respect to aesthetic experience, Hicks (ibid., p. 231) puts it as follows:

> As individual persons come together in an experiential moment, each reflects particularistic value centers. If this moment is one in which the individuals are responsive (answerable) to one another, an enriched experience is created. The particularity of one value center enhances that of another; as Bakhtin describes things, one value center (one individuated subject) envelops another, enriching the other with an outside perspective.

One's ethical sensitivity to an other is intimately related to the creative act of authoring self in other. One center of value, valuing another as an other is an act of authorship that is both aesthetic and ethical. Aesthetic seeing creates another consciousness (or center of value) and completing or finishing off this other to whom one is committed is an answerable or responsive act. Aesthetic experience is created in prosaic moments of answerable engagement, which are made possible by the aesthetic experience of completing the other. Out of the particularities of a dialogical relationship come both—and inseparably—the aesthetic experience of absorption in an other and the ethical experience of answerability to the other.

For Bakhtin, then, enriched, aesthetic experience is created from moments of answerability, the weight of which is located in the relationship between self and other in that moment. For him, the weight of lived moments of experience is felt in answerable engagement with a responsive other. According to Dewey, aesthetic experience involves the interpenetration of self and the world of objects and events, or self and other, according to Bakhtin. This interpenetration of two centers of value, involving what Hicks (2000, p. 231) calls "richly seeing," entails felt commitment to the other, seeing the other as a center of value.

The pragmatist aesthetic approach to understanding relations between people and technologies works best within a worldview characterized by creativity and dialogue. We are not presented with aesthetic experiences fully formed rather we make something of our encounters with jazz or technology. In the sections that follow we describe the process of making something out of what is given as situated creativity and we describe the world that makes situated creativity possible as dialogical.

Experience and the Creativity of Action

For pragmatists, creative action is always embedded in human situated freedom; the freedom to make something out of what is given, to construe and respond to the situations that one inevitably meets (Joas 1993, 1996). With creativity at its center, it might be useful to think of pragmatist ideas of action and experience as like the prosaic creativity of children playing. In play, children are not interested in achieving unequivocal ends and they overcome problems by imagining new ways of acting or by inventing new descriptions of the situation in which they find themselves. In the pragmatist model of action, the relationship between means and ends is radically reformulated such that action is both means and ends. Children play with paints not just to create pictures, but also to enjoy the experience of making colors and marks, and to have the tactile pleasure of feeling the texture of paint on their fingers. The child's experience of paint is that it is both useful and enjoyable. The two aspects are experienced as a complementary whole, part of the qualitative immediacy of a situation, with no need to separate them. Play, even adult play, is a context in which these unnecessary dualities—means and ends, use and enjoyment—are resolved. For example, people generally don't make love solely to reproduce. The action is useful, enjoyable, and creative, and the means and ends—making love—are indistinguishable. Play is also a very mindful model of action. Children and adults at play can imagine a variety of possible courses of action even while playing, and demonstrate a quiet readiness to experience and to round off experience. Both approach situations not in service of pre-set goals but creating goals and the means to achieve those goals in the height of their engagement with the world.

Let us think for a moment about how these ideas relate to our experiences with technology. People make practical distinctions between those technological tools that are simply a means to an end, where the technology is mere material at the disposal of our intentions, and those that can be both means and ends. For those that are mere means to an end, the potential complementarity of use and enjoyment is lost. We all make the distinction in different places. For some of us, a spreadsheet is merely a means to process numerical data: for others it a very enjoyable way of making sense of situations and events through creating and viewing patterns. For some, a chat room is merely a means of contacting people or getting information on a particular topic: for others, it is almost a way of life. While the boundary is in different places for different people, it is clear that the difference between what goes on one side of the line and what goes on the other can best be characterized in terms of the potential the technology offers for engagement in what would be, for us, a meaningful experience. To make space for this kind of conceptualization of experience with technology we have to be able to see potential in everything and be open to surprise at any time. This suggests a view of the world as an open, unfinalized, and unfinalizable place where every person and thing is always a dynamic process of becoming, always open to the future.

From Being to Becoming

With his commitment to unfinalizability, Bakhtin brings a deep sense of mystery to his treatment of experience, which is only challenged by a knowingness that forecloses on potential, the knowingness of stability and permanence that is "being." If I definitely know that a telephone is an auditory medium of communication, I miss the potential for making it a text-based or pictorial medium. Bakhtin's commitment to unfinalizability embodies values central to his thinking such as his concern for surprisingness, potentiality, freedom, and creativity. For Bakhtin (1984, p. 166), "nothing conclusive has yet taken place in the world, the ultimate word of the world and about the world has not yet been spoken, the world is open and free, everything is still in the future and will always be in the future."

Bakhtin's ideas about the world as open and unfinalizable resonate with ideas about matter as becoming and alive that we find in Ilya Prigogine's work on the thermodynamics of non-equilibrium systems. Prigogine's work, which is given an accessible treatment in *Order Out of Chaos* (Prigogine and Stengers 1985), argues that molecular systems have an irreducible element of unpredictability. They have a capacity to surprise that is not due to any shortcomings in measurement and that will not be diminished by any increases in knowledge. Molecules in far from equilibrium systems respond in exquisitely surprising ways to tiny shifts in the parameters of their existence and in relation to each other. Perhaps the best way of putting it is that they self-organize in ways that we could hardly have imagined. Prigogine and Stengers give as an example the appearance of chemical clocks. When we think of chemical reactions, we imagine molecules floating through space, colliding with each other, and reappearing in new forms. A chemical clock's behavior is different. Prigogine and Stengers (ibid., p. 13) put it as follows: "Oversimplifying somewhat, we can say that in a chemical clock all molecules change their identity *simultaneously*, at regular time intervals." It is as if they all simultaneously change color or shape following the rhythm of the chemical clock reaction. This is a description of matter as constantly becoming, a kind of non-deterministic order based on communication, that is characteristic of biological and social systems. In non-equilibrium systems, it is not just that it is impossible to calculate the trajectory of molecules rather that trajectory is not an adequate concept for their non-deterministic, irreversible behavior.

The important point for us about Prigogine and Stengers's and Bakhtin's work is that it describes what we tend to miss in the world because we have already finalized it in our minds. We tend to close our minds to the potentiality of the physical, biological, and social world, having already decided what everything is. Because of this, we fail to notice the essential creativity of our relationship with every "thing" that is. In a world that is always becoming, we create the thingness and eventness of the world, even physical reality that "is revealed to us only through the active construction in which we participate" (ibid., p. 293). This is not some kind of utopian statement about human creativity, it is simply a recognition that we have a hand in creating the world in which we live—good, bad, and indifferent. We exercise our creativity by giving shape to a world that is always open and unfinished. The material world described by Prigogine and Stengers is multiple, temporal, and complex, "seething and bubbling with change, disorder, and process" (ibid., p. xv). It, like Bakhtin's description of experience and Dewey's allusion to children's play, presents a world always becoming, and invites us to see technology as always becoming.

Embracing unfinalizability ensures that the pragmatist approach to the creativity of human action is not undersold. Pragmatist creativity is too easily read as a process of trying out different ways of thinking and acting that already exist. This approach to creativity, as revealing what is already given, seems natural in a view of the world as closed and stable where nothing is created whole cloth. However, as we have already seen, the pragmatist's worldview is dynamic and open and accommodating of the emergence of radically new ways of thinking and acting. In a world of change, the same action can have different meaning and significance, as the context is always different. In an open world, all action is creative, a fresh use of intelligence producing something surprising and new every time. Bakhtin's way of rendering action as creative is to locate unfinalizability in ordinary everyday processes such that they are always open to surprise, potential, and creativity. Thus, action retains its eventness by always being open to the future. It is never concluded, the potential it creates is always in the future, and its meanings are indeterminate. In such an open, free characterization of human action, action is always potential and always becoming, constituted dialogically in responsive relations.

Dialogicality

If pragmatist aesthetics requires at its center a view of action as situated creativity in a world that is always becoming, pragmatist creativity in turn requires a view of the world and the things in it as less stable and less entitative than many epistemologies allow. With the emergence of relativity and quantum theory, Bakhtin reflected on the possibility of any unity or truth in the face of what appeared to be constant change. In the new world being described by the physicists, unity could not be assumed. Following their lead, Bakhtin argued that in this world, nothing (or even no-thing) *is* in itself. By this he meant that any unity is always a matter of work and is always accomplished relationally or, to be more precise, dialogically. As Holquist (1990) described it, Bakhtin's appeal to dialogue is an attempt to develop a theory of knowledge for a time when matter is understood in terms of relativity and when coincidence between sign and referent cannot be assumed.

When we see molecules as separate entities interacting with each other, matter as static, a computer as an information-processing machine, the human body as bounded by the skin, an organization as composed of its members and resources, a community as already established, and social structures as pre-existing action into them, we are thinking monologically. All reification or finalization, whether it has to do with physical, biological, or social systems, is monological. In contrast, thinking dialogically involves being open to the relational processes that constitute molecules, bodies, communities, and personhood. Dialogics is sensitive to the particularity of felt life and to individual agency, even the agency in matter that Prigogine and Stengers allude to. Dialogically, cells and cell walls are understood in terms of the relations that constitute them, the cell wall seen as a process mediating between inside and outside. Dialogically any unity is composed of many voices in unfinalized conversations that cannot be reified monologically.

Dialogics and Dialectics

Bakhtin contrasts his dialogical approach with dialectics, which we met when reviewing Lave's work in chapter 2. Lave's dialectical account of cognition in practice, which has been quite influential in Computer-Supported Cooperative Work, describes activity in terms of the irreducible unity of person-acting-in-a-setting. Although dialectical accounts such as Lave's are oriented toward the interactions between people and the settings in which they find themselves, Bakhtin dismisses them as lifeless because they reify individual agency and particular evaluations diminishing the potential for real surprise and creativity. From the perspective of dialogics, the world is a lived event. Dialectically it is the mechanical contact of oppositions, things rather than people. The following quote from Bakhtin (cited on p. 57 of Morson and Emerson 1990) expresses his position on dialectics and clarifies what is original in dialogics:

Take a dialogue and remove the voices (the partitioning of voices), remove the intonations (emotional and individualizing ones), carve out abstract concepts and judgments from living words and responses, cram everything into one abstract consciousness—and that's how you get dialectics.

Any form of knowledge that takes the open-ended dialogue that is nature as described by Prigogine and Sengers and human activity and experience as described by Bakhtin and turns it into a monologic summary misrepresents its unfinalizable spirit. This is one of the reasons that Bakhtin turns to the literary novel for his exemplification of aesthetic experience—it is a dialogical methodology and embodies a dialogical approach to truth and unity.

If we describe John's experience at the Courtney Pine jazz session in terms of the properties of the improvising jazz musician, the emotional potency of music, and John's character or personality, we are producing a monological account that reifies particulars and particular people to types. If, however, we do it in a manner that is open to surprise and potential, that is sensitive to the different voices involved and to the emotional intoning of actions, and that makes space for emerging subjectivities—as a novel can— we are oriented toward a dialogical worldview. It would also be very easy to describe a nurse interacting with a patient and mediating her interactions with a patient care record in monological terms. It would be much more difficult to attend to the feeling, emotional responsivity between one particular nurse and one particular patient and between each of them and the variety of medical and lifeworld voices that people their interactions. But that is the kind of orientation that supports aesthetic experience, a dialogue between particular selves and particular others.

Dialogue, Self, and Other

In a dialogical worldview, understanding or making sense of an experience occurs in the tension between self and other. I only make sense of my self in terms of how I relate to others and to my own history of selves—the way I was and the way I would like to be—which are, like these others, always already in the present. In his introduction to Bakhtin's *Art and Answerability* (1990), Holquist notes that for Bakhtin aesthetic experience always involves a person perceiving an object, a text, or a person as something actively fashioned into the whole that it is. As the object, text, or person is not given as a whole but made whole in relational activity, consummation of the experience is treated as a shaping or finishing-off. Indeed Bakhtin goes so far as to treat it as an act of authorship. His emphasis here is on the unique perspective of the person involved in creating aesthetic consummation, the person perceiving, where perception is always from a uniquely situated place in the overall structure of possible points of view. The salient point in Bakhtin's characterization of aesthetic experience is that each person occupies a situation in existence that it is his alone. Perception from that situation is perception from a unique perspective. Bakhtin refers to this uniqueness of vision as a person's "excess of seeing," which is defined by the ability each of us has to see things that others don't see.

The uniqueness of our perception leads ineluctably to the aesthetic consummatory experience that prefigures all others, the consummation of ourselves in others. The paradox of our uniqueness, our excess of seeing, is that we are fated to need the other to consummate ourselves. As we all occupy a unique place in existence, we can share surroundings but not a field of vision. Each of us can appear in the other's field of vision but not in our own. I can look at my own body, but I cannot see myself doing so. What I can see about you that you cannot see about yourself constitutes my excess of seeing or my surplus vision over you. This surplus allows me to complete an image of you, to create a picture of the world in which you are located for me. For Bakhtin, this is the act of authorship. As I provide form and create an image of you, I relate to you as an author relates to a hero. From my excess of seeing, I create another whole consciousness, and I relate to this consciousness as a center of value different from my own.

Holquist (1990, p. xxix) describes the process as follows:

. . . the other is perceived as in the world, in an environment, while "I" exist in a world that enfolds me in a unique relation to my ends and is thus experienced as having an intimacy and reality different from that of the environment in which others are consummated as finite entities.

According to Morson and Emerson (1990, p. 185), this is the prosaic, everyday, aesthetic act on which more noticeable acts depend:

This essentially aesthetic act of creating such an image of another is most valuable when we seek not to merge with or duplicate each other, but rather to supplement each other, to take full advantage of our special fields of vision. In daily creativity— the real prosaic creativity on which more noticeable creative acts depend—you and I formally enrich each other and the world. Properly performed the aesthetic act in daily life involves a reassumption and a reconfirmation of one's own place after the other is encountered.

The self is not reducible to the temporal and spatial constraints that make consummation of the other possible. From its own perspective, the self is not located in space and time in the same way as the other. The other is in the world of beings and things, occupying finite space and time, consummated as a finite entity. Perceived in this way, there is a completeness, uniqueness, and unity to the other. From the perspective of the self, the other is so rounded out that it is a consummated, self-sufficient whole. In contrast, the self cannot see itself in that way. It is tied up in the incompleteness of its own story, unconstrained by time and space, unsettled. It suffers from a lack of vision with respect to itself. The excess or surplus of the other is required to make up for the self's lack and to consummate the self. The aesthetic experience for the self requires the other but also a return to self. It centers on the self, returning to itself to take advantage of its own surplus and outsideness. In this moment, the self is authored. Consummation of self entails a dialogue with the other—a meeting of two consciousnesses—that confirms the unique perspective and value of the self, allowing the self for a moment to experience unity and completeness.

In *Author and Hero in Aesthetic Activity*, Bakhtin portrays the relationship between the author of a novel and the hero in a novel as a metaphor for social relationships, particularly self-other relationships. He describes the author-hero relationship as a meeting of two separate consciousnesses. In terms of the aesthetic event or experience, he places great emphasis on seeing the other as separate from oneself—the hero as separate from the author, for example. Without this separation, it is not possible to treat the other as a unique center of value and to respond appropriately to him. Relationships therefore can be consummated only when those involved treat each other as separate centers of value. Hicks (2000, p. 234) suggests that Bakhtin, in his description of the relationship between author and hero, foregrounds "the ways in which others create the conditions for selfhood through the particulars of their affective and valuational response." For Bakhtin, the relationship of one consciousness to another consciousness, as an other, is constitutive of aesthetic experience.

The Sensuality of Self-Other Relations

It is important to see the sensuousness in Bakhtin's portrayal of one consciousness relating to another. For example, Hicks draws our attention to the sensuousness of Bakhtin's depiction of the constitution of selfhood in social relationship. She points to the emotional tone or shading that enables or "images forth" individuality. She makes her point with a quotation from *Art and Answerability* that evokes feelings, emotions, touch, connection, and separation:

As soon as the human being begins to experience himself from within, he at once meets with acts of recognition and love that come to him from outside—from his mother, from others who are close to him. The child receives all initial determinations of himself and of his body from his mother's lips and from the lips of those who are close to him. It is from their lips, in the emotional-volitional tones of their love, that the child hears and begins to acknowledge his own *proper name* and the names of all the features pertaining to his body and to his inner states and experiences. The words of a loving human are the first and most authoritative words about him; they are the words that for the first time determine his personality *from outside*, the words that *come to meet* his indistinct inner sensation of himself, giving it a form and a name which, for the first time, he finds himself and becomes aware of himself as a *something*. (Bakhtin 1990, pp. 49–50)

The self is constituted in the tones, lips, and responsivity of the others, as much as in their words. The elements of a dialogical relationship cannot be separated from each other. No element is abstracted from the aesthetic experience and reified as the signifier of dialogue, separate from the others. Unlike those who treat meaningful experience as a text, Bakhtin does not accept that the eventness of an event, the livedness of experience, can be reduced to text. Experience must be understood as an event, the eventness of which carries the weight of emotion, volition, and value. Devoid of that weight, as it is when treated as an object of cognition, experience is hollow. It is not lived experience at all. The moment of experience is lost.

There is a sense, in Bakhtin's description, of the weight of experience being in the body, or the dialogues within and between bodies: "The child receives all initial determinations of himself and of his body from his mother's lips. . . ." Bakhtin pays great attention to the embodiment (or, as Morson and Emerson put it, the enfleshment) of experience. He carefully draws attention to the physicality of bodies in a place, and to dialogue occurring between bounded entities. The body plays a pivotal role in dialogizing experience. The awareness of difference between one's own pain and discomfort and another's pain described by that other affirms a boundary between self and other. I can only imagine your pain; I can never experience it. The observable materiality of the beginning and end of other bodies is contrasted with the imagined or potential beginning and end of our own in an unsettling inner dialogue. Here, in a partial contrast with the pain example, I can observe other people being born and dying but I can only imagine my own birth and death. Another border, another dialogized experience, and these borders can be interpersonal or intrapersonal. Here is the weight of moment-to-moment, dialogical experience that Bakhtin wants us to notice. An embodied self, an organism participating in life, has no choice but to act, and no alibi for not acting, for not engaging, given its stake in all that is happening.

Conclusions: Aesthetic Experience and Technology

We began this chapter with a reminder from Geertz (1986) that cultural analyses must engage with felt life or experience if they are to connect with people's concerns; we ended it with an evocation of the sensory and emotional intimacy of relationships between particular selves and others. The pragmatic approach to experience is an invitation to hold up this intimacy and the rhythmic dance of aesthetic experience as the paradigm for experience with technology.

Following Dewey and Bakhtin, we also see the pragmatist position as a political act, the proper guard against the kind of reification of human-computer relations that emerge from many functional, sociocultural, and systemic accounts. It involves a series of commitments outlined in this chapter, including the following:

• a sustained commitment to the particularity and agency of emotionally and volitionally intoned action
• people doing and suffering, striving, loving, and enjoying, acting and being acted upon—a language that brings us into the realms of felt life
• the particular response formed in relation to and with others from which a sense of self emerges
• people making acts their own personal experiences through the particularities of interpreting, feeling, and making value judgments.

In order to take full advantage of the pragmatist approach to aesthetic experience in our inquiry into technology, we must begin to see technology in terms of situated creativity and dialogicality. This may not be very easy for designers and analysts who see their activity as bounded by the technological system with which they are concerned. Seeing technology as aesthetic experience requires that we see any boundaries between humans and technology as constituted by the dialogical relations sustaining them and that we see human-technology relations as always open and becoming. This is not presented as a utopian perspective on technology. We are aware that technology and even the language of becoming and dialogue can be used to enthrall and mystify as much as to clarify and open us up to the potential and surprise that we might otherwise miss.

Finally, we see the pragmatist position as a practical act. As well as putting the basic concepts for describing felt experience in place, it provides a methodology for making these concepts useful in people's lives. It offers aesthetic experience as the paradigm that illustrates how rich all experience can be because of its zestful integration of all the elements of ordinary experience. In this chapter we analyzed experience from two perspectives: (1) from the perspective of the internal dynamics of experience, which are described in terms of a rhythmic dance of cumulation, conservation, tension, and anticipation, and (2) in terms of the connectedness of aesthetic experience and its history and circumstances. Both provide us with tools for looking at experience to see where it falls short of what might be possible, tools which in this chapter have been used to generate indicative questions about people's experience with technology. In the next two chapters we will take this practical aspect a step further by inquiring into how an experiential analysis of people's relations with technology would look.

4 | The Threads of Experience

Emotion is the moving and cementing force. It selects what is congruous and dyes what is selected with its color, thereby giving qualitative unity to materials externally disparate and dissimilar. It thus provides unity in and through the varied parts of experience.

—J. Dewey (1934, p. 42)

In the previous chapter we discussed some of the main characteristics of a pragmatist approach to experience. As well as introducing the reader to pragmatism and to Dewey and Bakhtin, we drew attention to the role that aesthetic experience plays in their work. Dewey and Bakhtin use aesthetic experience as the paradigm of rich experience and both of them attempt to restore the continuity between aesthetic and ordinary experience. They are not interested in describing aesthetics as something grand and separate from ordinary experience, rather in using it as a tool for reviewing ordinary experience in all its potential value, meaning, and vitality. Our aim in this book is to present technology as experience in an effort to see relationships between people and technology in all their potential value, meaning, and vitality. In this chapter and the next, we describe those aspects of a pragmatist perspective that will help us with this task. We start by characterizing what we refer to as the four threads of experience.

The Four Threads of Experience

In order to be consistent with the pragmatist view of experience and inquiry outlined in chapter 3, it is important that we recognize the threads of experience for what they are. They are not fundamental elements of experience. Rather, they are ideas to help us think more clearly about technology as experience. They provide ways of talking about technology that heighten sensibility to people's experience of it. The four threads that we pick out from our reading of the pragmatist literature are the *sensual*, the *emotional*, the *compositional*, and the *spatio-temporal*.

The Sensual Thread

The picture Dewey paints is something like the following: It is through sense organs that living creatures participate directly in the world about them. The sensual thread of experience therefore is concerned with our sensory engagement with a situation, which orients us to the concrete, palpable, and visceral character of experience. It draws attention to things being grasped pre-reflectively as the immediate sense of a situation in which the wonder of the material world is made actual for us in the quality of experience. When the functions of the senses are fully realized to give this sense of the situation, the interaction between person and environment becomes participation and communication. Owing to the immediate and vital capacity of the senses to mediate communication between person and situation, any derogation of the senses narrows and dulls life experience.

Dewey describes a mechanic who has a *strong sense* of an engine and of the interaction between his tools and the engine. He can hear the slightest problem with an engine, and he can feel the rhythm of an engine running smoothly or a spanner turned a fraction tight. Not all mechanics have the same sense or sensory engagement. Dewey's hypothetical mechanic is an example of someone who has made what he does meaningful for himself—the situated creativity, which we described in chapter 3. This is someone who is "interested in doing well and finding satisfaction in his handiwork, [and] caring for his materials and tools with genuine affection" (Dewey 1934, p. 5). He is interested and committed, and he believes that the quality of his work and workmanship matters. His involvement and his sense of things make the work intrinsically meaningful for him. He does not have to think too hard about what a particular sound means, as he has a sense of "the meaning of things present in immediate experience" (ibid., p. 22). We have all experienced this kind of sensory engagement in our conversations with others. Engaged conversations are never just about the words; they are also about the sound of words uttered, the way in which they are intoned— words spoken lovingly, helpfully, or authoritatively from one person to another in a particular situation. And in any particular situation, it is never just the words spoken; it is also the eyes, the hands, and the body. Looking into another person's eyes as you speak to him is a different experience from looking away for both the speaker and the hearer. The same words spoken in the same way carry different weight when accompanied by supportively holding the other person's hand or touching him on the shoulder. We can see sensory engagement in the irreducible sense of immediately feeling unwelcome in a group, or feeling a room as cold and distancing, being comfortable or tense when operating a piece of technology, or feeling close to someone who is in fact miles away on the end of a telephone. We see it in mechanics who have a strong feel for engines, in mathematicians who sense pattern in numbers, in teachers and parents who know from a child's stance or tone of voice that something is wrong, in teenagers dancing to music that seems to control their very bones, and in dressmakers who work with their fingertips.

According to Dewey, industrialization has tended to separate work from interest and leisure and to compartmentalize aspects or phases of work so that people often don't have the kind of complete, satisfying meaningful experience that fosters engagement. In industrial societies, action, emotion, insight, and thinking are separated from one another; they are all separated from the senses; and the senses are separated from each other. In this context, Dewey (1934, p. 21) writes:

We undergo sensations as mechanical stimuli or as irritated stimulations, without having a sense of the reality that is in them and behind them: in much of our experience our different senses do not unite to tell a common and enlarged story. We see without feeling; we hear, but only a secondhand report, secondhand because it is not reinforced by vision. We touch, but the contact remains tangential because it does not fuse with qualities of senses that go below the surface. We use the senses to arouse passion but not to fulfill the interest of insight, not because interest is not potentially present in the exercise of sense but because we yield to conditions of living that force sense to remain an excitation on the surface.

A work docket passing a job from one department to another to facilitate finishing off work on a product that has already been started allows those in the second department to see the work that has been done without feeling it, and hear only secondhand reports. In this context, our sensory engagement is fractured or compartmentalized. Compartmentalization of the senses is inconsistent with the quality of experience that Dewey argues is important for human growth and development. For that, holistic engagement is required, with the whole person participating in the events in his world. Of course, for Dewey the ultimate compartmentalization that inhibits engagement and hinders full participation is the compartmentalization of the person into the body and the mind, the senses and the intellect, intelligence and feelings. A by-product of these compartmentalizations is the derogation of the senses and, as sense organs are the means of participation, a dulled life experience.

The importance of sensory engagement for our understanding of contemporary technologies can be seen in children's interactions with GameBoys and cyber-pets, in teenagers' appropriation of text messaging as their expression of perpetual contact with the other members of their communities, in teenagers' and adults' involvement in computer mediated relationships, and in the almost universal love affair with the mobile phone. Teenagers and adults, keen to participate in new forms of communication, overcome the constraints of the primitive input devices for text messaging on their mobiles. More than that, they make something sensual and expressive out of what seems like primitive text messaging. People caught up in the social worlds that they have helped to create in cyberspace can spend hours at their computers interacting with others. The body, the senses, and the physicality of the technology are intrinsic to interaction. Children playing with GameBoys demonstrate this most clearly. They often seem to crouch over this small object that they have grasped between their hands as their thumbs respond with great speed and dexterity to the sights and sounds of the game. Very often these children are so absorbed in the game that they cannot hear or see anything else around them. They are completely attentive, engrossed, intensely concentrated, and immersed or lost in an activity. Benson (1993) sees this kind of absorption as one of the pivotal characteristics of an aesthetic experience in which there seems to be a breaking down of barriers between self and object, even an outpouring of self into the object.

We are used to thinking of various technologies as computational devices, and to some extent we privilege the computational in our discussions of technology. In academic discourses, computers are seen as the zenith of the relationship between humans and technology. They help us to think. One day they might even do the thinking for us, and of course thinking is seen as the height of achievement. Turning the spotlight for a while from computation to engagement encourages us to look at technologies as artifacts that people can experience, that open up possibilities for participation in new actions, for engaging and absorbing experiences.

The Emotional Thread

Let us start again with the picture Dewey paints. Like his approach to the senses, his description of emotions resonates with creativity, change, and dialogue:

Joy, sorrow, hope, fear, anger, curiosity, are treated as if each in itself were a sort of entity that enters full-made upon the scene, an entity that may last a long time or a short time, but whose duration, whose growth and career, is irrelevant to its nature. In fact emotions are qualities, when they are significant, of a complex experience that moves and changes. . . . All emotions are qualifications of a drama and they change as the drama develops. (1934, p. 41)

The pragmatist use of emotion is different from our habitual way of thinking about emotions as things that exist independent of experience. We traditionally treat emotions, such as joy, hope, and fear, as entities that come on the scene fully formed. Yet no emotion exists independent of the particular circumstances connected with it and the character of the experienced event permeates the emotion, whatever name we give it. The joy of solving a problem is not the same as the joy of requited love. The frustration caused by an unresponsive partner is not the same as the frustration caused by an unresponsive computer. For Dewey, emotions are qualities of particular experiences. They are the color shot through the experience that holds all aspects of the experience together and makes it different from other experiences. The emotions at work in an experience belong to a self engaged in a situation and concerned with the movement of events toward an outcome that is desired or disliked. It does not exist separate from the person, the situation, or the feelings of the person toward the situation.

According to Bakhtin, a person's unique values and feelings with respect to a situation and the direction in which he sees it developing shade his actions. Action, in this sense, is permeated with what Hicks (1996, p. 107) called "the moment-to-moment 'oughtness' in which particular agents were responsive to particular situations of being." According to Bakhtin, this moment-to-moment oughtness invests each human act with an emotional-volitional tone and answerability, which is particular to the person, the object, and the situation and which is more like faithfulness than adherence to a set of norms. This dialogical interpretation of emotion is echoed in a more recent treatment by Martha Nussbaum, who argues that emotion views the world from the perspective of our goals, needs, desires, and values and she suggests that emotions are best seen as judgments of value:

. . . emotions are forms of evaluative judgment that ascribe to certain things and persons outside a person's own control great importance for the person's own flourishing. Emotions are thus, in effect, acknowledgments of neediness and lack of self-sufficiency. (Nussbaum 2001, p. 22)

Dewey, Bakhtin, and Nussbaum evoke people struggling for emotional unity and having a sense of their freedom and creativity. They also evoke a sense of the constraints of their commitments, values, needs, and goals, and of their need for others to achieve any unity. Thus, the emotional thread refers to value judgments that ascribe to other people and things importance with respect to our needs and desires. Our frustration, anger, joy, and satisfaction acknowledge our need for others in our struggle to achieve emotional unity. And as our relations with these others (people and things) change, so too do the emotions. In that sense, emotions are always becoming: lust can turn into love and ultimately satisfaction; frustration can turn into hope and joy as the drama develops.

In a research project concerned with how various individuals in a hospital construe and use information (McCarthy and O'Connor 1999), we found that nurses, doctors, and managers saw their work and their construction and use of information in terms of patient care. However, each of them construed patient care differently. An approximate account would say that nurses saw patient care in terms of a personal relationship between the nurse and the patient, and the information they valued helped them relate to and care for individual patients; that medical consultants saw patient care in a much more clinical light and valued information that helped them to look after the patient medically; and that managers saw patient care in terms of the effective treatment of as many patients as need treating, whether they are in the hospital or not, and valued information that helped them ensure that patients could be treated efficiently so that space could be made available for patients not yet in the hospital. This situation resonates with Bakhtin's treatment of events and persons as individually toned and emotionally shaded when "they are brought into correlation with a unique participant and begin to glow with the light of actual value" (1993, p. 47). Of course, a relationship between a nurse and a patient is not the same as that between manager and patient. Nurses can get to know their patients as persons; managers deal with patients as a group or collection most of the time. As we will show in the next chapter when discussing the merits of Mead's "generalized other," this does not necessarily imply that managers are detached from patients or have less concern for them. In this regard, we read the test that Bakhtin sets as insisting that managers treat patients as living and speaking, rather than as reified entities or mere statistics, not that they should necessarily meet and know every single patient. It is an emotional-volitional relationship with speaking and living others that gives an event its eventness or the quality of felt life.

At the risk of belaboring the point, we feel we should emphasize the implications of the emotional-volitional perspective developed in pragmatist thinking. That perspective asserts that what we would generally think of as cold computational processes—perceiving, thinking, reasoning, decision making, categorizing—are shot through with values, needs, desires, and goals. We do not perceive an objective representation of the world; rather, we perceive a unique version colored by our unique desires and values as experienced in the situation we are engaged in. This means that in experience there is no given system of activity. Activity entails feelings and a moral response that make different people's experiences with the same system, or even the same people's experiences of a system at different times and in different activities, radically different. Moreover, this is not a point about an individual's subjective state or private thoughts. It is not an argument that a situation can be different in different people's heads and hearts. That would be a trivial point in comparison. Remember, experience does not refer to these subjective states, but to the irreducible totality of people acting, sensing, thinking, feeling, and making meaning in a setting, including their perception and sensation of their own actions. It is not the subjective state that varies from experience to experience, but the totality of people acting and making sense of their action in a setting. According to Hicks (2000, p. 230), "this lived moment of intonings and responsive engagement was what Bakhtin described as the act or deed." Hicks further argues that Bakhtin "depicted acts of experience as meaningful only inasmuch as they are felt, known, and valued in unique ways" (ibid.).

The Emotional, the Sensual, and Sense Making

Before we move on, we should be clear about the relationship between the emotional and sensual aspects of experience that we have been discussing separately over the last two sections. Sometimes emotions are engendered through a sense of our own accomplishment or failure in response to immediate sensory reactions. A nurse who manages to master his or her sense of disgust at the sight of a badly infected wound or anxiety at the sight of blood is likely to feel a sense of pride and professionalism. A rock climber who exercises control over sensations such as fear or anxiety to reach the summit may feel a heightened sense of achievement. As we noted earlier, these emotional responses become part of the history of experience that colors our sensual response next time around.

Let us take some more prosaic examples. When you go to buy a mobile phone, you are presented with a stunning array of beautiful objects toward which you might feel attracted. But other issues that influence a choice of whether to buy a mobile phone or which one to buy include cost, functionality, and ease of use. Although you might get a thrill from buying the most beautiful one, it might entail a commitment to a higher monthly charge. In this context, the meanings ascribed to objects such as mobile phones are emotionally laden. They involve judgments of value. In terms of your needs, desires, and values, how important are cost, coverage, beauty, and fashionability to you? As Dewey and Bakhtin realized, judgments of value permeate these decisions.

Whether or not sensual attraction to an object or a person is welcome depends on our needs, desires, and values at that particular time. Such attraction could be unwanted and lead to frustration or disgust or it could complement the emotional-volitional content of the experience. Consider suspense movies. Here we are on the edge of seats feeling at first hand what it would be like to be stalked by a murderer but at the same time safe in the comfort of our home, insulated from real consequences. Such fear is produced, as Boorstin (1990) pointed out, by careful crafting of a compositional structure. To some extent such manufactured sensuality is enjoyable at an emotional level. That is why suspense movies are popular. In the case of a badly crafted movie, the suspense can become too much and the emotional response of boredom, disgust, or simple dissatisfaction with the quality of the film can lead one to stop watching.

Although we are writing about the emotional and sensual threads here as if they occurred separately in time and influenced each other through feedback, it is important to remember a core message from Dewey and Bakhtin that any experience is simultaneously sensual, emotional, and intellectual—

that is, relational. It attempts to capture something of the relationship between subject and object or self and other. At least to that extent, emotion is always directed at something or someone: boredom at a film, anger toward a friend who has let you down again, grief for the loss of a parent, joy in the presence of a baby, hope in the message of a leader. As Nussbaum clarifies, although emotions are often hot and urgent, they should not be confused with what we think of as animal or uncontrollable urges. This confusion arises from the unhelpful separation of emotion and thought in some philosophy and cognitive psychology, with emotion being hot and irrational and thought being cool and considered. This view does justice to neither emotion nor thought. The identity of any emotion is inextricably linked with how the person "having" the emotion sees the object or person toward which the emotional response is directed, and what he or she believes about that object or person. Nurses distrust the hospital information system because of what they believe it does to their relationship with patients. This is clearly an emotionally and intellectually intoned response.

The line we are trying to develop here is that the emotional quality of experience is an understanding or sense-making process, as is the sensual quality that we discussed earlier in the context of engagement. Our view of experience as adaptive depends on a strong characterization of the various aspects of experience as sense making but not all the same kind of sense making and not reducible to each other. We have already seen that the sensual aspect is concerned with the sense or meaning immediately available in a situation. Now we are suggesting that the emotional aspect is concerned with the sense or meaning ascribed to an object or person because of the values, goals, and desires we have.

The Compositional Thread

The compositional thread is concerned with relationships between the parts and the whole of an experience. If one is looking at a painting, 'composition' refers to the relations between elements of the painting and their implied agency, and between viewer, painting, and setting. In an unfolding interaction involving self and other, in a novel, play, or technologically mediated communication, it refers to the narrative structure, action possibility, plausibility, consequences, and explanations of actions. In Internet shopping, the choices that are laid out for us can lead us in a coherent way through "the shop" or can lead us down blind alleys. Attention to the compositional thread evokes questions: What is this about? What has happened? Where am I? How do these things go together? What will happen next? Does this make sense? What would happen if . . . ?

If we think of experience as the ordinary, everyday flow of events, many of which pass by us unnoticed, aesthetic experience stands out as satisfying, enlivening, and sometimes challenging. As we have already emphasized, it is not that some activities or events are intrinsically satisfying and others not; rather, the aesthetic quality of the event reflects the way in which person and event relate to each other.

Let us go back to one of our earlier examples: For some mechanics, working with an engine is just a way of making a living; for others, it is something to which they feel personally committed. The latter appreciate and care for their tools and are repaid by those tools. They enjoy their own handiwork. Perhaps they feel that it is a way of expressing themselves. The work is meaningful to them. They put themselves into the activity of caring for a car or a motorbike, and they are repaid by the enjoyment of an immediate sense of value and meaning. For those mechanics, working on an engine is more than a nondescript event in an undifferentiated flow of events. Each moment is movement toward an inclusive and fulfilling close, a consummated whole in itself, but also with reference to the whole to come.

But even a highly skilled mechanic could be forgiven for seeing one engine as just the same as another, one job as arbitrarily intruding on another. However, this would make for "uneventful" work, in which events and objects never clearly emerge from situations, precisely because the sense and meaning of those situations is never constructed. From our earlier discussion of experience as ongoing transaction between person and environment, it should be clear that what we might call the natural structure of experience is not pre-constituted. In some areas of life, a person's transactions with the world could lead uneventfully to the satisfaction of that person's needs and desires—for example, going through the motions at work in order to earn money to engage more fully with other aspects of life.

Faced with the potential arbitrariness of experience, a meaning-making creature or culture may try to bring a meaningful quality to experience. The doing that we engage in can be mindless or mindful. The more we attend to that doing, the more likely our experience is to be meaningful and of value to us. We can also make decisions about the beginnings and ends of experiences, which would dissolve some of the arbitrariness.

Jackson (1998) calls this "framing experience." By framing our experiences and giving ourselves as fully as possible to those experiences that we have deliberately framed, we begin to bring structure and meaning to them. We already do this in a number of ways, to a greater or a lesser extent. Some of us create a specific slot in our day for reading or writing. Others set an hour aside each day for a social lunch, during which we give our attention to eating and conversing, and make a serious effort not to be distracted— for example, by switching off our mobile phones. Yet others set time aside for playing with their children, probably between arriving home from work and getting the children to bed. We even call it "quality time." It can, of course, involve larger chunks of time, such as would be the case with a gardening project undertaken over a season. The fact that we distinguish between quality time and special projects on the one hand and just responding to events on the other suggests that we cannot make the effort to frame our experience all the time. Nonetheless, the point is that if experience is to be aesthetic, we have to put some effort into it by thinking about what we do and by providing a meaningful background against which the meaning of events can emerge.

An important question with respect to the meaningfulness of experience is whether some technologies facilitate framing, or even whether different technologies facilitate framing in different ways for different people. For example, for some people an hour playing with slot machines is a heightened experience with a clear beginning and end, and even a distinctive pattern of engagement. Imagine a person who buys a fixed amount of change to play the machines and is quite happy to leave when the change is spent. It may be that for such a person gaming machines offer an hour of pleasurable interaction every so often—that there is pleasure in the rhythm of involvement rising and falling during the hour and in the tension of each attempt increasing with the number of coins left. For another person, the same activity and technology might be meaningless and entirely absent of pleasure. This could be a person who simply cannot frame the experience because he can't end it, or it could be a person who can't see the point in even starting the experience because it makes no sense to him. Our earlier discussion of interaction with Macintoshes and Personal Computers offers a second example of the potential for technology framing experience. One way to read the two aesthetics is in terms of the way in which the structure of interaction with the Macintosh is meaningful for some people and meaninglessly arbitrary for others, and vice versa for the PC. For a user, working with files and folders quite like the paper ones they already have is a meaningful, framed experience. For a computer hobbyist, computer files are not like paper files, and the hobbyist isn't satisfied unless he has a working knowledge of what is going on beneath the surface. More than that, hobbyists seem to want their interactions with the computer to reflect that need, at least to the extent that they prefer abstract hierarchical file structures to files in folders in other folders.

It seems that meaningful framing of experience is transactionally accomplished with the effort of the person being repaid by the quality of some experiences. For me (John), setting time aside to visit the Tate Gallery in London was repaid by the experience of entering the Rothko Room for the first time. The small number of huge paintings, with their dark tones and fuzzy edges, created a sacred space and experience. The paintings, and especially the way they were hung together in one room, created the opportunity for a special experience. But a quick run through as part of a milling crowd could never complete the experience. It requires time and effort, a commitment to sit and be in the presence of the paintings in that room. It doesn't have to be an explicitly art-related moment to be aesthetic, nor does it have to be quite so intense an experience. For Peter, building a wall for the first time was also aesthetic and transformational. As an academic living in an area where people typically do their own building and maintenance, and with family involved in the technical aspects of building in the past, he found that this experience brought past and present together in creative fusion with an immediate sense of meaning and value. The intrinsic satisfaction of the work was met by the value of visibly participating in the culture of the neighborhood, a kind of ritual of passage into membership. Prosaic activities such as buying books and creating a home page can also be approached aesthetically. The important clarification is whether the tasks are completed in a relatively detached way as means of getting to an end from which one is relatively alienated or as activities that are personally meaningful, enjoyable, and approached creatively.

According to Dewey, aesthetic experiences are refined forms of the prosaic experience. As we have seen already, 'experience' refers to transactions between us and the objects and events that make up the world in which we act. When we are immersed in experience, the elements of experience so interpenetrate each other that we lose our sense of the separation of self, objects, and events. Distinctions between these elements are highlighted when something goes wrong with an experience or when we pause to reflect on the experience for some other reason. It is in the context of such a breakdown in experience that we isolate elements to try explicitly to make sense of what is happening. The aesthetic experiences we described above—our experiences engaged with paintings and computer systems—are readily characterized by our immersion in the transaction. We lose sense of the separation of the painting and ourselves. We are part of the painting and the painting is part of us. There is no gap to be bridged between person and object. In this context, aesthetic experience is used to shine a light on experience that falls short of the richest experience we can imagine and, in the process, to provide a model for design and evaluation.

The Spatio-Temporal Thread

All experience has a spatio-temporal component. An intense emotional engagement can make our sense of time change. A frustrating experience can leave us perceiving space as confined and closeting. Space and time pervade our language of experience. We talk of needing space to settle an emotional conflict, and of giving people time. Experiences of space and time are constructed through interaction. Time may speed up or slow down, pace may increase or decrease, spaces may open up or close down. Space and time may be connected or disconnected. In our construction of the spatio-temporal aspect of an experience, we may distinguish between public and private space; we may recognize comfort zones and boundaries between self and other, or between present and future. Such constructions affect experiential outcomes such as willingness to linger or to revisit places or our willingness to engage in exchange of information, services, or goods. Coyne (1999, pp. 174–175) also asserts the centrality of a temporal quality to experience:

Some grant that we can interpret time in many different ways, but the phenomenon of time itself is an absolute. History may be a construction, there is no returning to what actually happened in the past, and memory plays tricks on us, but our inability to capture precisely a past moment does not dissuade us from affirming our existence in a present with a past behind us and a future ahead.

For Bakhtin, all contexts are shaped by the quality of time and space that they produce. Although many philosophers took time and space to be fundamental, pre-existent categories of thought, Bakhtin's orientation was toward the quality of relationships between people and events on the one hand and their space-time on the other. He saw different genres in novels as containing qualitatively different senses of space and time. For example, Bakhtin describes the action in Greek Romance as occurring in adventure time, in which characters seem not to be affected by the passage of time or experience. The hero and the heroine, who are destined for each other from the beginning, do not change, mature, or even get older as a consequence of time or their experiences. There is no reason in the internal logic of these novels why the adventures that occur could not be longer or shorter or composed in a different order without doing damage to the sense of space-time being conveyed. However, within each particular adventure in the story, the sense of time is heightened. Things happen in the nick of time, and action becomes intense and irreversible. Though the action in many such stories occurs in a city, on a mountain, or at sea, the particular city, mountain, or sea does not seem to matter very much. Time and space are, according to Bakhtin, "undifferentiated' in these novels. They are just the background for the story.

In the nineteenth-century novel, the detail of historical time and place permeates action and experience. In these novels, character and personality are shaped in important ways by the particular time and place in which people live. What a person can do, think, or feel is strongly related to the values and customs of a specific, changing place. Many of the women in Jane Austen's novels, for example, are characterized as testing the limits of the conventions of their time and place. Here we get a strong sense of the struggle for personal meaning in the tension between identity and normativity that we see as commonplace now. It is expected that teenagers rebel and that people struggle against the constraints imposed on them by their circumstances. In the nineteenth-century novel, people change as a consequence of their experience and we cannot predict from the outset whether the heroine and hero will get together at the end. What happens in between is crucially important in this regard. In contrast with the Greek Romance, where characters are propelled through space-time by fate and chance events, characters in the nineteenth-century novel try to take initiative and control over their fate.

In the novel of emergence, people and the world in which they live exhibit a genuine sense of "becoming," or change and development. Neither the people nor the world in which they live are given ready-made; rather, they are created by the efforts and actions of specific people living particular lives. Although the characters in a novel of historical emergence are saturated by the time and place in which they live, they are not determined by it. On the contrary, they retain initiative, even to the point of trying to shape the time and place in which they will live. These characters live into the future, imagining how the world might be, not satisfied with being and doing but always striving toward becoming, making the new world with their own efforts. The novel of emergence, especially when contrasted with the treatment of space-time in earlier genres, raises issues of potential, creativity, freedom, and initiative in a way that takes account of the fullness of time, the inner connectedness of past, present, and future. In the fullness of time, the past and the present are not finalized, for they are always playing into or becoming a future.

In the novel of emergence, the realization of a person depends on a complex relationship between a rich interior and a rich exterior life. The novel of emergence produces heroes with unrealized potential and demands looking to the future. Indeed the future penetrates deeply into the heart of a novelistic hero who is shown more as what he could become than what he is. The characters in a novel of emergence cannot be produced by history, systems, conventions, or dogmas, because the major contribution of the novel of emergence is to recognize potential: the potential of emergent histories and the potential of the individual that can be found nowhere else. Here the unfinalizability and dialogicality of experience are made visible as we see the past and future in present objects, events, and situations.

We contrast qualitatively different characterizations of space-time in different novelistic genres in order to make visible the salience of space-time in felt, lived experience. As ways of seeing, valuing, and expressing human experience, the novelistic genres described above make visible experiential contexts in which people are respectively indifferent to time and place, constrained by it, and always creatively connecting past, present, and future. As cultural memories for ways of seeing and valuing, they reveal a cultural-historical unfolding of prosaic experience from the disconnected monological to the deeply involved dialogical. Morson and Emerson (1990) help us to push this way of seeing a little further by proposing a range of questions about any experience that try to uncover the space-time quality of that experience. Their questions include the following:

- Are actions dependent to a significant degree on where or when they occur?

- What kind of initiative do people have? Are they beings to whom events simply happen, or do they exercise choice and control? If the latter, how much, and of what kind?
- Is time open with multiple possibilities, or is it scripted in advance?
- Depending on the degree and kind of initiative people have, what kind of ethical responsibility obliges them?
- What kind of creativity is possible?
- Does social context change? If it does, in what ways? Are time and space shaped by events that take place in them?
- Do personal identity and character change in response to events, or are they fixed? If they change, how, when, and to what degree?
- Are people understood as entirely "exterior," or is there real "interiority"? If there is real "interiority," of what kind is it?
- How does the past impinge on the present, and what is the relation of the present to possible futures?

As we have seen, Bakhtin's treatment of the novel as a way of seeing, valuing, and expressing experience brings various qualities of experience into view that might not otherwise be apparent. Contrasting genres shows us how the quality of the space-time in which we live has implications for whether we experience life as emergent or as determined (with every moment full of potential or already determined). Moreover, the novel of emergence reveals the dialogicality of experience as potential, enabling us to see the past, the present, and the future together in a moment.

Analyzing Experiences with and through Technologies

In order to clarify the value of a pragmatist approach to analyzing people's experiences with technologies, we will now take a closer look at some examples. The first comes ready made. As mentioned previously, Jon Boorstin is a Hollywood screenwriter and filmmaker who has written about people's experiences of Hollywood movies with a view to describing what it takes a create a good film experience. His framework for analyzing film experience echoes what we have just presented as the threads of experience. It involves a description of three ways of seeing movies, which closely relate to the sensual, emotional, and compositional threads. It is important to note how Boorstin treats these not as separate components but as different ways of seeing in which the relationships between the different ways describe the experience.

Three Ways of Seeing a Movie

Boorstin (1990) suggests that the key to understanding how we respond to film is to understand that we experience or watch movies in three ways. Each way has a distinct pleasure and magic associated with it. Boorstin refers to his three ways of seeing as the voyeuristic eye, the vicarious eye, and the visceral eye. He suggests that as we watch a movie, the three compete within us.

Boorstin's *voyeuristic eye* is a bit like our compositional thread. It is a way of experiencing film in terms of the simple joy of seeing the new and the wonderful. It is the consummatory pleasure of watching for its own sake. "The voyeuristic eye" refers to getting up close to things and really looking at them but becoming bored as soon as the experience of seeing the newness of the thing has run its course. Boorstin gives us the prosaic examples of people watching fireworks or a group of children huddled around insects. With fireworks, we are captivated by the amazing display of color, explosion, and pattern until it seems to us that we are seeing the same thing over again. A great fireworks display adds one new visual experience on top of another until the climax, never holding us too long at any level. Likewise children watch insects for ages, seeing how different they are from us and from each other, and how differently they behave. But once a child has watched a bit too long, familiarity breeds contempt.

As the mind's eye, the voyeuristic eye can be quite skeptical, and it requires a high level of plausibility and credibility. When it experiences events that seem implausible, it is inclined to disengage. What appears on the screen must contain surprise and plausibility to seduce and enchant the voyeuristic eye. There is no magic without a new look at things, but that new look must make sense in the world being experienced, even if it is a fictional or fantasy world. As we have already seen with respect to novelistic genres, even fictional worlds have a quality of space-time that contextualizes everything that happens in them. If we see something that seems impossible in a certain space-time, we are inclined to be disappointed. If we are inclined to think "That couldn't happen," our engagement with that cinematic experience is threatened.

In the early days of cinema, the voyeuristic eye was seduced by the magic of the projected moving image. As the projected image became passé, more was required: talk to go with the action, more and more precise synchronization of talk and action, highly precise editing, adherence to a more sophisticated grammar of cinematic action that took account of how the audience would fill in the gaps. As we viewers become more experienced with a medium, it takes more to enchant the voyeuristic eye. However, designers should bear in mind that less can be more enchanting as long as it gives us something new and wonderful. For example, Boorstin describes films by Charles Eames as miniature masterpieces because they make us see anew simple objects such as spinning tops. These short films do this without story, characters, or even a point. They stand or fall in terms of voyeuristic pleasure on the back of the visual logic threading through the images.

The *vicarious eye* is attentive to the emotional substrate of action rather than to its internal logic and plausibility. It may be an even more powerful factor in our experience than internal logic, because we can make allowances for what seems illogical if we are made aware of an emotional truth underlying it. The vicarious eye sees with the heart. It is a way of seeing that is informed by our own sense of incompleteness and also by our sense of the other's incompleteness, our need to matter to others, and our need to please others. It enables us to respond to the slightest shift in other people's feelings. This kind of seeing depends on the emotional-volitional intoning of action that we discussed earlier in this chapter and is pivotal to the dialogicality and answerability of experience that we discussed in the previous chapter. It is the kind of seeing that has us investing part of ourselves in another person and that moves us.

Whereas the magic of film can be threatened voyeuristically if a viewer feels "That couldn't happen," it is threatened vicariously if a viewer feels "That character wouldn't do that." It is not just the consistency of the world created in the film that has let us down, it is a person in whom we believed and with whom we engaged emotionally. On the other hand, when we are won over by a character who fulfills his or her promise, anything implausible in the action can be overcome by the conviction that "Yes, that character would do that." But fulfilling promise is no easy thing. For that we need the depth and complexity of character that has us wanting to be that character and at the same time to judge him. We don't become intensely emotionally involved with caricatures. Intense emotional involvement requires the tension that is part of seeing the other as another center of value who sees the world in his own way, a center of value with whom we want to identify and disagree simultaneously. Of course this is the kind of aesthetic relationship friends have with each other or a parent has with a child.

So vicarious seeing is a very personal kind of seeing in which what is seen matters deeply to us. It is seeing into the face and eyes of the other, the emotional space that conveys his deepest feelings, needs, and desires.

But film also shows us that even the most fulfilled character cannot be seen separately from the world created in the film. For the vicarious eye, the basic unit is not the beat of the story but the moment of the character. In great moments, story time stands still and the pleasure of the new and wonderful is irrelevant. But a film cannot be enchanting if it is made up of great moments alone. The editor has to create a rhythm and movement between the voyeuristic and vicarious to keep us engaged intellectually, emotionally, and valuationally.

The *visceral eye* is attuned to first-hand experience of thrill, joy, fear, and abandonment. Here the character is a conduit for the viewer's feelings rather than the other way around. Unlike the vicarious eye, the visceral eye is not interested in characters in the empathic sense; it is interested in having tokens for our sense of thrill or fear. As we feel the thrill and fear of people on a roller coaster, we are not empathizing with them, rather we are having our visceral experience through their activity. However, it is a thrill or fear cosseted by the knowledge that it is not actually you that is being attacked by an alien or free-falling from 10,000 feet. As character is not empathic in the visceral experience, it is closer to montage than story, narrative, or connectedness. It consists of moments of gut reaction, and we viewers are carried along by those moments as if on a roller coaster.

Of course the magical experience can have visceral, vicarious, and voyeuristic elements together and competing with one another. In film, visceral alone can't be enough. We build up resistance to every thrill the director creates for us so that (as Boorstin puts it when evaluating the visceral aspect of the magic of film) twice as much comes off as half as effective. The visceral impact of films like *Psycho* and *Alien* depends as much on the characters we identify with as on the thrills of the action. The visceral shock of the shower scene in *Psycho* depends on Hitchcock's manipulation of the story to that point such that a tale of love and embezzlement becomes a tale of murder. He builds up to the visceral moment by playing with our voyeuristic and vicarious pleasures.

Boorstin does not have an analytic category that corresponds to our spatio-temporal thread, but he considers in some detail how filmmakers can manipulate people's experiences of time and space. By careful editing they can make moments seem like hours and create a sense of three-dimensional space on a flat screen:

Philosophers may theorize about subjectivity, but working filmmakers try to learn exactly what it means to say that time is flexible, a function of our inner clock. They study how long a second really is, and how short, and what makes it feel one way or the other. They know that what we see isn't really what's out there because they've learned how spatial perception varies with angle and focal length and lighting, how "true" colors are a figment of lighting, and context, and even the glass of a lens. They know there is no "real" sound but only a better or worse approximation of what our ear expects. (Boorstin 1990, p. 198)

Boorstin's analysis of the magic of movies suggests that, in a media-savvy world, a combination of wonder at the new, sensuous interaction, and emotional response to characters is required to create an experience. Boorstin's analysis develops from an understanding of the play of appearance as dialogical, with multiple perspectives on novelty, emotional tone, and sensuousness in constant interaction with each other against a shifting magic standard. It shows us that even our prosaic experiencing and seeing can be active and highly differentiated.

In recent times we have begun to see approaches to technology design that are clearly geared toward augmenting user experience. As is the case with the experience of watching movies described by Boorstin, we see in many of these technologies a combination of wonder at the new, sensuous interaction, and emotional response.

Making Stories in POGO World

Another example of people interacting with technology is POGO World (Rizzo et al. 2003), an information-technology environment designed to empower children in the creative process of storytelling. The system has a number of tools that the children can use to create and edit a story. They include the beamer (which acts as an interface between the worlds of physical and virtual objects and allows children's drawings, toys, and other objects to be digitized), the cards (which allow virtual objects to be stored, named, and moved to other tools), the mumbos (which are used to move and modify foreground elements on the screen), the settings (a silver mat surrounded by leather cushions and the other tools), and the sound twister (which allows the children to activate sounds by inserting a sound card into the mat).

The design team observed narrative activity in the classroom before the POGO environment was set up there, then evaluated the POGO environment's effect on narrative activity while it was in place. In evaluations, teachers proposed some structured activities in which they specified timing, content, and dynamics and some free activity in which the children themselves organized the processes for creating the narrative as they wished. In the initial video analysis of the processes and analysis of the narrative productions using POGO, the combination of the threads of experience was apparent.

In the initial exploratory stage, there was a strong emphasis on sensory experience, often focusing on things that children had seen, heard, or touched. They might be objects that they found in the forest, at the seashore, or even in the classroom. Children brought personal objects into the classroom, and exploration of sensory interaction with them and little vignettes about them formed the basis of story construction. With POGO, this included turning these objects into virtual objects, which were then employed as elements of a story, using the beamer, the cards, and the sound twister for example. These tools were also designed to be satisfyingly sensuous: a mixture of gestural, manipulative, visual, aural, and material.

Later in the process, children reflected on the initial experience upon which their story was based and analyzed it by expressing it orally and in drawings. POGO facilitated recombining elements and displaying them in real time on the screen so that all the children could see what was going on and could participate in the process, some kneeling on the mat producing sounds and others gathered around the beamer manipulating elements of the story.

When pulling the story together, the children were extremely creative, making new connections among the story elements by manipulating the tools and exploring the flexibility of the tools in representing and structuring the story. Shy children were able to get involved in this process by quietly creating background, which then became part of the story, rather than being directly involved in verbally negotiating the main story line.

Although analysis of children's experience with POGO World is not complete, it is clear that when they are creating stories with it there is a sense of wonder at both the environment and the functionality of the tools. There is a strong emphasis on the sensory aspect of story and interaction with the digital technologies, which children seem to enjoy. It is also possible to see a sense of order or composition in the activities children engage in, both in the sense of there being a recognizable series of stages and a useful process of role definition or emergence. The analysts did not report in any detail on the emotional thread of children's experiences with POGO; however, in view of the interaction between children and a wonderful new environment and the strongly intersubjective nature of the process they were engaged in, it would be inconceivable that an analysis of emotion would not reveal more about the experience.

We can use the threads to analyze experience in POGO World, either to unpack some of the informal observations made in the previous paragraph or simply to walk through the environment thinking about what is and what might be.

Reflecting on the sensual thread directs us toward the sensory aspects of POGO World: the wonderful silver mat and leather cushions; children crawling around on mats eliciting sounds that they have stored; images projected anywhere, including on the children's bodies; and the strongly sensorial objects with which the children interact. It also poses questions about the sensuality of virtual objects. Can they be touched and rolled like the mumbo, manipulated like the beamer, and crawled over like the sound twister? And do they facilitate children's sharing these sensory experiences, as the tools do? The emotional thread directs us toward values, needs, and desires that lead us to ascribe importance to other people and things. In the design of POGO World we can see attention to children's needs for social interaction with other children, creative action, physical contact with others and with their environment, moving around and doing, and stimulation. It also seems from the evaluations that the children can enjoy a shared sense of satisfaction having created a story together using these tools—or frustration if they find it difficult to do so. They also get a chance to empathize (or not) with other children's feelings— for example, when it comes to sharing tools and objects and when deciding on roles.

Reflecting on the compositional thread in POGO is particularly interesting. Though we can see how the tools might form a kind of coherent whole (an information-technology environment as the designers call it), and though the activity of making a story seems to have a recognizable shape to it, the details of who does what and when can be determined by the teacher or left up to the children. In other words, answers to compositional questions such as "What is this all about?" seem to inhere in the tools and the environment, whereas answers to questions like "What happens next?" have to be set out by teachers or negotiated by the children. It would also be useful to inquire into the sense that teachers and children have of each part of the experience. Does each part feel like a whole in itself and in relation to the whole to come? Is using each of the tools to store and manipulate elements of the story fulfilling in itself, and does it also feel like an integral part of the whole activity of creating a story?

The spatio-temporal thread directs us toward the sense of space-time in the experience. We can see in POGO an exciting, adventurous shared space for children and teachers, a space in which they can have fun and learn, a space constituted by texture and technology. It would also be interesting to explore children's sense of time when working in POGO and even comparing it with their sense of time in the classroom without POGO. In terms of the fullness of space-time, we can see that there is plenty of scope in the design of this environment for the emergence of situations and characters together.

Taking the threads in combination, we can develop a sense of what the experience of interacting in POGO world is like or might be like. They suggest areas for design and evaluation and for interpretation of the children's and the teachers' experiences in the environment.

The two experiences of technology that we have described have helped us to illustrate how the threads can be used as tools for analyzing experience. So far in our analysis we have tended to talk about experience as if it had a well-defined beginning and end—for example, watching a movie from opening titles to closing credits, or, in POGO World, going into the classroom interacting with the tools and coming out at the end of a lesson. As we will see in the next chapter, approaching experience in this way alone is rather limiting. Dewey, as well attending to these discrete experiences, emphasizes the importance of thinking about the continuity and cumulation of experience over time. Nonetheless, as we have seen, it can still be useful to view experience as discrete events. Viewed this way, it leads to questions such as whether an experience was memorable, happy, sad, or satisfying. In terms of people's experience of technology, these are useful questions to ask, and Dewey offers some help in how we might approach such questions in his characterization of what he calls an experience.

Analyzing an Experience

Dewey referred to segments of ordinary experience marked by a sense of wholeness, unity, and fulfillment as *"an* experience":

We have *an* experience when the material experienced runs its course to fulfillment. Then and then only is it integrated within and demarcated in the general stream of experience from other experiences. A piece of work is finished in a way that is satisfactory; a problem receives its solution; a game is played through; a situation, whether that of eating a meal, playing a game of chess, carrying on a conversation, writing a book, or taking part in a political campaign, is so rounded out that its close is a consummation and not a cessation. Such an experience is a whole and carries with it its own individualizing quality and self-sufficiency. It is *an* experience. (1934, p. 35)

One question that characterization of an experience leads to is whether the experience has run its course to fulfillment or *completion*. The experience must come to fruition or at least feel that it is at a natural end. In POGO World, children might have a sense of the fulfillment of a POGO experience because they have successfully completed a story using the tools, or perhaps because, even though they haven't managed to finish their story, they got to use a tool they had been waiting to try. Or perhaps the sense of fulfillment could simply be due to having worked well with other children and teachers.

For Dewey, in order for an experience be complete it must be possible to differentiate it from other experiences—to see it as unique. Each experience is a whole that "carries with it its own individualizing quality and self-sufficiency" (Dewey 1934, p. 35). The individualizing quality of the experience differentiates it from what went before and after and also from other experiences that might be considered similar to this particular experience. Some days in POGO World, children might be very enthusiastic, perhaps because they get to work with a tool that they have come to really enjoy. Other days might be quite frustrating perhaps because there are too many children and too few tools and the teacher is too controlling. Either way, such days have a uniqueness about them.

In addition to completeness and uniqueness, *unifying emotion* is necessary for experience to become *an* experience. For Dewey, emotional unity gives experience an aesthetic quality, even when the experience is not predominantly aesthetic in character, and emotions are the quality of an experience. They change as the experience changes. They can be clear or fuzzy. They move with the experience as well as holding it together. Imagine the children on their first day in POGO World feeling a mixture of excitement at exploring this new environment and some of them being a little fearful and not knowing what is expected of them. But on the next day, having already become comfortable with the tools and with using them to make stories, the children might be more relaxed, perhaps feeling just as excited but worrying less about what it is all about. On their second attempt, some children may still be uneasy with the tools, they may not have managed to really understand how to use them. Whatever the particular emotion, the point here is that the quality of an experience, the thing that holds it together, is the emotional tone. According to Dewey, the emotions at work in an experience belong to a self engaged in a situation and concerned with events moving toward consummation. Without this emotional engagement, any experience would lack unity and would fail to be *an* experience.

Conclusions: The Continuity of Experience

In this chapter we have described the threads of experience, carefully positioning them so that they are seen not as fundamental elements but as a pragmatic tool for thinking about experience. We have seen how Jon Boorstin uses a very similar approach in his analysis of film making. We have also demonstrated, with the example of children making stories in the educational information-technology environment POGO World, how the threads can be deployed as a means of sensitizing design and evaluation to various aspects of experience. Though this can be very useful, on its own it provides too narrow an analysis of an experience that begins with the opening titles and ends with the credits. If we were to leave it at that, we would make the same mistake that Laurel (1991) did.

Laurel's analogy between theatre and human-computer interaction raises some important points about experience and engagement, but they tend to be limited to the time and space between onset and conclusion of an event. For example, when she identifies action potential as a particularly important quality that contributes to engagement, her analysis is bounded by the beginning and end of a play. Action potential, which refers to the set of possible actions that could happen at a given point without loss of coherence, is considered to be very high at the start of a play and gradually reduces as we move toward the finale. At the same time, the continual revealing of events generates in the audience a set of expectations about what the play is about, what might happen and, more important, what they would like to happen: "The shape of a play can be visualized in terms of the pattern of emotional tension created in its audience. Typically tension rises during the course of a play until the climax of the action and falls thereafter." (Laurel 1991, p. 81) These are just a couple of examples of Laurel's concepts' being bounded by the beginning and end of an activity or an event. It is hardly surprising that her analysis takes this form, in view of her reliance of the analogy with the audience's experience of a play. Nonetheless, it is a shortcoming.

When discussing the continuity of aesthetic experience in chapter 3, we made it clear that for Dewey experience is more than what happens between the beginning and the end of an activity. For Dewey, the internal dynamics of aesthetic experience connects it with its circumstances and history through a continuous interplay between past, present, and future, each shaping and renewing the others. Our experience of a play or a movie is not confined to what we do and what we undergo for the two hours we are in the theatre. It includes the recommendation from a friend or a reviewer that enticed us to go in the first place and that sets up expectations that color our experience for those two hours. It also includes reflections on how we will talk about it with friends. Now our analysis must follow Dewey's conceptualization of aesthetic experience and include connectedness and continuity. Reflection on those processes takes us in the next chapter to an analysis of the processes through which we make sense of our experience—before, during, and after—and to a consideration of the continuous transformation of self through experience.

5 | Making Sense of Experience

We have used our relationships with technology to reflect on the human.
—S. Turkle (1995, p. 24)

We have sought out the subjective computer. Computers don't just do things for us, they do things to us, including our ways of thinking about ourselves and other people.
—S. Turkle (ibid., p. 26)

Experience does not come to us ready made. The quality of an experience—whether it is well rounded or fragmented, for example—depends significantly on our readiness to experience and to round off experience in a present. The personal meaning of an experience depends significantly on the sense we make of it given our particular history and disposition. One of the characteristic features of being a person is the urge we have to interpret and understand our experience (J. Bruner 1990, 1991, 1996). As creative, dialogical, meaning-making creatures, we bring as much to any experience as a designer, a filmmaker, or a friend brings. We make something of what they give, we make it in dialogue with them and with others, and we do it at the time, before, and afterwards.

As we sit in a cinema, we may find ourselves thinking about the film we are watching in terms of other films we have seen. Sometimes, especially if the film is not engaging us, we try to work out what is wrong with it. Whether the film engages us or not, we talk about it with friends and read reviews and commentaries. In a social gathering, we ruminate on what somebody has said to us and what it means, and afterwards we wonder what it might have meant. We ask friends what they think about something that has happened to us, or somebody new we have met. We reflect on the actions we make and the decisions we take. And very often an experience that seems to have been stored in the vaults is taken out again and revised—

for example, after one has split up with the person one met and got involved with a year ago despite friends' advice to the contrary. We keep diaries or write stories. For some of us, when experience seems incapable of expression in words, we paint or make or do something. In short, people seem to have a strong need to express and make sense of their experience, do it in many different ways, and never finish it off.

Becoming aware of or constructing a self is a particularly salient feature of making sense of experience. Making sense of a film or a jazz session, at the time, before, or afterwards—laughing at a film with the whole audience, or being caught up in the music at a session and suddenly noticing that others are not—is a dialogical event that gives rise to something new: an observation, a thought, or a feeling that tells us something about ourselves and our relations with each other, and with the world we live in. Sherry Turkle's 1995 book *Life on the Screen* documents the increasingly important role that computers play in shaping this sense of who we are. The most obvious place in which this happens is in people's interactions with others in a variety of cyberspace communities. For example, in collaborative virtual environments people can present themselves as different characters and can meet a variety of people in a variety of situations. Turkle sees this as "people turn[ing] to computers for experiences that they hope will change their ways of thinking or will affect their social and emotional lives" (ibid., p. 26). But people may also construct themselves in subtler ways in their interactions with computers. One example that we have already discussed is the way in which some people are very committed to PCs and others to Macs. Another is the way in which "different people make the computer their own in their own ways" (ibid., p. 267) some using it as no more than a word processing machine, others connecting to a wide networked world with it, still others using it to support such everyday activities as shopping and coordinating social events. In general, one's unique response to technology—even if that response is not to use certain technologies—changes one's way of being (or becoming) a self.

As is always the case in pragmatist thinking, there is no self without other. Therefore, in the process we are describing, whether it relates to making sense of experience in a computer-mediated social environment where the presence of others is obvious or in a growing preference for the Mac or for doing our grocery shopping over the Internet, becoming a self always happens in the context of dialogue with others.

Self and Other Making Sense of Experience

Before we further explore pragmatist approaches to self and other making sense of experience, let us make the discussion more concrete by briefly describing some research on teenagers making sense of their experiences with text messaging. What they do and how they reflect on it with each other and with researchers exemplifies important aspects of relations between self and other in making sense of experience.

Teenagers' Text Messaging

Kasesniemi and Rautiainen (2002) interviewed 1,000 Finnish teenagers in depth about their mobile phone use. With respect to teenagers' use of text messaging, they identified a number of practices that typified the way in which these teenagers understand and use text messaging and particularly how it expresses their identification with each other. The main practices that they identified are message collecting, chain-message circulation, and collective reading and composing. In an ethnographic study carried out in an English secondary school, which involved observation and interviewing, Taylor and Harper (2002) also found many cases of message exchange and message collecting.

Although mobile phones are often marketed as personal and private, teenagers read messages to each other, circulate messages among friends, compose messages together, and even borrow messages or parts of messages from each other. Sharing messages with each other can even involve swapping phones to read each other's messages. Allowing other people to read their messages is often a sign of trust and friendship, sometimes even of intimacy. Interviewees told Kasesniemi and Rautiainen that it tends to happen between partners and very close friends. Some couples look back over messages together to revisit good and bad times in their relationship.

Kasesniemi and Rautiainen and Taylor and Harper also found that for teenagers who save and collect messages, text messages and memory become intimately entwined. Take the following extract from one of Taylor and Harper's interviews with Susan, for example:

Yeah, Peter sends me loads of nice messages and I want to keep them all. It's so sad cause he sends me so many nice ones and I have to delete some. I feel horrible. . . . And like, I really don't want to give the phone back because it's got so many little memories and things on. And it's not the same having them written down . . . cause it's not from him anymore. . . . I really hate deleting messages that are nice you know. Like when someone's said something that's really sweet or just like really personal or something.

Susan attached strong emotional significance to keeping the messages in their original form: ". . . it's not the same having them written down . . . cause it's not from him anymore. . . ." Transforming the electronic messages into her own handwriting loses something of the signature of the sender. For Susan, transcribed messages become detached from the particular sender and the particular act of sending. Taylor and Harper see this in terms of the message's being a kind of gift. Think about giving and receiving gifts: the importance of the occasion of giving, the gift wrapping, the gift card, and the setting are integral to any object becoming a gift. The way giving and receiving gifts makes you feel about yourself. The sense of somebody else caring enough about you to give you something that is personally meaningful and special. The pleasure of giving a gift that the recipient loves. Taylor and Harper see personally significant text messages in a similar light. The whole ritual of sending and receiving, and the importance of the wrapping (i.e., a phone) in which the gift was received, is an important feature of the experience.

There is little doubt that text messaging influences how teenagers feel about themselves. Perhaps it is a modern form of rebellion against another generation and of carving out a space that they can call their own. And there is little doubt that text messaging can be very personal for them, often mediating intimate relations and becoming a repository for precious memories and gifts. The most important point for us is the way in which experiences with particular friends, relationships, and even phones become entwined in the sense some teenagers make of this technology. In using and making sense of their experiences with text messaging, some of these teenagers consummate self and other in what seems to be a very personal and particular way. This raises questions about the role of community in pragmatist thinking on self-other relations.

Community, Technology, and Self

As we noted in chapter 2, the notion of community has been quite influential in technology and information studies in recent years. The take-up of work by Lave and Wenger has put the design and use of information and interactions with technology into a community context (see Brown and

Duguid 2000; Rheingold 2000). This work suggests that information and technologies are always caught up in community practices. For example, the mobile phone can be seen as a tool that mediates community practices such as information exchange, social chat, and branding, and users of the mobile phone as people finding their way as participants in a community. It is not so much that it is a good thing to participate as that participation is inevitable if we want to be fully human. For example, although Lave and Wenger (1991, p. 116) recognize that conflicts, contradictions, and dilemmas are experienced in participation, they argue that they can only be resolved in situated, community practice:

Conflicts between masters and apprentices . . . take place in the course of everyday participation. Shared participation is that stage on which the old and the new, the known and the unknown, the established and the hopeful, act out their differences and discover their commonalities, manifest their fear of one another, and come to terms with their need for one another. Each threatens the fulfillment of the other's destiny, just as it is essential to it. Conflict is experienced and worked out through a shared everyday practice in which differing viewpoints and common stakes are in interplay.

Thus, Lave and Wenger's commitment to "the partially given character of an objectively structured world" (Lave 1993, p. 21) inhibits their contribution to dealing with questions about the production of community, practices, and identity to which Walkerdine (1990, 1997) and others give primacy. A pragmatic approach to community, of the sort we find in Dewey, Mead, and Bakhtin, addresses the process of emergence of community more directly. And although we agree with Emerson's (1993) analysis of the differences between the way in which the American pragmatists and Bakhtin would approach those questions, we feel that a pragmatist reading of both that does not get caught up in which better represents reality points to their complementary usefulness.

Mead's and Bakhtin's Concepts of Self-Other Relations

As G. H. Mead (1934) is the American pragmatist who most explicitly engaged with the question of self in society and relations between self and community, we will focus on his and Bakhtin's contributions in this section. In both cases we will place their concepts of self-other relations in the context of their overall projects with a view to extracting something useful from both for our current project.

Mead and Bakhtin have been treated as similar in their emphasis on the sociality (Mead) or dialogicality (Bakhtin) of human experience. Both assume that increased differentiation or diversity is accompanied by increased cooperation. Both see all activity as having a communicative quality. Both see mind and self as emerging from social activity. Both conceptualize thinking and consciousness as something like internal conversation and, crucially, selves as existing only in definite relationships with other selves. For both, I can only develop a sense of my self in the context of my relating with another person. My sense of self is something like a creative response to their response to me. All this common ground notwithstanding, Emerson argues that "Bakhtin ends up more radically and unsentimentally individualist than his American contemporary" (1993, p. 6) and suggests that the contrast between them can best be seen in their respective models of the self. We would add that those models of self must be considered in terms of the projects they serve.

Mead, like most of the American pragmatists (including Dewey), saw his project as a long-term one of building up communities and institutions— educational, democratic, occupational, legal—that would improve people's experience. Because an element of this project was to construct and renew institutions so that community could carry forward any gains and not repeat mistakes, the span of an individual life, never mind of particular moments, could not be the main focus. Mead was therefore inclined to emphasize the communal aspects of the self and because of this is often mistaken for describing a self that is shaped by processes of socialization. However, the picture he drew of the self was more complex than that.

Mead described self as emerging from living communally with other individuals, as an individually distinctive member of that community. For him "selves only exist in definite relationship to other selves" (1934, p. 164), but they are not shaped by community or those other selves. Mead's social self is not just the creature of convention and socialization; it can also transcend the idealization of community, step out of it and criticize it. And, at any stage, it is capable of impulsive responses that seem far from social or socialized. For, as well as an object self of learned conventions and other people's attitudes, there is also a recognition in Mead's writing of an aspect of self, the "I," which is the source of spontaneity that can surprise the person themselves as much as other selves. This is the immediate response of any organism to the attitudes of others. However, as a revisionary pragma-

Bakhtin has a three-part model of the self that includes the following:

- "I-for-myself"—how my self looks and feels to my own consciousness
- "I-for-others"—how my self looks to those outside it
- "the-other-for-me"—how outsiders appear to me.

These are singular categories where the other is always one particular other. Like Mead's "I," Bakhtin's "I-for-myself" is impulsive, unsocialized, potentially recalcitrant, and always somewhat dissatisfied with itself. But Emerson (1993, p. 6) argues that Bakhtin's "I" "is even more lonely, isolated, mute, and incapable of expression" and that Bakhtin's other is intensely personal. Thus, whereas Mead relies on organized communities for the construction of the active self, Bakhtin does not assume the existence of organized communities. Whereas Mead's "me" can learn to play the role of generalized other, Bakhtin has no generalized other at all. Instead he builds self on particular interpersonal relationships and this requires two parts in place of Mead's "me": a part that sees those relationships from the perspective of my self and a part that approaches the relationships from the perspective of other. According to Bakhtin, the self is created intersubjectively in dialogue with the particular, personal other.

For Bakhtin, the liberated person is not dominated by one truth or one view of the world; rather a liberated person has access to multiple truths. If we think of each individual as a unique and singular center of value, Bakhtin argues that when they come together in activities in which they are responsive to each other—sensitive to each other's thoughts, feelings, and values and trying to take account of each other's thoughts, feelings, and value in action—an enriched experience is created. The particularity of one value center envelops the other, enriching the other with an outside perspective.

In pragmatic terms, it seems to us that Bakhtin can be read as describing one kind of very rich aesthetic experience and holding it up as paradigmatic. He would try to make sense of Susan's and Peter's experiences of text messaging by looking closely at their particular technologically mediated relationship. He would explore the emergence of Susan's subjectivity in her expression of her experience of Peter's messages; the sense of Susan becoming in her emotionally intoned responses to these messages, her feelings toward Peter's kindness and her feelings toward the message as an utterance worth remembering in all the particularity and weight of the act it performs.

tist, the point of Mead's theory of self is to suggest how things 1
improved and life experience made more fulfilling. In this re
emphasized responsible and diverse participation in community a:
to greatest fulfillment. Becoming such a responsible self involves nc
reacting to other's arbitrary and individual responses to me, but al
ing to others' attitudes toward community activity, invoking "the
ized other" as well as particular others and a sense of owne:
community activity.

For Mead there is no yielding up of individuality in his pragmatic
munity activity, as individual and community are constituted in i
sonal action situations. In fact, Joas (1993, p. 23) argues that
achievement is to radically change the way we look at the problem c
ject that communicates with itself and with others. In an interp
action situation, actors are themselves a source of stimuli for their p
They must therefore attend to their own actions since these actior
reactions from their partner and become conditions for the continua
their own actions. In such situations, not only is consciousness funct
required, so is self-consciousness. Social interaction and individu
reflection are functionally coupled in interpersonal action, and a s(
self is created in such situations. Therefore, the creation of social or(
example in the construction and maintenance of communities of p:
does not require like-mindedness or normativity. Neither does it re(
process of becoming like the other, the master, or the member. It re
interpersonal action situations and human communication that
autonomous, self-organizing people.

Where Mead and Dewey saw the value of emphasizing communit
ticipation, Bakhtin saw the value of emphasizing individual dial
moments. Bakhtin resisted prioritizing social structures such as comm
because of the danger of trivializing individuality, subjectivity, and th
logical moments. In terms of making sense of experience with techn(
this eventually comes down to a subtle but important difference in the
in which they imagined the self-other relations to which we have {
some priority for the last couple of chapters. Whereas for Bakhtin self-(
relations always involve a particular other, for Mead not only may the c
be generalized; it is also important for society that the other is general
To address the particularity of the other, Bakhtin has a complex mod(
self that is worth briefly outlining here.

While the foregoing is the kind of analysis of experience and sense making that we have been advocating throughout, it seems unnecessarily restrictive to exclude any use of a generalized other and community life, and not very pragmatic if they offer something useful to the analysis. Bear in mind from our discussion of the background to Bakhtin's work in chapter 3, his resistance to social structures is a guard against Stalinism and other forms of totalitarian thinking that foreclose on experience. The cost of such an extreme guard is that it makes critical evaluation of social structures extremely one dimensional, with oppression only articulated in terms of the limitation on interpersonal contact. A pragmatist account, such as Mead's, which accepts the relevance of our experiences of institutions such as education, the law, and democratic structures, and of generalized others such as people of other races and nationalities, allows for a more richly dimensioned critical evaluation. In the context of such an account of felt life, Bakhtin remains as a constant provocateur forcing the objective, reified, environment to speak. To borrow from another philosopher, we read Bakhtin as insisting that institution are treated as living, perhaps as something like MacIntyre's living traditions ". . . historically extended, socially embodied argument, and an argument precisely in part about the goods which constitute that tradition" (MacIntyre 1981, p. 207). Such an account would enable us to consider critically Susan's and Peter's experiences of mobile phone branding, and their experience of institutions that bring people together such as a mall or a club, without allowing these institutions to remain silent.

Following Mead and Bakhtin, we see making sense of experience as always self-referential and involving us changing our way of becoming. It involves creative, dialogical processes that construct self, other, and the voicing, living traditions in and through which self-other relations occur. It also involves constructs from the past and future that become present in particular dialogical moments. In the remaining sections of this chapter, we will concentrate on describing the variety of ways in which we actually make sense of experience in practice.

Making Sense of Experience in Practice

Attending to the ways in which we make sense of experience has the potential to broaden an analysis of experience in two directions at once, both of which have already been implied and will be made analytically explicit. As well as describing any particular experience by inquiring into sensual, emotional, compositional, and spatio-temporal aspects, analysis must also attend to the history and future, the before and after that are folded into the present experience and that are themselves changed by the present experience. For example, how our anticipation of a new film from a favorite director colors our seeing that film and how the relationship between anticipated and actual in that case colors our approach to future films by the same director. As well as nodding toward a broader temporal context, the analysis must also make explicit the social or interpersonal context of sense making. For example, the filmgoer's dialogue with the film director, reviewers, the voice of film promotion, and friends who may have already seen the film.

We will start with some basic distinctions, which speak to where meaning resides and whether it always has to be socially constructed. Dewey provides a differentiated treatment of meaning that helps us understand the variety of ways in which activities can be experienced as meaningful. His treatment of meaning also highlights the temporal and cultural dimensions of his conceptualization of experience. Just scratching the surface of what Dewey has to offer in this regard, we find distinctions drawn between *intrinsic* and *extrinsic* meaning, and between the *sense* and *understanding* or *interpretation* of an experience.

Intrinsic and Extrinsic Meaning

Intrinsic meaning refers to the value of the event for the person engaged in it. It is an expressive, aesthetic meaning, which is enjoyed for its own sake. Imagine you are out for a day's hill walking and you come to a high point from which you can see for miles around. You just sit down and enjoy it. It doesn't matter much where you are, what the weather is, or what precisely you are looking at. Experiencing a panoramic view—just simply experiencing the view, the breadth and depth of it, the airiness of it, the perspective and expanse of it—can be moving, exhilarating, and fulfilling. It is meaningful in itself, enjoyed for its own sake. There is a danger that this example implies that the culmination or end of some activity is the bit that is intrinsically meaningful, and that is not what is intended. For many walkers, the couple of hours rhythmic walking up the hill is also intrinsically meaningful, enjoyable and fulfilling in itself, not just a means to get to the top. Following Bakhtin, we might say that intrinsic meaning refers to the emotional-volitional shading of the event:

The world in which an act or deed actually proceeds, in which it is actually accomplished, is a unitary and unique world that is experienced concretely: it is a world that is seen, heard, touched, and thought, a world permeated in its entirety with the emotional-volitional tones of the affirmed validity of values. (Bakhtin 1993, p. 56)

The intrinsically meaningful experience is meaningful in its own expressiveness and consummation and that meaning is enjoyed for its own sake.

For me (John), the intrinsic meaning of Internet book shopping is in engaging with the richness of a labyrinthine world of books I had never even imagined. In contrast, the extrinsic meaning of Internet book shopping is not in the intrinsic joy of the labyrinth but the usefulness of Internet book buying, the practice of shopping as a means to an end. The extrinsic meaning is that meaning put to use for a purpose outside the immediate experience that you are engaged in. Walking up the hill in order to get to the panoramic view, not really getting much out of the walk itself, again throws the focus on the end to which this walking is a means and so highlights the extrinsic meaningfulness of the experience. In many cases the wall between extrinsic and intrinsic meaningfulness is paper-thin and it even moves over time. I find Internet book shopping enjoyable for its own sake and I also shop on the Internet in order to find books that are useful for my research. I find hill walking enjoyable for its own sake and I also walk up hills just to get to the top. When I started shopping on the Internet I am fairly sure I did it in order to buy books that were difficult to find elsewhere. It is only later that I began to enjoy searching the labyrinth itself. Likewise when I started hill walking, it was probably to get to the top and the intrinsic meaningfulness of the walk came later.

Sense, Understanding, and Interpretation

Dewey describes another quality of meaning that helps us to understand relationships between experience and meaning: the sense of a situation. Shusterman (2000) refers to the *sense of a situation* as *understanding* and contrasts it with *interpretation*. One of the main distinguishing characteristics between understanding and interpretation is whether the meaning making involved is linguistically mediated or not. According to Shusterman, interpretation is primarily a linguistic activity carried on in reflection on experience and understanding is more immediate and non-linguistic. In making this distinction, he argues as follows:

To interpret a text would be to produce (at least mentally) a text. Understanding, on the other hand, does not require linguistic articulation; a proper reaction, a shudder, a tingle, may be enough to indicate that one has understood. Some of the things we experience and understand are never captured by language, not only because their particular feel defies adequate linguistic expression, but because we are not even aware of them as "things" to describe. They are the felt background we presuppose when we start to articulate or to interpret. (Shusterman 2000, p. 134)

We will return to interpretation later when we discuss reflection on experience. In this section we will continue to focus on the kind of understanding that is immediately present in the sense of a situation. It would be tempting to call this aspect of experience "feeling" rather than understanding, but Dewey was careful to distinguish between understanding as the *immediate sense* of an experience and the psychological predicate of feeling that goes with it. According to him, a situation is a whole because of its immediate pervasive quality. He argued that although a whole situation can be said to be sensed or felt, it would be a mistake to reduce the situation to those sensations or feelings. On the contrary, Dewey's holistic position leads him to argue that the meaning of the whole permeates the parts and qualifies their meaning. Therefore sensations, feelings, and emotions have to be described in terms of the sense of the whole situation with which they are associated.

Our sense of any particular situation depends on previous experience and reflection. Objects and situations attain a meaning for me in my ongoing experience with them and reflections on them. As meanings developed through reflection are absorbed by the object or situation, the sense of that situation changes. For example, a beautiful mountain view may invoke feelings of awe on our first visit or when we return after many months but that sense of awe can be lost if the place is visited every day. It can also become overridden, as Dewey pointed out, by instrumental meanings such as seeing the mountain as something to be traversed. Thus the sensual aspect of an object or situation is constructed and open to change, just as much as its compositional, emotional, and intellectual aspects.

Not only is our sense of any particular object or situation influenced by previous experience, it is also constructed in the particular moment of its occurrence. Shusterman's distinction between interpretation and understanding is not meant to render understanding passive. On the contrary, according to Shusterman, although understanding is not the kind of reflective thinking involved in interpretation, it is nonetheless an active structuring, not a passive mirroring. He forcefully argues that active, intelligent structuring is not limited to cognitive interpretation. The active, intelligent structuring we see in understanding the sense of a situation involves intelligent habits, sophisticated and complex bodily responses, and emotions. A racist gesture or remark can evoke a wide range of sense-making processes from "gut reaction" to upset, distaste, and fear, without any conscious, thoughtful reflection. The active, selective processes involved in producing a sense of the situation in which the remarks are made—picking out the person who made the remark and the look of hatred on his or her face and noticing the supportive attitudes of others in the same room—does not require conscious, purposive, deliberate thinking, rather pre-reflective and immediate seeing.

Being pre-reflective and immediate does not make understanding simple and without variation. Remember that we are describing an active process of selection and structuring influenced by past experience and mediated by habits, emotions, and bodily responses. This is clearly not simple. Let us extend an example from Shusterman to clarify this point. Shusterman notes that when he is at a beach and hears "Surf's up" he immediately understands what is said. To people who surf, hearing that the surf is up opens up a situation in which going surfing is possible and there may even be an opportunity to go ride a big wave. If I hear "Surf's up" and I am not a surfer, it does not have the same connotations at all. Even if I am a surfer but I feel tired or find the waves on this beach too challenging I can still understand the words without interpretation but not be excited at the prospect of surfing on this beach today. For a surfer, in a particular place and time and in a particular state, "Surf's up" can be challenging and exciting. For another surfer, or for the same surfer at a different time, "Surf's up" can be challenging and frightening. Here the sensual and emotional aspects of experience become very closely allied.

As with the contrast between extrinsic and intrinsic meaning, Dewey is not trying to drive a wedge between sense and meaning. In fact, his position is that over time our experience is enriched by reflection, by thinking and talking about experience. Specifically, Dewey suggests that our sense of a situation—the meaning directly experienced—is enriched by reflection and the meaning that signification supplies: "In the course of experience, as far as that is an outcome influenced by thinking, objects perceived, used, and enjoyed take up into their own meaning the results of thought; they become even richer and fuller of meanings." (1929b, p. 134)

The immediate sense one has of a chat room is infused with meaning if one has thought about it and is not just habitually and mindlessly participating. The nurse's sense of patient care is also enhanced by her reflecting on it. The temporal and transformational dimensions of experience are apparent in Dewey's treatment of the relationship between sense, meaning, and reflection. This also draws attention to the risk in assuming that what appears to be the same situation at two different times is indeed the same situation for the person involved. Thinking and talking between the two events may well have changed the situation. Any object in the situation may have been invested with meaning it didn't have before. It may also be connected to other objects and events in ways in which it has not before. A nurse attempting, for the first time, to enter patient details into a new information system is not in the same situation second time around. In the meantime she may have become aware of the ways in which the new information system results in a redistribution of work. Simply reflecting on her experiences during the day may have heightened her awareness of potential meanings of the new information system. Or discussing the day's work with colleagues may have heightened it. No matter how it happened, the information system, as an object, is invested with new meaning second time around and, as a consequence, her immediate sense of it is different.

Reliving Experience and Putting It into Circulation

E. M. Bruner (1986) noted that the relationship between experience and expression of experience is inherently problematical and dialogical. Thinking about and talking about experience changes it and Bruner adds that experience in turn shapes our expression of it. Earlier I (John) wrote positively about my experience of book buying and the Internet. Would my expression of that experience have been structured in the same way had my credit card number been stolen as a result of the transaction or had the books never arrived? In writing about my experience, I relive it and recreate it. I do what Victor Turner called "putting experience into circulation."

In writing about or performing my experience, I am making something else of it. I am making sense of it and I am ensuring that the meaning I have worked hard to make doesn't just disappear. As researchers interested in people's experiences with technology, we further circulate our interpretation of those experiences with a view to creating conceptualizations of technology as experience. The anthology edited by Bruner and Turner (1986) contains many different examples of people making sense of their experiences and putting those experiences into circulation including: making artistic or craft objects that express something of one's sense of self; literary expressions; performing dramas; making murals; and having carnival. E. M. Bruner notes that "stories, as culturally constructed expressions, are among the most universal means of organizing and articulating experience" (1986, p. 15).

Narratives of Experience

Narratives of experience deserve particular attention because of the pivotal role they play not only in the way in which we make sense of our experience but also for the way in which they can shape our felt, lived experience. As well as being an important medium for putting our experiences into circulation, narrative also permeates the experience as it is lived and dominates the process of making experience meaningful for ourselves afterwards. There is a sense in which we actually "make" the experience by recounting it, as the expression of experience is both structured by and structures the experience. E. M. Bruner (1986, p. 5) captures something of this dialogical character of recounting: ". . . experience structures expressions in that we understand other people and their expressions on the basis of our own experience and self understanding. But expressions also structure experience, in that dominant narratives of a historical era, important rituals and festivals, and classic works of art define and illuminate inner experience."

Narratives of experience are not mirrors of what "actually" happened. They are selective interpretations, constructed for a purpose and an audience. We decide where to start and end, what to emphasize and how to frame it and in doing so we often feel the gap between experience and telling. Nonetheless, these stories are self-referential. Even though we might not feel totally comfortable about how we do it, we have to position ourselves in the story. By expressing ourselves to others, we show something of how we feel about the experience being described and also how we feel about ourselves in that experience. In showing ourselves in this way, we seek the kind of recognition that leaves us feeling understood, and perhaps even worthwhile. In this dialogically responsive sense making, we consummate self and other, according to Bakhtin the paradigmatic aesthetic experience.

Narratives are also multi-layered including "not only action and feelings but also reflections about those actions and feelings" (E. M. Bruner 1986, p. 5). Julian Orr's (1996) account of the "war stories" told by photocopier technicians beautifully captures these qualities of recounting experience. They talk about their work experience to other technicians, telling them the stories of their day, specifically how they coped with any troublesome problems. Often the stories are about diagnosing a very tricky fault and will include details such as "red herrings" that initially took the technician away from the proper diagnosis. Occasionally, the stories are about how a particularly troublesome customer was handled. As well as carrying information relevant to diagnosing particular problems, they are also expressions of how members of the community should stand in relation to those problems. They carry in them expressions of concerns that are seen as acceptable within that community. Orr's analysis is that "technicians tell stories to make sense of the diagnosis confronting them, to bring their prior experience to bear on their current problem, and to preserve what they have learned" (ibid., p. 140). In recounting their experience, they make sense of it for themselves and create a knowledge resource that is socially distributed through the oral culture of the technicians.

An important point about recounting experience is that the telling of the experience seems to fold itself back into the lived experience. As we live through experiences, we already have a sense of the social context in which we will recount and make sense of those experiences. As E. M. Bruner (1986, p. 15) put it, there is a double consciousness in experience as we both participate and report. We are involved in the experience, but even as we are involved we are already witnesses with one eye to the past and another to the future. In a sense, we live an experience in the light of how we are likely to recount it to others. J. Bruner (1990) was also aware of this, arguing that narrative is both woven into the experience in action and is a form of its representation in our meaning making. In the everyday experience of going to the movies, we see the film in part with an eye to what our friends would make of it, whether we would recommend it to them, and what it would say about us if we did recommend it and they saw it. Similarly, we buy a bottle of wine, not to drink alone, but to drink with someone else. Our choice of wine is made in the light of our experiences of what we take to be the attitudes, values, and preferences of those others. In some critical sense then others, through their recounting to us and through our recounting to them, live with us in an experience. But they do so reflectively, we are not simply conduits for other people's interpretations, we make sense of experience by overlaying the interpretations of others with our own. The experience is, as Bakhtin (1993) would say, *interanimated* with the voice of self and of others, and our reading of experience takes account of these other voices in preparation for a recounting.

The Temporality of Living and Reliving Experience

So far in our discussion of reliving experience and putting it into circulation, we have run the risk of oversimplifying the temporality or the temporal quality of experience. It seems to suggest that we have an experience and then afterwards relive it and tell others about it, perhaps as story. However, we have already set down a number of markers against such a discrete view of the continuity of experience and against a simple "clock time" approach to the temporality of experience—a distinction also made by Coyne (1999) in his discussion of the pragmatics of anticipation. It might be worth recalling a couple of these markers now.

When writing about narrative of experience earlier in this chapter, we suggested that as well as being the main form for recounting experience, narrative penetrates experience as it is lived and felt. For example, when I am involved in searching the Internet for holiday accommodation, qualities of narrative help shape the experience. As I search, I am wondering what to do next, what kind of person would develop such a tacky web site and whether I would want to stay in a hotel run by such a person, or whether my wife and I would be likely to enjoy ourselves in a very formal hotel. So it is not just after the event that narrative shapes experience.

Earlier in this chapter and in chapter 3, when discussing the continuity of experience, we described the notion of each experience taking something from what has gone before and thereby modifying the quality of what comes after. It is as if in each dialogical, experiential moment images, feelings, and ideas from the past and future are made present. As I search for accommodation, in that moment, I have a sense of the kinds of hotels we like from our past experiences and I have a sense of the kind of holiday we would like to have from conversations we have already had about it.

What we require here to do justice to the complex relationship between past, present and future in experience is a move away from any notion of time as being like clock time. Instead we must see all time—past, present, and future—in terms of what we bring to and take from an experience and the continuity of experience. We have seen how we make stories of experience and how stories make experience. We must also be aware of how stories from the past and the future, from particular people and from culture, interpenetrate in experience. As well as being concerned about what we will tell friends about the movie that we are watching, we are also engaged with stories they have already told us about this and other movies. As we engage with both our expectations from past experiences and our expectations of future experiences, the gap between expectation and experience emerges in a feeling of, for example, dissatisfaction or pleasant surprise.

The temporal quality of our experience is not just related to the type of experience we are having. For example, we don't just bring experiences of past and future films into a movie with us, we bring our experiences of the day we have just had and the day we expect tomorrow to be. Our expectations, and the quality of the felt experience, are likely to be different when we go to the movies having had a particularly awful day at home or work than when we go after a great day. Moreover, the feeling that we should really be at home preparing for what is likely to be a very demanding day tomorrow brings expectation of something in the future into the present experience of watching the movie.

Making Sense and Making Self

We humans want to understand and interpret our experience. It is part of who we are and how we become in the creative, dialogical world in which we live. We live in a world that is not given to us whole cloth and so we have to make something of it. One of the most impressive features of making sense of experience is the always-emerging self that it evokes for us. In the process of making sense of our experience we get a sense of part of who we are. For example, the realization, only dawning as you recount your experience, that something or someone is very important to you. The tiny query that this realization raises about your current priorities. A once-occurrent dialogical event informing relations with an other and triggering a voice in the interanimation of discourses that is the always-becoming self.

Technology plays a role in making sense and self in our experiences with it. And not just in the more dramatic worlds of cyberspace and Internet-mediated social interactions explored by Turkle but also in interaction with more prosaic technologies. For me (John), my sense of myself as someone who supports small local bookshops is interanimated by discourses on the values of global capitalism, the importance of choice provided by small specialist booksellers, and the centrality of a personal relationship in choosing which books to buy. These discourses, however, might be accommodating of an Internet bookseller who appears to try to develop a buyer-seller relationship with me based on an understanding of my reading preferences, provides specialist choices, and seems to support small specialist booksellers. If my book buying activity moves from the small local bookshop to an Internet seller who present themselves as engaging meaningfully with some of these discourses and has other qualities of interest to me also—e.g. speedy fulfillment of an order—my sense of my self is subtly changed through dialogue with that bookseller. Though I have in fact appropriated Internet book buying into my life, I have more resistance to the idea of being a mobile phone user. At the moment, I don't have and I don't want to have a mobile phone. The idea that people could contact me wherever I am doesn't appeal to me at all. And even if I switched it off, the thought of another bank of messages building up is not attractive. But there is another aspect of my resistance that is not really about practical concerns. I simply like being the odd one out, the one resisting the marketing onslaught and the growing pressure always to be connected and perpetually in contact. Quiet, privacy, and the possibility of being alone for a while are high on my list of values. My experience with (or should I say without) a mobile phone is fed by those values and in turn supports and develops them. In this sense then, the mobile phone experience cuts against how I see myself.

Other people are also involved in this process of making sense of self. For example, to the man across the road, Peter is a guy who works in computer science and who can help him install a new computer. For that particular person, with his particular problems, Peter is comfortable allowing himself to be construed as the neighborhood computer expert. However, at work, where he is surrounded by people far more technically skilled, he would be uncomfortable being construed as a technical expert.

The above examples show how we make sense of ourselves as we make sense of our experience, how we make sense of the technology in relation to our selves, and how we make sense of our selves for others. In these ways, we appropriate technology and others into our own life and allow ourselves to be appropriated by them.

Making Sense in and of Experience: A Tool for Analysis

As was the case when we described the threads of experience in chapter 4, we find it helpful to take something that is whole and dialogical and to express it in a form that runs the risk of suggesting something other than wholeness. While it may be risky to address individual sense-making processes apart from the whole, in our experience it is the only way to render this work practically useful for talking about technology as experience. With this caveat in place, we refer to six processes of sense making. There is no implication of linear or causal relations between these processes. It is conceivable, for example, that in anticipation of some future planned action we reflect on the consequences of that action engendering a certain sensual response. Or it could be that how we recount our experience to others may change how we reflect on it. Any suggestion of linearity here would be a gross oversimplification.

Anticipating

Anticipation or expectation is a continuous process in experience. When visiting a company web site for the first time, we do not arrive unprejudiced. We bring expectations, possibilities, and ways of making sense that we associate with offline experience with the brand. Although anticipation suggests something that is prior to the experience, it is important to remember that it is not only prior. The sensual and emotional aspects of anticipation and our expectation of the compositional structure and spatio-temporal fabric of what follows, shapes our later experience. It is the relation between our continually revised anticipation and actuality that creates the space of experience.

As an example, let us consider the children using the POGO World environment that we described in chapter 4. When looking at the sense they make of their experiences with POGO, it would be useful to consider the sense they have of themselves as children and as students, their relationships with the teachers who direct POGO use, and the values and emotions they have with respect to the school environment in which POGO was deployed. How do they feel about school? How do they feel about their teachers? How do they feel about their classmates? What does POGO do to the anticipations created by those feelings? What feelings do they bring from one POGO session to another or from using one POGO tool to another? Do they expect to be freer to express themselves? Do they have a developing sense of how POGO fits into their experience of making stories and of school?

Connecting

Connecting refers to the immediate, pre-conceptual and pre-linguistic sense of a situation encountered. In the spatio-temporal aspect this may be an apprehension of speed or confusing movement or openness and stillness for example. Sensually, connecting may engender an immediate sense of tension or perhaps a thrill of novelty. Emotionally and compositionally, connecting may engender nothing more than a sense of relief or anticipation at something happening.

We might inquire into whether the children in POGO World feel at home there or whether they feel threatened by such a different environment. Do they get a sense of being in a playground, or is their sense still of being at school, or is it some unique amalgam of the two? Are they thrilled initially, and if so does that wear off? Do they have a sense of being somewhere that is child friendly?

Interpreting

Interpreting an unfolding experience involves discerning the narrative structure, the agents and action possibilities, what has happened and what is likely to happen. The process of interpreting may evoke a sense of the thrill of excitement or the anxiety of not knowing. At an emotional level, we may feel frustration or disappointment at thwarted expectations or we may regret being in this situation. On the basis of our interpretation falling short of our anticipation, we may reflect on our anticipation and alter it to be more in line with our interpretation. Can we make sense of the experience in space and time? Do we know where we are, where we have been, and where we have to go?

Do the POGO children have an initial sense of what they and others should be doing? Is it confirmed? If it isn't, do they become anxious about it, or are they inclined to explore and inquire? How does their interpretation of the various tools and activities change over time? How do they interpret their teachers' roles in POGO, and indeed how do they interpret their own? And do those interpretations change over time?

Reflecting

At the same time as interpreting, we may also make judgments about the experience as it unfolds. We may try simply to make sense of the things that are happening and how we feel about them, or wonder whether there is progress or movement toward completion. From an emotional perspective, we may relate events to motivation and to whether we have achieved any sense of fulfillment. How does the experience tally with our anticipation, and how do we feel about being in this situation and this time? From a sensual perspective we wonder why we are anxious or bored. This is like an inner dialogue that helps us meaningfully to recount our experience to others, the anticipation of which may help us to reflect.

As children in POGO World begin to reflect on the experience, we may see them feeling fulfilled or frustrated, satisfied or disappointed. They may also try to work out why they are disappointed or frustrated. We may also see them trying to work out how to use the tools and reconsidering what a story is in the light of their use of the various tools and media.

Appropriating

By appropriating, we mean making an experience our own by relating it to our sense of self, our personal history, and our anticipated future. If it turns out to be an experience we identify with or want to experience again, the center of our personal universe may have shifted slightly. Moreover, by imagining the experience in the context of a past and a future, we may give it a meaning that is more personal to us. Does the unique sense of immersion in undifferentiated color when a first-time scuba diver descends into "the blue" change who he is and how he wants to be seen? Do the compositional aspects of an experience relate positively to a person's sense of self? Does one feel that it is morally right or socially acceptable to go shopping at a virtual supermarket? In the experience of using a mobile phone, do new possibilities for action in everyday life become apparent, or is the experience yet another concession to an undesirable technological future?

Do some of the children in POGO World feel excited at having made a significant contribution to making a story or at having shown a teacher or fellow students how to use the tools? If so, does this make them more confident about themselves in school generally? Does using POGO change children's perception of themselves as students and learners?

Recounting

Recounting is fundamentally dialogical, involving telling the experience to others or ourselves. Like reflecting and appropriating, it takes us beyond the immediate experience to consider it in the context of other experiences. Recounting gives us the opportunity to savor the experience again, to find new possibilities and new meanings in it and this often leads us to want to repeat the experience. And as a dialogical process of making meaning, recounting facilitates our accommodation to the valuative responses of others. As we tell the experience, it can change depending on the moment-to-moment response of the other.

Look at the POGO children telling each other what they have been doing. Do they get excited about it? Do they feel good about the way other children and teachers react to their recounting—"I know I saw you doing that, you were very good"? Or do some of them feel ticked off for dominating the process? As the children talk with each other about POGO is there any sense of children learning things about POGO that they had not noticed when using it? Are they getting new insights and ideas that can be used the next day?

Conclusions

The relationship between experience with technology and the sense we make of it is clearly not straightforward. There are many twists and turns on the road and in this chapter we have taken some of them. In exploring self and other making sense of experience, we encountered some of the subtlety and complexity of pragmatist approaches to self-other relations. In exploring the variety of sense-making processes, we have seen how time seems to fold back on itself with past and future becoming present in an experience. We have encountered self as something like multiple, complex voices always becoming. We have seen that self, sense, and experience interpenetrate each other, and that the coherence required for a story that is convivial in the telling sometimes shapes the experience.

Part of the work of this chapter and of chapter 4 was to describe a set of ideas to help us think about technology as experience. In chapter 4 we described the four threads of experience. In this chapter we described some of the processes people use in making sense of their experience. Both descriptions were intended as reminders of what to look for when approaching technology as experience. However, it is important to note that the threads and the sense-making processes must be understood in the context of the sensibilities to felt life that we have also developed in chapters 3–5. As an additional reminder, these sensibilities are

- the situated creativity of action that makes visible the personal involvement of people creating both goals and means in the height of engaged activity,
- the openness of experience that encourages us to see the messiness and the process that underlie order,
- the weight of answerability that enables us to see experience as simultaneously aesthetic and ethical,
- the holism and unity that require us to avoid reducing the relational and multi-layered quality of felt life,
- the sensory engagement with a situation that orients us toward its immediate, pre-linguistic sense and its reflective interpretation,
- the emotional-volitional character of experience that makes visible the feltness of self-other relations,

and

- the continuous engagement in experience that helps us understand how the past and the future interpenetrate the present.

Thus, for example, our emotional response to a film must be understood in terms of the dialogical sensibilities outlined above. With that in mind, we move on to some concrete case studies.

In the next three chapters we illustrate the ideas we have developed over the last few chapters with concrete, particular case studies. Our aim is not to introduce new concepts or even to further develop those we have already introduced; it is to illuminate some of them by relating them to accounts of concrete experience. The case studies are drawn from our reflections on experiences with Internet shopping, procedure following, and ambulance control. In gathering them together in this way, we are not assuming any shared characteristics or common basis for analysis. All we are saying is that we have had sufficient involvement with these contexts to attempt to describe and interpret some of the experiences. In the process we hope to show how the concepts we have introduced sensitize us to particular aspects of experience.

6 | An Online Shopping Experience

As we have argued throughout the book, central to our approach to analyzing experience is an emphasis on the felt life of personal lived experience, retold through narrative and analyzed in terms of the sense that individuals make of the experience. But we have also emphasized that sense making is a process of continual engagement within a culture and at the intersection of self and others. In keeping with this emphasis, the main part of this case study is a personal account of the experiences that Peter had going online to buy wine. But before we present this narrative, we explore some of the collective meanings that wine buying, the Internet, and e-shopping has in our culture. These collective meanings provide a background for the narrative. The personal story includes a description of the values that the people involved place on buying and drinking wine and their ideas about the Internet and Internet shopping. With these values in mind, it continues with an account of what it felt like to go online at Virginwines for the first time. The story that unfolds is not always a happy one; many problems with the site were encountered. The story takes place in December 2000, which is important because the Virginwines web site has been improved since then.

The concepts and ideas that we have drawn together in chapters 3–5 are as much about a way of seeing experience as they are about describing it. Our aim has been to give the reader a sensibility to what we mean by experience so that we can look at people's interaction and see new and interesting things. Thus, in the story we are about to recount, we have tried to provide a vivid description of what happened and to minimize conceptual analysis. The aim is for readers to *see* the felt life for themselves and to draw their own conclusions. But the concepts we have introduced do have a role to play beyond simply raising sensibilities. They can be used as a way of crystallizing important aspects of the recounted experience (see, for example,

Wright, McCarthy, and Meekison 2003), and this provides a deeper insight into what's going on in the story. Thus, in addition to the firsthand, present-tense narration of the story, there is commentary and discussion that relates some of the ideas developed in chapters 3–5 to the experience of Internet shopping described.

In what follows, the data are from notes written at the time of my (Peter) first experience of Virginwines. But there is also reflective and commentary text interposed with the "at the time" data. The "at the time" data are reproduced in a distinctive font.

Shopping Culture and the Anticipation of Going Online

Shopping in one form or another is an activity we all engage in at some time or another, some more willingly than others. It is not difficult in the case of shopping in a bricks-and-mortar store to provide a description of the aesthetic experience of the activity. Most of us can recall and recount shopping expeditions that have been variously frustrating or satisfying. We can remember long queues at checkouts, the push and pull of crowded stores, the difficulty of choosing just the right gift at just the right price. We can also remember moments of enchantment and the feeling of being presented with so many items that we always wanted but never knew we wanted.

For many, shopping on the Internet is still something of an unknown experience. But the very rapid growth of this form of shopping means that not so long ago there was much discussion of whether it was "safe" to give personal details and credit card information over the Internet. Even now, such concerns preoccupy many non-users. For many, there is also something of a mystery over how one practically goes about things in, for example, an online supermarket. Will items be laid out on virtual shelves? Will you be able to see tins of beans and other products on the shelf? Will you still buy vegetables and fruit first and finish with wines and beers so that grapes get squashed? How do goods get delivered? What if nothing turns up or something is missing or damaged? This lack of continuity between bricks-and-mortar and online may be a source of curiosity for some people and a source of reluctance for others.

These and many other experiences of shopping form a continuity of meanings that influence our anticipation of what it would be like to shop online. This leads us to have expectations in terms of what might happen, how we might feel about it, whether we will find it satisfying and whether we will identify positively with the experience. But our expectations of online shopping are not simply based on previous shopping experiences, they are also shaped by our previous experiences with the Internet in general, the browsers and computers we use and how these are connected. They also involve other Internet experiences we have had or we have been told about. There are questions about how reliable the service might be, particularly from people who connect from home via a modem. Such people may already have experienced slow download times and periodic web site, browser, and computer crashes. While such unreliability may only be mildly frustrating when browsing an online magazine, it might be decidedly worrying when one is in the middle of paying a £100 bill with a credit card.

Thus, there are a host of culturally received meanings and values at the intersection of shopping, the Internet, and e-shopping that influence our expectations of what it would be like to buy wines online.

A Personal Story about Buying Wine Online

My wife and I are not in the habit of buying expensive wines. We have occasionally bought a case of wine by mail order for Christmas with a group of friends to get a bulk-buy discount. But apart from this, we buy wine at the corner shop or the supermarket. We drink wine regularly but we still see it as something a little different. My bookshelf has a 1986 copy of the *World Atlas of Wine* bought for me as a present by my wife, and a 1989 copy of Oz Clarke's *French and Rosé Wines* donated by my uncle. I've always been intrigued by the ability of experts to identify wines in blind tastings, but I probably couldn't tell a Cabernet from a Merlot without looking at the label. I once bought my wife a course of wine tasting night classes for her birthday present. She enjoyed it enormously and developed the ability to detect a "corked" bottle of wine. But even now, she prefers to buy good wine at inexpensive prices rather than to "lash out" on expensive wines. While I might spend £6 on a regular wine she would be more likely to spend £4.

I am not connected to the Internet at home, only at work. There we have fast connections and a dedicated web server. I've never experienced modem delays and the unreliability of home use. From innumerable experiences of Amazon.com at work, I have a generic idea of Internet shopping. It is usual to begin by entering the web site, and it takes a moment to orient yourself to the layout, and to what is going to happen. If it is your first visit to a site, you may have to register by providing personal details but usually not credit card information at this point. After the initial introductions you must browse or search in order to find something you wish to buy. When you have found what you want to buy, you place it in a shopping basket or trolley. Eventually you must move to buy, whereupon, if you have not already done so, you must hand over personal information, including credit card details. This includes information about where and how the goods are to be sent. After confirming your purchase and your details, you can leave the site. Often an email confirming your order and delivery details follows. Some time later, the goods arrive.

I first experienced the Virgin web site in December 2000. This was partly out of academic interest—I was looking into branding and e-commerce at the time— but also out of curiosity to see what it would be like to shop online beyond Amazon. For me, as for many people in the UK, the Virgin brand is associated with Richard Branson, a handsome, wealthy and very English balloonist, who dared to take on not only Coca Cola but also British Airways to bring customers something better and cheaper. Personal experiences of the Virgin brand are mixed though. I remember booking a flight on Sabena to Rome only to find the Brussels-Rome leg being run by Virgin Express. There was no food or drinks available on board even to buy. Similarly I have memories of innumerable Virgin train journeys between York and Bristol hampered by delays and the feeling of old, slow, and unreliable trains. I often take this journey with colleagues from work and we have standing jokes and stories that are recounted each time we make the journey. What was my first encounter with Virgin on the Internet and in particular Virginwines like?

First Impressions of Virgin Online

When I enter the Virgin.com site my immediate feeling is one of surprise at the variety of things that Virgin are involved in (flights, trains, wine, books, financial services, etc.). I am also surprised at the absence of Richard Branson. I kind of expected a picture of him but in fact there are no images of him on the home page. The site is red, part of the Virgin brand image, which looks fine on a coke can but connotes a slight sleaze here. I am also surprised and eventually annoyed by the number of windows that pop up automatically, telling me about Virgin products. My curiosity is aroused by an advert for an attractive holiday venue but this is obliterated by another window trying to sell me books before I have the chance to read it. Each page spawned gives me a feeling of being under time pressure and I feel a need to escape to where I can be in control. A window pops up to offer me free entry into a competition in exchange for my email address—that seems both premature and cheap. I move on to Virginwines.com and get much needed relief from the garish red, the time pressure, and pushy advertising.

Episode 1: On First Entering Virginwines

On entering the Virginwines site I am presented with the promise of "exotic wines at supermarket prices." I'm encouraged by this—it fits with how I see myself and my wife and I have a curiosity to find out more—exotic is an interesting word to use in the context of wine. The ways forward here are clear: you can browse, you can use a wizard to make choices for you based on a profile of yourself (but this will take time and require me to make decisions about myself I'm not ready for), or you can buy mixed red and white cases off the shelf. There's also a wine magazine, something called "my cellar," and something called "recommendations." It is not clear how these latter two would work on first go, but they suggest possibilities of a personal touch if I should ever return.

I have a sense of being at ease and the customer promise makes me feel looked after. Apart from cost there seems to be very little reason not to buy something. But, on the matter of cost, it is not clear whether wine is bought by the bottle, case or part case, whether there is bulk discount or what delivery charges there will be. I press on.

On Moving to Browse

When I begin to browse, contrary to my expectations and to my pleasant surprise I find that the wines are not categorized in the traditional way according to country, color, and price. Rather, they are classified by tasting sensation or drinking occasion, for example: *huge reds, fragrant but dry whites, glugging wines, lunchtime reds,* and so on. For each of these a price band can be selected (£5–£10, £11–£15, and so on). Clicking on an image of the bottle in a category leads to a detailed and often sensual description—for example, "If you consider yourself a sensual animal then this is the perfect wine to complement your sexy nature: a stirring rush of peachy tropical fruit aromas. . . ." Associated with each description are comments from other customers and from the retailers. When I click on one bottle, I get the following message from the retailers:

This is one of those wines where we bought the lot and thought—oh my goodness its not enough. . . . We're almost 100% sure it's the soft redcurrant fruit flavors . . . that does it for most people.

And the following comments from customers who had bought the wine.

Christina: It went down a treat not enough in one bottle. Must remember to buy again.
James: Drank half a glass. The rest went down the sink.
Shaun: Really enjoyed this one. Remember to buy again.
Anon: And you thought turps was bad.

For me, these comments reinforce the feeling that I am among people like myself, and not the victim of a hard sell. It also enabled me to get beyond the bottle labels and exotic descriptions to hear what the wine actually tasted like. This emphasizes the sensuous aspect of the wine-drinking experience. James and Anon's negative comments don't put me off buying that bottle. On the contrary, I am curious to find out who was right and whether some people had just been unlucky enough to get a corked bottle. I feel at home and happy to buy.

Wine drinking is primarily a sensuous and a social experience. Few people drink wine alone. We buy wine for its taste, the effect it has, and what it contributes toward a social occasion. Thus, often enough, when we buy wine we are buying with others in mind. These aspects of the wine-drinking experience are hard to mediate in a bricks-and-mortar store with the formal language of label descriptions and the racks of wine carefully categorized by country of origin, color, and price. But in the story so far we see how Virginwines, through a rather unconventional approach to structuring its product range, has broken the genre of the bricks-and-mortar store to offer an interesting development that mediates the sensual and social characteristics of the wine-drinking experience in a different way. At the same time, by cocking a snoot at the received wisdom on how to talk about wine they are identifying with certain kinds of people. By breaking the generic convention in this creative way they are expressing a different value system and, as a consequence, a definite sense of individuality. This value system is consistent with values expressed by the Virgin brand itself—innovation, fun, and value for money. They have also achieved this by making the site into what might be thought of as a dialogical space. Customers' comments are there alongside retailers', which puts the retailers on the same level as the customers. It is almost as if they were at your party telling you why they had bought this particular wine for you. The values expressed and the tones of voices are persuasive and not authoritative. Other drinkers are also characters in this space. Consistent with a dialogical perspective, their points of view do not always agree, but foster curiosity and trust, which is so essential to an online business.

The Start of the Problems

For some time before getting involved with Virginwines, I had been experiencing trouble with my computer at work. The technical support staff blamed this on the fact I was using a Macintosh on a network tailored for PCs. There was no official technical support for Macintoshes and thus any help was heavily intoned as a favor. I'd had trouble printing, and the computer was crashing more frequently than it had been.

As I begin to put bottles into the trolley, I experience long delays. Each time there is a long delay, I am completely preoccupied with whether or not my computer has crashed. I'm not sure what the problem is. If it is the bad design of the Virginwines web site, I may feel I ought to think differently about buying wines from them. On the other hand, if it's just a network problem beyond the control of Virgin or my department it wouldn't be so bad. On the other hand again, if it's a development of my ongoing problem with Mac compatibility, I will feel obliged to talk with the technicians. I'm not sure which problem I would prefer it to be. I decide to move back to the home page to see whether I can find any information about costs or payment. I get an even more severe delay and then nothing. My browser appears to be frozen. I click on another open application and frustration gives way to anger as, after two hours of activity on the site, my Macintosh crashes completely. There is a sense of irony too as all those earlier delays, which I had been apprehensive about but dismissed as paranoia, turn out to be narrowly avoided crashes after all.

Reflecting on what the problem is, I have to ask myself whether this was a "one-off" problem perhaps to do with the time of day and unusually heavy traffic on the site or whether something was wrong with the web site. But Virgin is a big company and should have invested in decent servers and decent designers. Worse still, maybe it's my Mac. Whatever it is, something has intervened to subvert my idea of buying "exotic wines at supermarket prices" at the click of a button. I don't get the wine this time; instead I get a computer problem; and what was going to be a good story to tell my friends turns out to be a horror story or a bad joke. But I have to reserve judgment on Virginwines (although I have my suspicions) until further information is available and I have both the time and energy to try again.

The Virginwines experience recounted up to this episode had been a story of two worlds. The first world is the world of the Virgin web site (a dialogical space in which people can talk about and buy wine); the second world is one in which people drink wines bought through the first. But these worlds are not separate. On the contrary, the interesting thing about them is their interpenetration. Part of the tension that arises in online shopping, and why issues such as trust emerge, is because the world of the shopping transaction in which products are bought is separate from but connected to the world where those products will be delivered, consumed, and paid for. But more important, in this episode we see a third world that enters the experience: the world of computer tools. In the earlier episode this world had been a transparent one, but as the story progressed it became a world in which technology emerges as a broken object. In this world, the user has to try and understand how the technology works and how to get around the obstacles placed in his way by the technology. But in trying to creatively respond to these problems, the individual is faced not only with a complex and messy technical problem, but also with the need to act in the ethical and social world of diverse agents, purposes, and responsibilities. A world where Mac users are taken as outsiders, where technicians have the luxury of favor, and where what you decide to do has consequences, weight, and answerability.

Episode 2: Virginwines at Bedtime

Since I am reluctant to give Technical Support any more leverage for their argument about getting rid of my Mac, I return to Virginwines some days later in the evening assuming there might be less traffic and it might be okay. Initially there is a much faster response than I remember but soon the telltale signs of empty windows and long download times return. With each click now there is a perceptible delay. Having invested effort to be here in the evening I continue despite my better judgment. With growing apprehension I select wines for the basket and wonder whether I will get to the end of this transaction before the crash, and if not, what will happen to my basket—will it be empty when I return? Will I have to start over again?

The "exotic wines at supermarket prices" soon becomes an object of cynicism, disappointment, and frustration, when having selected the cheaper wines in the £5–£10 range, I am told it is out of stock (and remember, each selection is very anxiety provoking, as each click is accompanied by delays promising a crash any second). What you see is not what you can put in your basket. This happens more than once and I am forced "up-market" in my choices. At one point I unthinkingly resize the window so I can read all of the content leading to an appalling delay and I kick myself for being so forgetful—the world of broken technology is in my face. The stakes are high now because I have made a number of choices and if the system crashes I'm not sure I will be able to remember what they were. As I press the back-button to go to a new shelf, the system finally does crash. On reflection I feel cheated by the funky descriptions, the comments, the presence of the retailers and the customers—it all seems a sham. But I still don't know whether it's my fault or theirs. Surely those customers would have made some comments about the site if their experiences had been as bad as mine. Or am I getting a very edited version of their views? Are they genuine customers at all?

This episode captures something of the way in which acts and utterances take on different values and intonations as experience unfolds. Things that were earlier understood as well intentioned or conforming to our own values and desires can later be seen as cynical when new events unfold. Promises become broken promises and eager anticipation turns to disappointment. Trust and confidence in the whole situation can be eroded by such changes. We also see how the quality of time, action, and the movement toward completion is compromised by the ever-present fear of a system crash. It is as if the very expectation of finishing the transaction at all is open to question.

Episode 3: A Colleague's PC

I go back again, this time on a friend's PC in a different part of the office. I have had to ask Technical Support for access to this machine. I have mixed feelings. I hope using the PC doesn't make the difference, because I don't want to get rid of my Mac and I don't like PCs. On the other hand, I'd really like to believe that my first feelings about Virginwines were the right ones. In a short time the site does crash on me, but throws me out only as far as the Virgin home page, and when I re-enter I see my basket is as I left it. Thus, there is some perverted sense of progress. I press on in a state of high anxiety feeling like I'm walking in a minefield. The ever-present danger of the crash adds to what would otherwise have been minor annoyances about the structure of pages like, for example, having the descriptions of the wine on one page and the prices on another, one anxiety-ridden click away.

Eventually I move to buy but I am still completely in the dark about whether I am buying by the bottle or case. Wines are individually priced suggesting by the bottle or part case, but I guess it would be absurd to be allowed to buy one bottle? Although perhaps not if it were a very expensive bottle. I am very unsure at this stage, wanting the wine on the one hand and yet asking myself whether I want to trust this outfit with not only my money but also my credit card details.

When I press "go to basket" all is apparently revealed. There is a clear list of the steps required to complete the transaction: Who you are; claim a voucher; where to send it; final check; done. I can also see that there is only a modest delivery charge making it entirely feasible to buy say, a half case and for it still to be cost effective, but scrolling down the page a message indicates that a case is the minimum quantity. Thus, I change the amounts of a couple of bottles to make it twelve and in the process I somehow manage to add a whole extra case of wine to my basket. Now I have to adjust the quantities in the basket to get rid of the items from the extra case. I do this by setting the quantities to zero like I would in the Amazon trolley. But when I go back to the total price it is still exactly the same! I eventually see a message telling me that I cannot select less than one bottle, rather I must check the "remove" boxes and press update but when I do this nothing happens. At this point, my mind is down at the level of variables and program code trying to work out what the program is doing. What have they done to get this to happen? Then I get an insight; you have to have more than one item selected before you can remove it—a superb programming bug!

Finally, after working with the Virginwines web site for about 5 hours over three days, I move to pay and to my astonishment and disgust I receive the following message:

Warning . . . the information you have submitted is insecure . . . if you are submitting credit card numbers or other information you would like to keep private, it would be safer for you to cancel the submission.

I feel angry, disgusted, and betrayed. Up to this point, the comments of the sales staff and customers that I have read have been persuasive and welcoming. But this message is authoritative and strident and quite at odds with the tone of the other comments. It's even at odds with other similar messages on other parts of the Virgin site such as "Please read the small print because it came from our lawyers and was expensive." What's this message telling me? "Don't trust us after all at least not where money's concerned—we're not really serious and we're sorry we've wasted your time." The message doesn't just appear once but each time I move to a page containing personal details.

Broken technology emerges again here and we are taken into the world of the web programmer as we try to figure out why the program is behaving so oddly. But the more significant feature of this episode is the way in which my sense of what the web site *is* was subverted. A significant discontinuity in my experience has occurred. Before this was a social space that was friendly warm and welcoming. The retailers had worked to bring themselves into what Bakhtin calls the zone of familiar contact—part of the dialogical space that put them on the same level as the customers. But now the tone of their voice is authoritative and, by connecting to a quite different speech genre of legal responsibilities and disclaimers, manages to negate the trust that was being built up. After this episode, I had a very strong feeling of being let down.

Moving to Completion

As I move through the detail of paying for the wine I am brought back into the real world. What is my wife going to think when a case of expensive wines turns up on the doorstep? What if there is no one in and it gets delivered to the neighbors? In their eyes, are we the kind of people who can afford to have wine delivered by the case? Do I want to be that kind of person in their eyes? I decide to send the case to my wife as a gift with a suitable note. That way, it will be a surprise and potentially a one-off perhaps saying less about any commitment to a change in lifestyle.

I feel a sense of incompleteness about logging off at the end of the transaction. I have felt this when logging off at Amazon too. I have paid by clicking on the confirm button, but in contrast with a bricks-and-mortar shop there is neither a physical exchange of goods nor a "Thank you." This lack of closure is ameliorated to some extent by the arrival shortly afterwards of an email confirming the order, its cost, and a likely delivery date. There is also an offer— "20% off a future case"—not for me but for a friend to whom I should forward the email along with the code number it contains. This seems like a nice way to share the experience; on the other hand, it also seems like a way to make me an unwitting salesman. As a gift, the voucher is compromised for me by the desperate nature of the experience I've just had. Could I possibly be mean enough to inflict an experience like this on a friend? In the end, I do send it to a friend—

but someone who, if they have as bad an experience with the web site as me, would see the funny side of it.

Episode 4: Afterwards

A few days later, the case arrives. I have primed my wife to expect a surprise. When opened, the gift tag with the message is duly found, but she also finds a receipt indicating the cost. I tell her my nightmare story, which makes the present seem more special, and the anticipation of the first bottle more acute. Sadly, however, the tasting notes (remember "if you consider yourself a sensuous creature . . .) that had been so central to making the wines special when they were chosen are not included with the case. I go to my workplace with a list of the wines we have bought and print out each web page (remembering the delays with each click). A few days later I receive a voucher giving me a 20% discount on a case. Taken together with the case I have already bought, that would bring the bottle cost down to those elusive "supermarket prices." What's more, I only have to click on one button this time to complete the transaction. Thus, I decide to buy to help resolve my problem with the unexpectedly high cost of my first case.

In these episodes, we see how the experience runs its rather uncertain course to completion. But whether or not this counts as a fulfilling experience cannot be answered in a simple way. Events that should have helped consummate the experience such as the tasting notes, the gift voucher and so on become points of difficulty and parody. In one way the experience was fulfilling since I received and enjoyed the wine. But the anxieties and frustration involved in achieving this were felt to be undesirable. On the other hand, the very fact that the experience was less than problem free provides interesting material for recounting. What was difficulty, anxiety, and hardship at the time becomes heroic adventure in the retelling.

There is also a further example in this episode of the meeting of two worlds and the ethical weight of this meeting. The voices of others and my construction of what they will make of my conduct comes over clearly in the description of how I creatively negotiate the meaning of the arrival of a case of wine. I leave open the opportunity for my wife to creatively respond on her own terms to the act. Issues of identity and loyalty are apparent in my self-questioning about what this act says about myself for my neighbors.

Some Important Themes

In chapter 5, we concluded by identifying a number of key concepts in our account of experience. This case study has helped illustrate a number of these.

Holism and Unity

The case study shows us how the creative activity of sense making occurs at a number of interpenetrating levels. A practice-based approach might have treated the activity of wine buying as separate from the activity of using the Internet as a means of buying wine. However, in our account we saw how the activity of wine buying and the activity of using the Internet as a means of buying wine might be seen as interpenetrating worlds: the world of wine buying, the world of online shopping, and the world of technology. How we make sense of the technology that participates in the experience of online shopping cannot be separated from how we make sense of the act that is Internet shopping itself nor from the act of wine buying. As Dourish (2001) points out, the meaning of experience is multi-layered. But what is clear in this case study is that these are not so much layered as interpenetrating worlds of meaning. These worlds interact dialogically through the voices of others for me and the voice of I for others. There is another important sense of holism and unity in this account too. In the wine-buying story there are equal measures of the sensual, the emotional, the intellectual, and the ethical. This holism and unity is the kind that Dewey and Bakhtin speak of most strongly.

The Emotional-Volitional Nature of the Act

By making the emotional-volitional nature of the act central to our account of experience, we focus on felt life as the concerns, fears, confusion, ambivalence, interests, desires, and expectations that permeate our sense making. But our dialogical account of sense making also commits us to seeing such things as emerging through continuous engagement of self constituted as a center of values coming into contact with a situation involving others as equal centers of value. The emotional-volitional nature of action commits us to seeing engagement as a continuously open and free act of creativity that the individual is thus answerable for. This creative construction of self and other is found in the intersection between imagined possibilities and the actual working out of events.

In the case study, we saw how, for me, the initial desire for a simple and satisfying experience quickly yields to frustration as the hoped-for goals become unobtainable. But the crashes I experienced meant more than simply an inability to achieve a goal. They meant that I might have to enter into negotiations with technicians and even give up my Macintosh. The answerability for the act extended far beyond the immediate means-end construal of the situation. Likewise, the act of purchasing wine online bore the weight of other relationships, those with my partner and my neighbors for example. I am answerable to these others even in such a seemingly solitary activity as buying wine online.

The Sociality of Experience

Answerability links to another central feature of our account of experience: sociality. For us, sociality of experience is a commitment to Bakhtin's idea that sense making is always at the boundary of self and other. This comes through in a number of ways in the case study. The way in which I bought wine with others in mind and the extent to which I reflected on actions as saying something about myself for others are clear examples of this dialogicality, echoing Bakhtin's distinction between I for myself and I for others. My engagement with the voices of others (retailers and customers) on the web site was another way in which dialogicality was made visible. The fact that both customers and retailers spoke in particular tones encouraged a sense of belonging for me. The site literally became a dialogical space in which differing individuals entered on the same plane and presented very different perspectives on the same things. These voices contributed to a sense of the Virginwines web site as a center expressing certain values quite consistent with the values expressed by the Virgin brand itself. Technicians and colleagues also enter the experience in value-laden ways.

Unfinalizability

But dialogicality also commits us not only to seeing the other as a center of value but also seeing the process of sense making as open and one of continual becoming. In the case study, the inherent openness of meaning is manifest in a number of ways. The understanding of system problems as delays early in the experience becomes transformed into narrowly avoided crashes later in the experience. Dire warnings about the risk of transferring credit information led to doubts about the sincerity of those early comments. Trust can be seen as a project simultaneously under construction and erosion in this case study. As we described in chapter 4, Brenda Laurel discusses engagement in terms of the suspension of disbelief and willingness to enter a mimetic context. But these examples speak to a broader sense of willingness and mimesis than Laurel had in mind. They speak to an unwillingness to continue *as if* those voices were sincere. In addition we can see that the boundary of the technical system itself is open and unfinalized. The computer, the browser, Internet servers, program code, new PCs, different offices at different times—all of these enter the frame as the experience is made sense of.

The Quality of Aesthetic Experience

The story of my experience of online shopping and my part in the creative act of movement toward a consummation is clear. But we can also see how the experience is one of a struggle for completion in the face of difficulties. Difficulties that were, on reflection and recounting, not part of what Dewey would call the intrinsic meaning of the task. Finding the correct piece to fill a gap in a jigsaw puzzle is an intrinsic part of the activity. Finding a missing piece by searching toy cupboards is not. The system delays, the crashes, the lack of clarity over how to pay, the irony of the wine turning up as a gift but with the receipt enclosed and the absence of the tasting notes, all point to problems with the intrinsic meaning of the Virginwines experience for me. In particular, they point to problems involving a number of Dewey's conditions of an aesthetic experience described in chapter 4.

The intellectual and emotional build up that goes along with positive experiences, the curiosity that drives us on to want to know more, the uncertainty that is gradually resolved as the experience unfolds, and the growing sense of a consummation were absent in this experience. While the motivation to go on must clearly have been present, this was not intrinsic to the circumstances of the experience. Though I clearly had a desire for a case of these wines, the means of fulfilling that desire seemed like fighting battles on a number of fronts. The reason for this lack of cumulation lay in the inability to make progress. Each new episode with the exception of the last was a return to the start point with nothing accumulated except frustration and uncertainty. Energy, in terms of moving toward fulfillment, was dissipated with each crash and with each technical problem. The meaning of events within episodes was not built upon, instead questions arose that could not be resolved even as a way of going on. Like, for example, knowing how to pay and what the purchasing unit was. But, even so, the question of fulfillment for me was not a simple one. The experience was fulfilling in as much as I received and enjoyed my case of wine. In another way too the very fact that the experience was less than problem-free, provided interesting material for recounting. The fact that wine could be sent as a gift with a message but turns up with a receipt clearly indicating the cost. The fact that the tasting notes that had been so central to the experience of choosing were not included in the case when it was delivered. All of these qualify the experience as a fulfilling and satisfying one even if they can be made into a joke when recounting to self and others.

Conclusion

In this, the first of three case studies, we have taken a prosaic experience with technology and used it to exemplify what it means to talk about technology as experience. We have tried to provide a vivid account of a particular individual's experience to make visible what we have been referring to as the felt life of experience with technology. We tried to do this first in as direct a way as possible by avoiding the technical language we have been developing. But then in the above discussion we have tried to relate what we have seen to the theoretical account we developed in chapters 3–5. The fact that we can do this is evidence to us that the concepts we have introduced in those chapters are valuable as a way of seeing experience, not just as a way of describing it.

In earlier chapters we argued that there is no way out to felt life through theory, only through the individual experience. There is no God's-eye view of felt life. To paraphrase Geertz, without experience, theories can float several feet above the human ground. In order to engage with the rough ground of felt life, we must engage with actual experience. The case study in this chapter has sought to show how the felt life of a particular experience of technology can be made visible. What we gain from such visibility is insight into the variety of experiences with technology and since this may be construed as a story of difficulties rather than joys, it is an insight into what the particular web site in question might become rather than what it is.

7　A Pilot's Experiences with Procedures

In this chapter we explore the issues of the construction of self and identity as they emerge in the dialogue between individuals and organizations or communities of practice. In chapter 2, we argued that practice-based accounts of community and identity do not give enough weight to individual experience. Instead they emphasize a monological account of identity as normativity. We pointed to Hodges's (1998) account of the struggles she experienced when trying to become a teacher. In this chapter we focus on an individual who is already a trained and experienced commercial airline pilot. His story is not so much about a peripheral newcomer wishing to become a legitimate and central member of a community. Rather, it is about the creative, continuous, lifelong construction of self as a member of many communities and the way in which technology figures in that process. Bowker and Star (1999, p. 295), following Dewey, argue that someone's illegitimacy "appears as a series of interruptions (anomalies) posed by the tension between the ambiguous (outsider, native, stranger) and the naturalized (at-home, taken-for-granted) categories for objects. Collectively, membership is about managing the tension between naturalized categories on the one hand and degrees of openness to immigration on the other."

Bowker and Star argue that technology is about classification at all levels of granularity. In order to write a computer program that works, we must identify all possible combinations of inputs, and for each different combination we must specify precisely how the program should respond. It is finalization through classification. Similarly, in order to rationalize a work activity, we must first identify the different types of activity and the different types of tasks the workers do. The same process of classification is at the heart of work design and computer programming. It is no surprise, then, that the rationalization of work begins by classifying and ends by automating.

The classification system we are concerned with in this chapter is the system of emergency operating procedures for a commercial aircraft. Commercial aircraft are complex systems, and like many such systems they are easy to control when they are working correctly but much harder to control when things go wrong. Consequently, the people who manufacture, regulate, and operate commercial aircraft have defined a set of emergency operating procedures, which they write down in manuals and reference books or build into automated warning systems. These procedures classify every possible type of failure that the designers can imagine and associate with each failure a well-defined series of steps that pilots should follow in order to safely recover from the failure.

The operating procedures are intended as a rationalization of the work aimed at identifying what Taylorism might have called "the one best way" of dealing with each emergency and thereby reducing diversity of operator responses, the likelihood of human error, and the cost of training. In view of this orientation, it is not surprising that pilots are required to follow these procedures carefully and suffer various forms of reprimand if they are found to be deliberately or even accidentally violating them. Many organizations and authorities contribute to the definition of these procedures. These include, the aircraft manufacturer, the regulatory authorities (e.g., the Civil Aviation Authority in the UK and the Federal Aviation Administration in the US), and the operating companies (e.g., British Airways and Continental Airways) that buy and fly the aircraft. Elsewhere, we have shown that, as a consequence, standard operating procedures constitute centers of value that are interanimated with many voices, and we have explored the paradoxes, tensions and contradictions that emerge in the use of these procedures (Wright and McCarthy 2003). We shall revisit some of those issues, but in the main, we want to take a different perspective on the data here.

The data we will present comes from an interview with an experienced commercial pilot whom we shall call Captain Roy. Before the interview, we had been talking informally to Captain Roy about procedure following, and he presented us with a copy of the emergency operating procedures for one of the aircraft he flies regularly. The pages had been heavily annotated by Captain Roy. We did a content analysis of these annotations to identify what information was lacking in the procedures. This was a revealing exercise (see Wright, Pocock, and Fields 1998; McCarthy, Wright, Monk, and

Watts 1998) but not nearly as revealing as the interview in which we explored where the annotations had come from, how they were used, and what would become of them. This interview revealed the felt life of being a commercial airline pilot, the situated creativity of working within a regulated work practice, where finalization and conformance rather than openness and creative freedom is the underlying value system but where individual action is also valued and carries moral weight. In this context, an individual is continually identifying himself as both an outsider and an insider through the technology of his practice.

The Story

In what follows, excerpts from Captain Roy's interview are presented in a different font. The interviewer's comments are presented in italics.

Annotating QRHs

Captain Roy's story of the annotations begins with his early training to become a pilot. A modern pilot's working life is dominated by procedures of many kinds. There are the so-called normal operating procedures. These specify the kinds of checks that must be carried out at various critical points in a flight, such as take-off and landing. In addition, there are emergency operating procedures to deal with hazardous failures, such as engine fire or generator loss. Of course, *normal* operating procedures become very routine during day-to-day work but *emergency* operating procedures are different because emergencies during day-to-day flights are very rare. A pilot might go through his whole career without ever having to experience an engine fire in real life. Procedures appear in many contexts and artifacts for a pilot. They appear in cockpit computers as advisories, they are written in quick reference handbooks (QRHs) kept on the flight deck, which are always supposed to be consulted when an emergency occurs. Procedures are also to be found in other technical manuals on the flight deck and elsewhere. But the technical manuals are not so much for consultation in a real emergency as for training and learning. Captain Roy's activity of annotating his procedures began in response to his desire to gain mastery over the emergency procedures and the documents and technology that present them. He wanted to gain mastery by making sense of not just "what to do" but "why to do." This information does not always appear in the quick reference handbooks, but is more likely to be found in other more comprehensive volumes:

All the annotations are to be found in the manuals somewhere—it's a sort of collation exercise to bring it all together. In the books there are the checklists and then there's an expanded checklist which tells you what the problem is. You might have say "APU fuel valve" in the checklist—I just wanted to know what that was, and you go deeper into the book, and it says "valve not in commanded position." I just tried to get lots of bits of the manual all together in one book.

Thus, this activity of bringing the bits together is a creative, sense-making exercise. Captain Roy is appropriating the inscribed procedures he may one day be required to enact. And in this process he is creating a new artifact: his annotated quick reference handbook. Here Captain Roy, the reader, is a writer in a process of creative construction. He has taken this writing to its logical conclusion: since he acquired a computer at home, he has used his annotated QRH as the source for a new word-processed document, which he refers to as *QRH for Dummies*. This professional-looking document has a number of usability features he is very proud of:

Yes, well what I've done now is put it all on computer now in a nicely colored book [indicating a book titled *QRH for Dummies*]. In a way, if you had a problem you could get all the books out on the flight deck, search through the indexes and try and find references on every little bit in each different manual, but [that] would take you for ever. So mine is really a time saving device that brings it all together.

My customized QRH has a cross referenced index at the back with page numbers, so you can find things quickly. I've noticed in the simulator people scratching around looking for these drills all over the place.

But the kind of mastery over the procedures that Captain Roy's *QRH for Dummies* represents, the design-in-use and situated creativity it points to, is really only the beginning of his story.

Simulator Training

Books and manuals are one source of information about what to do in an emergency. Another important source is the training that pilots receive in simulators. As one might expect, this is a highly important part of training to become a pilot, but simulator training is more than this. Even qualified pilots have to regularly visit simulators to have their competencies reassessed for aircraft they are already qualified to fly. In addition, they visit simulators to get new qualifications to fly new types of aircraft. In the simulator, pilots are (among other things) given emergencies to deal with.

These are serious exercises for which Captain Roy prepares by reading his *QRH for Dummies*:

Simulator revision. . . . It's brilliant for that. It jogs your memory. . . . I try to memorize most of it anyway before I go in the simulator.

But Captain Roy's experiences of simulator training, both as a novice and now as a full-fledged captain, bring to light another dimension of the business of following procedures. When a captain takes part in simulator sessions, the trainers regularly set up situations wherein by following the QRH procedures he will crash the aircraft:

. . . just about every time I go in the simulator I learn something which I think is wrong. You know, why was I not given that information on day one? I feel sorry for people that have just come onto the aircraft. I was flying with a guy the other day who's just come off the Airbus. He's done six months on the 757, and he's going for a command course next week and I was chatting to him on the flight deck about certain things that I've learned over the years, and he hadn't a clue what I was talking about, and he's going to be a captain next week, you know. You might not get that problem in a simulator, and these are not things that are written down in the books anywhere, but if it happens for real he won't know about it.

So what are the main reasons you think he won't know about it?

Well, the only way I've gleaned it is from being put in this situation in the simulator where some instructor has realized that this is a bit of a "gotcha"—with this failure you don't get this, for instance. And I've been caught on it and I've come home and written it up, and I can't for the life of me understand why they don't publish all this sort of stuff. And I've said this to trainers over the years and they go a bit quiet, and they don't seem to understand what you're talking about.

Thus, as well as bringing together information from a range of technical manuals, *QRH for Dummies* is also a creative response to these simulator-based learning experiences:

After simulator sessions, I always write up my notes on the simulator and add anything that I've learned onto my "dummy" QRH. . . . One of the "gotchas" on the left AC bus failure is that you lose the equipment cooling on the captain's instruments. Now bear in mind you've got a lot of messages come up with a left AC bus failure (a lot of insignificant stuff that you can deal with later), and one more creeping in doesn't become apparent. So while you're doing this checklist which it says here, what happens is the instruments on my side overheat because they've got no cooling. A message does come up and says "Equipment cooling overheat" and the next thing, I'm flying along and all my instruments disappear—they all go blank. Now that's not very nice really! You've lost half your electrics and half of a lot of other stuff and then your instruments go blank! I think the QRH perhaps mentions it way, way back at the end of the checklist, but in mine it says at the

beginning "A left AC bus failure will cause equipment overheat after about one minute"—
in which case you'll have to select alternate equipment, won't you?

The "gotchas" raise interesting issues about community membership. Captain Roy is, by title, a fully qualified and legitimate pilot. At the same time, what Bowker and Star refer to as the "anomalies and tensions" brought about by his experiences mark him off simultaneously as both more and less legitimate. His experiences of the "gotchas" mark him off as lacking in the eyes of his trainers. Yet at the same time his surplus of experience relative to other soon-to-be captains mark him off as a relative old-timer in the eyes of these newcomers. This simultaneity of membership has a dialogical feel to it—there is no one relationship that locates Captain Roy on a single path to community membership. Rather, it is a multiplicity of relationships whose meanings are different depending on the perspective taken.

Captain Roy's response to the tensions this multiplicity implies is a simple one. He wishes that the "gotchas" were all written down so that everyone knew them from day one. This is the motivation for *QRH for Dummies*:

You know, if I was a chief pilot (perhaps in an idealized world), I'd like my pilots to know all the "gotchas" from day one. OK, they may not have time to read all this stuff, but I've always quite fancied writing a book on the "gotchas." I mean, the training department would kill me, but I can't understand why someone doesn't.

Different Airline Companies Have Different QRHs

As Captain Roy's story continues to unfold, a new dimension of emergency operating procedures begins to emerge. Captain Roy has not always worked for the same airline company, and he has discovered that some companies' QRHs are better than those of other companies:

At that stage I had been 757 captain for one summer season with Company X using that checklist. [He taps on the aircraft manufacturer's original QRH.] I was then on a non-flying job during the winter. Then I joined Company Y, flew the first season using this checklist, and that first winter I thought I would find the time to start composing my own [checklist], and when I did, quite a few people wanted copies of it. But you've got to be careful not to start distributing copies of the thing, because the training department would go bananas because its not approved, etc., etc. It's very much a personal thing that I don't actually spread around.

There's nothing in mine which conflicts . . . although actually . . . something like a loss of thrust on both engines is an interesting one. Because the manufacturer's checklist assumes that their drill which is given starts one or both engines, but there's nothing there to say what to do if you don't get the engines restarted. The Company Z QRH has a procedure for starting the engines using the APU when you get to low level, and I've got that in my book. . . .

This panoply of experiences with different procedures in different companies is a real part of what it means for Captain Roy to be a pilot. His identity as a pilot is intimately bound up with it. But his experiences are also a source of frustration when they lead to expectations about what can be achieved that are not borne out in practice:

When I joined Company Y, I was dismayed to find that they used the manufacturer's basic checklist, whereas I had been used to the Company X expanded one which had a lot more information on it, so I decided then to start putting more and more stuff on it, and its just got better and better. I've had a lot of people at work want copies.

The feeling of dismay here is an emotional-volitional response to a situation where he knows things could be done better and aren't and yet at the same time he is required to operate within the standards of the company for which he currently works. The use of less than the best procedures becomes a moral issue for Captain Roy both as a statement of company values and as a personal question about what to do:

But as far as your company's concerned they're using the manufacturer's standard-issue QRH? Yes, and I think that's criminal. It may be because we're a brand new company. We've only been going a year and a half, and we've merged with two airlines since we started. And the training department and powers that be are probably well overloaded anyway. But I know Company X use this [indicating the manufacturer's QRH] as well, and they've got no excuse because they've been going twenty years or so. . . . But I think leaving people with this standard checklist is a bit disgraceful really.

Thus, it appears there is no final word on what to do in an emergency. Different companies have different emergency procedures, simulator trainers show you where even the best procedures let you down, and your personal experiences may lead you in many different directions. So what should pilots do when faced with an in-flight emergency? The official answer to this question is, of course, to follow the procedures of the company they currently work for. But such a simple-minded rule seems to float several feet above the felt life of Captain Roy. He knows that a particular procedure may be less than adequate, and that he could improve the situation by following his own QRH. Whether or not he follows the company rule, he is making an ethical choice brought on by the weight of his own experiences, and he is answerable both to himself and others for that decision. His use of the word 'criminal' highlights the heavily ethical nature of this response.

Captain Roy takes his QRH with him into the cockpit, even though the QRH provided by the company is supposed to be used at all times:

The actual pilots with the training department would be horrified if they thought I'd get that out during a flight, obviously because its not an approved book at all. But what I actually do is I take it with me, and if I have a problem (I had one the other day) I do the proper drills from the normal QRH, and then I would get mine out just for further reading.

So on the flight deck, you've got your original copy of the QRH. Are you prescribed that you must go for that one?

Oh yes, I'd always do the company book—the proper QRH first. . . . The Company Z QRH has a procedures for starting the engines using the APU when you get to low level, and I've got that in my book, so in that case, having done the manufacturer's checklist I'd probably get out mine and do the drill for that.

So in effect you've followed the letter of company law?

Yeah, as far as it goes.

But, as you were mentioning there, you've got the company book and you take your own onto the flight deck?

Absolutely. I would now feel very uncomfortable having left [his version] at home—I feel very comfortable having all that extra information sitting next to me on the flight deck, and I've used it on quite a few occasions, and it's been very useful.

Thus, in some sense Captain Roy's *QRH for Dummies* is a security blanket. Having it along with him "just in case" makes him feel comfortable. But it is also a source of tension. It marks him out as both an insider and an outsider, in Bowker and Star's terms. He is an outsider inasmuch as his intention to use *QRH for Dummies* places him outside of what is acceptable to his company, but an insider inasmuch as it represents for him a lifetime of experience as a pilot in many different communities and through many different practices.

Some Important Themes

Making Sense of Procedures

Much of what Captain Roy described in his interview can be seen as making sense of operating procedures. This has many dimensions. There is the very practical one of bringing together all the different sources of information in order to get as many different perspectives on the procedures as possible. This involves finding what information is missing in the various descriptions, and trying to put together some comprehensive accounts. Such sense making includes trying to find answers not only to the question "What to do?" but also to "How?" and "Why?" But there are other dimensions to this sense-making process. It is not just a case of bringing together information from different sources; it is a case of valuing and critiquing that information on the basis of Captain Roy's lifetime experience of simulator training and flying for many different companies. It is this accumulation of skills and knowledge that fuels the construction of meaning and ultimately motivates the activity of producing *QRH for Dummies*. This accumulated experience provides the means by which Captain Roy can make sense of his situation. But making sense of his situation involves resolving the dilemmas and tensions that result from the discrepancies between the different views of what should be done in the event of an emergency, and hence it has an emotional and a moral dimension. In all these dimensions, the sense-making process is one of finding a way of "going on."

Finalization and Situated Creativity

For Bowker and Star, identity is something constructed at the interstices of many communities of practice all of which are continually in flux. There is nothing stable here, only a process of construction. But, for them, there is also a sense in which this process of construction is somehow predetermined by the communities and the taken-for-granted categories that reside in them. It is as if the categories are pre-existent and the individual has no choice but to play into them. In contrast, although we see identity as constructed at the boundary between self and others, it is not simply a matter of resistance in the face of pre-constituted categories. Rather, it is more a case of creative reconstruction in response to finalization by others. For us, Captain Roy's story seems closer to this dialogical view. It is not so much a story about individual suffering in response to a preordained institution of rules and regulations. As we have seen throughout the excerpts from our interview with him, Captain Roy does not allow the meanings of his experience and actions to be determined by organizations and institutions. Rather, meaning arises as a creative response to the potential of his current situation as the organizations and classifications attempt to finalize him. Captain Roy is defining himself in relation to these others and by reference to his lifelong experiences as a pilot.

Where Bowker and Star might see procedures that are immutable creating the suffering and "torque" that define what an individual is, Bakhtin would see procedures as the means by which an individual can redefine himself and create something other. This creativity manifests itself quite literally in

Captain Roy's design and production of *QRH for Dummies*, an artifact designed to enshrine his experiences and put them into wider circulation.

Centers of Value and Responsivity

The QRHs are centers of value for Captain Roy. They are multi-voiced and authoritative. For Captain Roy, just like any other pilot, failure to follow procedures in the event of an emergency risks various levels of reprimand. But paradoxes arise because, as a statement of what to do, the manufacturer's QRH is not the final word, as evidenced by Captain Roy's experiences. There are many versions of what to do, and some are better than others. As such, the tensions between Captain Roy's concrete and situated experience of QRHs and procedure following and what the manufacturer's QRH says inevitably draw a response from him. They draw a response to each of the voices, each of the centers of value. He wishes his fellow pilots would be taught the "gotchas" from day one. He can't understand why trainers don't write a better book. He sees it as criminal that the operating companies don't write a better QRH. For himself, then, these tensions draw out the felt need to create his own version of the QRH. Through this process, he can achieve some unity in his experiences with the operating procedures.

Engagement, Oughtness, and Answerability

Captain Roy's situated creativity is born, in part, of the emotional-volitional nature of his engagement with the business of flying. Like the mechanic we described in chapter 3 and 4, Captain Roy loves his work and gains aesthetic satisfaction not only from flying but also from mastering his materials. In short, Captain Roy's experience of being a pilot is one of engagement. But there is also a real sense in what Captain Roy described of his life of not just *being* but *becoming*. There is a strong sense of continual growth and change. The project of constructing *QRH for Dummies* is a continual one. Each time Roy goes into a simulator he may find something new, and he is continually on the lookout for QRHs from other airlines.

The felt life of Roy's work as a pilot is clearly one that Dewey would describe as tension-filled. He feels an answerability not only to his passengers, but also to his company, the regulators, the training officers, the other pilots, and himself to do the right thing. This oughtness, and the contradictions it implies, leads to compromises: writing *QRH for Dummies* but not using it in the simulator or circulating it to colleagues, and not "feeling comfortable" without it on the flight deck but always consulting the "official version" first. There is also a sense of responsibility for his fellow pilots who are newcomers to flying certain types of aircraft. These compromises are born of respect for the authority of others under which he works and of certainty that they do not know everything that he does.

Bakhtin argues that for individuals to be in a dialogical relation, each needs a surplus of vision over the other. This is the only way in which they can achieve a creative understanding. The individual is differently placed yet sufficiently connected to allow him or her to enter into dialogue. Through dialogue, each side experiences something new. In Captain Roy's case, the authorities clearly have a particular perspective on the activity of flying a commercial aircraft which is different from yet sufficiently close to Captain Roy's prosaic experience to make dialogue potentially meaningful for both parties. The irony here, of course, is that the institutions within which Captain Roy is operating have what Bakhtin might refer to as an authoritative form-shaping ideology. In such institutions, individuals are subjects of analysis and control, not participants. Activities and individuals are finalized, outcomes are determined in advance, and control is exercised over what the other is required to do. Creative understanding is impossible, because individual and authority cannot enter into dialogue as differently placed equals with the expectation that both authority and individual will learn and change their ideas as a result of the dialogue.

The Sociality of Experience

The social and dialogical nature of experience and sense making permeates this case study. We find it in the multi-voiced nature of the QRH document. We find it in Captain Roy's accounts of simulator trainers, captains he has met, and pilots to whom he has spoken about his *QRH for Dummies*. Most fundamentally, the very existence of a QRH in the life of Captain Roy points to the dialogical character of what Captain Roy does. The QRH is a statement by others as to what Captain Roy should do. For Bowker and Star this might amount to a statement about what it means to be a commercial airline pilot—it is a naturalized artifact of that community, after all. But, as we have seen, for Captain Roy being a pilot is more about creatively redefining the boundaries of what ought to be done.

But a further striking aspect made apparent by Captain Roy's story is what we referred to in chapter 5 as "putting experiences into circulation" by recounting. *QRH for Dummies* represents for Captain Roy a statement of the accumulated experiences of his life as a pilot (at least with respect to his experience of procedures). He wrote it as much out of a concern for others as for himself. He remarks that other pilots who have seen it have really wanted a copy, and he has tried to make it into something that others would find useful and usable and that would give them something better and more valuable than they currently have. But this desire to share his hard-won experiences with others is thwarted by the institution under which he works and, more important, by the respect and to some extent fear he has of that institution.

Conclusion

In the first of our case-study chapters, we gave a very personal firsthand account of shopping online. In this chapter, we have presented a different approach to analyzing experience based on biographical data. We asked Captain Roy to explain where his annotations had come from and why he had made them. In short, we asked him to tell us a story about himself and what he had done. The interview data that flowed out of this simple inquiry startled us in many ways. How Roy described what being a pilot was like differed greatly from our naive conceptions.

We had naively assumed that procedures were the last word, and that dealing with emergencies was simply a matter of choosing the right procedure and filling in the details. Of course things could go wrong, pilots might choose the wrong procedure, and procedures might be inadequate, and we knew that pilots sometimes had to work around the procedures because the procedures couldn't possibly specify every contingency. We understood that there was more to following procedures than reading the words off the page. We had read the ethnographies—well summarized by Dourish (2001)—about the difference between work as prescribed and work as practiced. Indeed, we made sense of the annotations that Captain Roy had made on his QRH as inscriptions of the extra knowledge that the pilot brought to the situation in order to make the procedures work. Shortly after we first presented our analysis of Captain Roy's annotations at a conference (Wright et al. 1998), we were invited to submit a journal article based on our talk. We felt a need to get more background information. Steve Pocock, who was working with us at the time and was a friend of Captain Roy (it was he who had obtained the annotated QRH and done the initial analysis of the annotations), agreed to interview Captain Roy. What emerged from that interview was the data presented here, and elsewhere in more detail (Wright and McCarthy 2003). We were totally unprepared for the radically unfinalized and messy world of "gotchas," different versions of QRHs, official and unofficial versions and the dilemmas that ensued.

When we gathered to discuss the data, we were sure that they were highly significant to our understanding of procedure following and that they would be of value to the academic community and to the aviation community. They seemed to challenge some very deep preconceptions about what procedures were. Yet we never managed to produce a journal article. From the practice-based orientation we had at that time, we simply had no way of articulating what it was we saw in the data. There was "no way out" from practice theory to the felt life of Captain Roy. The language of cognitive psychology, situated action theory, and activity theory simply failed us. Deborah Hicks (1996, 2000) shed some light on what we were searching for with her conception of "moment-to-moment oughtness," but it was not until some years later, when we embarked on the research for this book and read Dewey, Shusterman, and Bakhtin, that we began to have the language necessary to begin to express what we saw in the data. We needed the ways of seeing that the language of Bakhtin and Dewey gave us in order to be able to make sense of it.

Shusterman's notion of reader as writer gave us the first clue to how we should proceed with the analysis. Bakhtin's concept of unfinalizability and the dialogical nature of self-other relations seemed to provide us with what was missing in Bowker and Star's account of classification. Dewey's conception of sense making and continuous engagement helped us understand the motivation for QRH for Dummies. What we took from all this was that Captain Roy's story is a story about identity and felt life, about what it means to be an airline pilot. Identity for Captain Roy is indeed "about managing the tension between naturalized categories on the one hand and degrees of openness to immigration on the other" (Bowker and Star 1999, p. 295). But it is also about more than mere management. It is about a creative, ethical, and aesthetic response to the tension that is the felt life of Captain Roy as an airline pilot. It is a process of continual construction through engagement.

This case study is unlike the others in two significant respects. First, in contrast with the previous two cases, we have very few firsthand accounts of what the experience of ambulance control is like. Second, whereas each of the previous cases focused mainly on one person's experience, here we are concerned with two very different experiences of ambulance control in two very different settings. There is a sense in which this case could be seen as an attempt to check some of the limits of our approach. How do we describe the felt life of ambulance control when we have not asked the ambulance controllers with whom we worked how it feels? And how well can the concepts and ideas that we brought together in chapters 3–5 deal with diversity in experience, insofar as ambulance controllers in different settings have different experiences of ambulance control?

The previous case studies were based on reflection and recounting—an author making sense of an Internet shopping experience for himself, and an author being told about an experience of procedure following by the person making sense of the experience. But this study only occasionally encounters reflection or recounting; it is based largely on situated observation, with an occasional brief discussion of what a particular action meant. This is more like Dewey looking at a mechanic at work and making inferences about the intrinsic meaningfulness of the engine for the mechanic. In the case of ambulance control, we may be able to make similar inferences about the felt quality of lived experience, such as the frustrations and satisfactions that ambulance controllers experience, the sense they make of their work, and emotional responses that reveal something about the things they consider important. There is no magic in what we are trying to do here. It is just like what we do in ordinary, everyday encounters when we get a sense of a person feeling disappointed or one person valuing friendship more than another. We regularly make judgments about people's felt experience in social interactions: why not bring these aesthetic sensibilities into our research?

It is important to be clear at this stage that we are not dealing with anything like an experimental or controlled comparison of the experience of ambulance control in two settings. As we will describe later, there are many differences between the two settings that we studied and we are not concerned with making any claims about the specific relationship between the settings and the experiences. When we carried out this study, a few years ago, we were simply interested in getting a sense of how workers ostensibly doing the same job—getting ambulances to the scene of an emergency—experience the job differently in different settings. It was exploratory and illustrative then and it still is now. The point of including both settings in this case study is to illustrate how our approach to analyzing experience can help us to pick out differences in experiences between them.

It might be useful to begin by briefly describing the background to the study and the two settings. After that, we will develop a description of the felt experience of ambulance control in both settings in order to illustrate the value of our approach even when observation is the main source of information. Of course, it will not be possible or necessary comprehensively to describe ambulance control in this short case study. Rather, our approach will be present an account of a few minutes of ambulance control in each center that seems to us to capture the sense of ambulance control in both. Although these accounts are not representations of any single call in these centers, they imaginatively draw on aspects of the work or moments of activity that we find interesting with respect to the felt experience of ambulance control in these settings. Finally we will present a short discussion that brings our observations and descriptions back to the concepts that inform our approach to felt experience, with a view to making explicit our use of some of those concepts in this chapter.

Two Contexts for Ambulance Control

In this case study, our understanding of experiences of ambulance control is based on research that started in October 1995 and continued for about two years (McCarthy et al. 1997). For about 18 months of the two years, a colleague of ours made visits to two very different ambulance-control centers, which lasted many hours at a time. This involved a series of extended periods sitting in with ambulance-control staff while they carried out their duties. A number of issues that arose from observation were subsequently followed up with staff through open-ended interviews. Tapes of a number of emergency calls were also collected and transcribed to provide further insight into the work. Since ambulance control involves a wide range of activities that we could not cover comprehensively, our analysis focused on the most critical activity performed by the ambulance-control staff, dealing with emergency calls and locating the scenes of emergencies.

As we noted above, this research deliberately involved two very different ambulance-control centers. Center 1, which is situated on the grounds of the main hospital in the region, serves a population of 410,000, nearly one-third of whom live in the main city in the area. Center 1 schedules the activities of sixteen emergency ambulances, five reserve ambulances, and one control unit. The five reserve ambulances, the control unit, and five of the emergency ambulances are stationed in the city; the remainder of the emergency ambulances are distributed across the county. The normal staffing of center 1 at any one time is one controller. All controllers have several years' experience working on ambulance crews before moving to control. Center 2 covers a much larger geographic area, with a larger population and a larger fleet of ambulances. It serves a population of 2.2 million people, 80 percent of whom live in a dispersed conurbation. Center 2 controls 110 accident and emergency ambulances located at 21 ambulance stations and six substations, many of which are in town centers within the conurbation. On a typical day, center 2 deals with more than 500 emergency and urgent calls. During peak operating periods, the personnel in center 2 include three ambulance dispatchers, three radio operators, six to eight telephonists, one team leader, and others who provide technical and planning support. The telephonists and radio operators are recruited directly into center 2 without ambulance experience. A small number of dispatchers have worked on ambulance crews, but most have no direct ambulance experience.

In both cases, 999 calls are directed to the control center via a Telecom operator, located at one of several centralized switchboards, who makes some initial identification of the area the call has originated in and subsequently directs it to the appropriate control center. The individual receiving the call then aims to establish both the precise location of the caller and the nature of the emergency. In both settings, once an ambulance has been selected for dispatch the relevant details of the job are normally passed to the crew on the radio. There are, however, many differences in the way calls are dealt with within each control room. In what follows, we present the experiences of the controllers in each of the two centers as interleaved episodes. This helps emphasize the similarities and differences between them.

Dealing with Emergency Calls

Jane sits at her desk in center 2 watching her space and talking with the women next to her. She is one of seven call receivers sitting in a row, all young women, all wearing telephone headsets with an earpiece and a microphone. Some of them are talking to callers and typing at the same time. Others are chatting while waiting for the next call. Each has in front of her a telephone handset, a bank of telephone-line buttons, a keyboard, and a screen. The bank of buttons is divided into blocks and color coded according to the source of the call they signify when they light up. The screen displays a blank form. One of the buttons begins to flash red. That red light is what makes this job different for Jane. It gives it a sense of urgency and importance that was lacking in her previous job. Two of the receptionists reach for the button. Jane presses it first and is on again. It's the telephone operator. She gives the caller's number to Jane: "795442." "Thank you," says Jane. She takes an emergency call more or less in stride now, but she can still remember how anxious she was the first time she pressed the red button for real.

Jane presses Return on her keyboard, and a number and a time stamp are assigned to the form on her screen.

"Ambulance service?" says the operator to the caller, partly informing, partly querying, as if to double check that she is ready.

Jane hears another voice. She registers a purposeful but slightly anxious woman speaking: "Hello love, emm, it's Mrs. Phillips speaking. I think my husband's took some tablets."

Jane types the woman's name. She's down to business again, clicking now on the address box. She took the name as a matter of form, not even thinking about it, but it's the address that really matters. Without a precise address, the ambulance could end up anywhere. This has been drilled into

Jane and the other call receivers during training. Whatever else, get the address right. Especially when it's an emergency, her business is to help get the ambulance to the emergency as quickly as possible, and that means getting the address spot on. No ambiguities or confusions.

"Right. What address do you want us to come to?"

"Forty Seven Chequers Close."

"Number forty seven, which road again?" Jane is typing as she talks. It is almost a tic at this stage. Jane always gets them to say the address twice, no matter how clearly she heard it the first time. It's a way of checking that it has been said and heard correctly and that it is genuine. (Hoaxers often give a different address the second time.) But Jane is not really aware of checking. It's just what she does now. She sees another button flash red. It stays on for a moment too long. All the receptionists are busy. Jane feels a trace of the anxiety she felt in her early days. But somebody has picked up the new call, and Jane picks up with Mrs. Phillips again. "Chequers Close. C H E Q U," says the caller.

As soon as Jane has typed "Chequers Close" and pressed Return, three addresses appear on her screen. This call is going the way of most calls, and Jane is in the flow now, talking and typing, checking and entering all the while, echoing the address to rehearse it as she types and to check it with the caller as it goes in. She prefers calls like this—ones that go according to plan and where the caller sounds in charge of the situation at the other end. When she has a caller who is not in control, who needs calming down so she can get the information from them, Jane is always left with the nagging feeling that she didn't do all she could or as well as she could have. Has she spent too much time with the caller and delayed the ambulance? Could she have got the information more quickly? Did she miss a detail about the address or the emergency while concentrating on the caller?

"Chequers Close, and that's where please?"

"Em, Castletown."

Castletown—a precise match on the gazetteer. That's the most important part of the job, and it's finished.

"I thought he was just drunk, but I think he's taken some tablets."

"Right. You know what he's taken?"

"Em, it's a sleeping tablet."

"He's taken some sleeping tablets . . . plus alcohol. Has he been drinking?"

"Yeah."

Jane types "alcohol and sleeping tablets" in the free field on her screen and fixes the job, sending it to one of the dispatch teams behind her on the other side of the room.

"All right, Mrs. Phillips. We'll get somebody to him."

"Right, thank you."

"Thank you."

Jane settles back in her seat for a moment. Another one done. She has been doing this job for a year now, so it is mostly fairly routine to her. At the beginning she felt tense every time she pressed the red button. This was an emergency, and if she got the details wrong somebody's life could be at risk. She had had a couple of weeks' training, but this was for real, and the tension was not the tension of learning and examination; it was the tension of a performance where getting it wrong could affect somebody's chances. But now there is little tension with most calls.

Even on an off day, all Jane has to do is follow the computerized form. She can move around the form any way she likes, but she prefers always to take it from the top. If she follows the same order every time, there's less of a chance of missing something. Following the form is comforting in that way. Make sure that you have the name and address and some indication of the problem, and off it goes to the dispatch team. Most of the time Jane likes that comfort of routine. Doing something that matters but without too much pressure. A clear beginning and end to each call. Not too many surprises, though there is the odd difficult call where the caller doesn't know his exact location. The caller might be using a mobile phone, or calling from a phone box in an unfamiliar area, or too distracted to give a clear address. Jane tries to coax relevant information from the caller. It's a challenge, and it creates a bit of pressure from time to time. It breaks the routine.

Another thing that breaks the routine is a hoax call. There are a few every week. Sometimes a hoax caller is a real nuisance, drawing the call out and wasting ambulance time. But an ambulance has to be sent even when there is suspicion about the call unless the call receiver gets the caller to admit that the call is bogus. The more experienced receptionists are very good at spotting bogus calls and at getting the callers to give themselves away. Jane feels she should be better at it. She loves telling the others when she has spotted one, and she is disappointed whenever she misses one. What is it? Is it the voice? Or the way they give the details? Or background sounds?

Jane knows that it is all of these and more. She has been told what to watch out for, but she can't quite feel it as well as some of the others yet.

In center 1, Tony is sitting at a large, old office desk, chatting with a driver who has just popped in to say hello after dropping a patient at the hospital. This room is dull and functional. There are a couple of maps on the wall, one either side of the desk and a computer to the left that doesn't look overused. There is a filing cabinet in the corner and a telephone and a radio system on the desk with a tape system next to the radio console. There are two pads and two pens on the desk. One of the pads looks official; the other, the one nearer to Tony, is a notebook.

Tony is in regular contact with all the drivers, and he knew most of them before he got his present job. Like all the controllers here, Tony was an ambulance driver for eight or nine years before he became a controller. He has been a controller for six years now, and he feels that he knows the job inside out and backwards at this stage. As a controller he never really feels under pressure. There's no pressure like trying to get through heavy traffic to a heart attack or trying to keep somebody going until you get to the hospital. Of course there are times when the calls mount up and he finds himself chasing drivers to get back quickly or to do a double pickup. But because he knows the guys and has done the job, he feels comfortable pushing them. It was something that worried him a bit when he went for the job, but now he feels okay about it.

When there is a lot of work on, it can go one of two ways. Either Tony is driven mad by obstructive rules, technology, and people or he gets into a real flow. He can get really irritated by the things in this job that just shouldn't happen. Last week, two ambulances were out of action because of minor bumps. They could easily still do the job, but the rules say they must be checked by a mechanic before being sent out again. Other times it is poor radio reception. Or a driver or a caller not pulling his weight, not being helpful, or demanding the impossible. But there are times—rare but brilliant—when Tony feels a deep satisfaction at the clarity of his communication with callers and colleagues, respectively reassuring and directing, and the creativity with which he arranges pickups to hit all the right spots at the right times. Of course it's still about getting patients to hospital, but when this happens Tony feels a bit like a jazzman, moving things on at a pace, coaxing, provoking, improvising, drawing improvisation out of the others, and pulling it all together in a piece that feels just right and just on the edge. Although it happens rarely, when it does Tony becomes totally absorbed in what he is doing. He can't see why the busy spells can't be like that all the time, and that makes him cross with his bosses and anybody else who seems to put obstacles in the way of his doing the best job he can.

The phone rings and a button lights on the phone. Tony picks up the phone and presses the button.

"Hello, ambulance service."

"Yeah, this is the operator here. There's someone looking for an ambulance there between, um, Carrigside and Easton. That's yours, is it?"

"It, yeah, that's, er, between Carrigside and Easton?"

Tony is trying to pin down the location. He knows all the city locations but isn't as confident about country ones. He feels uncomfortable when an outsider can tell that he doesn't know exactly where a place is. He feels that they would expect an ambulance controller to know. As he queries the location, he starts to write it in his notepad.

"Yeah . . . near . . . it's beyond Ballylea. It's near some railway gates."

"Yeah, okay, give it to me now." Ballylea means more to him, but he still hasn't pinned it down.

"Right, you're through to the ambulance now."

"Hello."

"Hello, this is ambulance control."

"Yeah, um, Frank O'Brien here speaking."

"Frank O'Brien is it?"

Tony is writing. He can sense the uncertainty in the caller's voice. Although Tony loves talking with people and being able to help them, trying to understand the callers is often the hardest part of the job. Trying to pick up what is urgent and what is not, how bad the injuries are, where exactly they are. People often panic in an emergency, and many people calling for an ambulance are anxious even if there is no panic. You can expect that. And you feel a need to engage with them personally. But you still have to get enough out of them to get an ambulance to the scene and to decide how urgent it is when ambulances are in short supply. Tony thinks Frank is going to be one of the more difficult callers. He sounds really nervous.

You can tell what kind of a caller you have in a few seconds. Some are very confident and businesslike. They have the information rehearsed so well that you hardly have to ask for it. ("My name is. . . . I need an ambulance urgently. My father has collapsed and he has a heart complaint. We live at. . . . It's just beyond the shopping center on the left.") All you have to do is slow them down a little to give you a chance to get all the details. That's great. Tony feels confident from the start of one of these calls. But already his confidence in Frank is limited. Even though he has handled many such calls, he still finds that his attention heightens as soon as he hears any uncertainty in the caller's voice. His sympathy is with the caller, but he knows he will have to concentrate hard.

"That's right, yeah. There's been an accident here at the Imphric railway gates in Ballylea."

A crash. Tony expected as much today. It's always that way over a bank holiday.

"It's midways between Carrigside and Easton. At the railway gates where again? Imphric?" Tony is writing again.

Jim, the ambulance driver sitting across the table, whispers "I know where that is, Tony." Tony nods to Jim. He has heard him. He is pleased that he does not have to push Frank further for directions.

"Well actually you're wanting the railway gates at, uh, you know, it's known as Imphric railway gates."

"Any idea how many people are injured, Frank?"

"Er, there is one."

"How many people are injured?" the caller asks someone at the scene.

"There's a couple injured, but there's one girl I think's, er, kind of seriously injured."

As he talks to the caller, Tony is continuously writing in his notebook. If he was sure of dealing with one call at a time this would not be strictly necessary, but he knows that it is possible that as soon as he puts down this call another will come in. When you get a busy spot like that, writing good notes is essential, so it is best to get into the habit. Anyway, he wants always to feel ready. He also needs to have a fairly precise record for the call receipt book and log book later, and detailed notes make this much easier.

But it's more than that. It's as if Tony is building up a picture of the scene. The notes help him to create a clearer picture of where it is and what's going on there. The location. The injured. The people milling around, trying to help. Each piece adding to the others to make for a clearer picture of the scene. Little notes to help him complete the picture and pass it on as clearly as he can to the ambulance crew. When he was a driver, he hated arriving at a scene and finding that it was totally different from what he was led to expect. No matter how experienced, an ambulance crew must be prepared for a bad accident and possible fatalities. Tony knows this. He imagines himself arriving at the scene, so he always tries to give the crew a clear picture. He almost has a picture of Frank for them now, so that they will know who to talk to when they get there.

"Okay. Anybody trapped, Frank?"

"Pardon?"

"Is there anybody trapped in the car?"

Tony is a little impatient. It happens no matter how hard you try.

"No, there's nobody."

"They're all out of it?"

"There's nobody trapped here at all."

"How many. . . . ?"

Tony can hear some checking between the caller and other people at the scene.

"No. Okay. How many cars involved, Frank? Do you know?"

"There were two, there were two cars."

Frank's edginess makes Tony work twice as hard for every bit of information. Tony is used to this; every second caller is anxious. That's understandable; they are ringing for an ambulance, after all. And time is flying for them. Although Tony knows that they have been talking for less than a minute, he also knows that this can seem much longer to the caller. Tony tries to work with them. He tries to calm them down, reassure them. It's only when they are calmed a little that you can get the information you need. The older controllers always emphasized this when he was training with them. They used to tell him that the hard part of the job was to get the right information out of the caller. You had to stick with the caller for that extra minute to get the information even if it meant a slight delay in dispatching the ambulance. As far as they were concerned sending the ambulance to the wrong place, or to vaguely the right place but without the information needed to get to the spot, was the big no no. Your job was to make sure that didn't happen.

"Okay, what number are you ringing from there, please?"

"Ah, well actually this is, er, a car phone."

"Right, and the number is oh double eight and your phone number."

"Oh. God! Oh eight oh eight eight. I only I only have that."

Frank is getting more worked up by the minute. Tony doesn't want to push him, but he needs the number in case it should be necessary to call Frank back to reassure him and the others there that the ambulance is on its way, or to get clearer directions, or to check how people are if the ambulance is delayed.

"42731," the operator cuts in.

"42731," says Tony, checking.

"Thanks very much," Tony says to the operator.

"Okay."

"Okay, Frank. Hello."

"Okay, Frank, I have it so it's roughly halfway between. . . ."

"You can't miss it because there's a good share of cars."

"Okay, thanks. I'm sending somebody to you now Frank. Okay. Bye."

"Okay, yes. Bye.

"Thank you very much," says Tony to the operator.

"Okay."

Back in center 2, the scheduling system has passed Mrs. Phillips's call to Fiona, one of the dispatchers sitting behind Jane. It is marked as an emergency when Fiona sees it. She has three emergency calls to dispatch now, and she works through them in the order in which they arrived. When she gets to Mrs. Phillips's call, she assigns ambulance 12. Andy, the paramedic on that crew, lives near Castletown, so he should be able to take advantage of any shortcuts and help avoid any traffic problems. Ambulance 12 is about due a run anyway; the crew has had 10 minutes since its last call.

Fiona writes "12" in one of the boxes on a sheet she has next to her. This sheet is her way of keeping track of what crew has been out, when they returned, and what crew is best positioned to answer a call. Fiona tries to ensure that each crew gets a fair share of the work and that she can take advantage of their local knowledge. The official systems don't give her the information she needs. At one time it did, but when a new version was brought in it failed to provide information on ambulances returning to station. Management went on about how efficient the new way would be, but it took no account of what Fiona and the drivers know, what areas they are familiar with, how people feel about getting a fair share of the load. That really annoyed Fiona. (Do they think we're stupid?) So the first thing Fiona does at the start of a shift is pull the relevant missing information together on her sheet. She radios the crews, letting them know that she is on duty and checking who is in each ambulance. She notes their initials next to the ambulance number on her sheet. For the rest of the shift, ambulance 12 or 18 or 9 is a particular crew to her. She knows most of the drivers and paramedics, where they are from, and what area they are most used to, and she tries to dispatch them to that area during the shift. They expect this from her, and in return they would try to do anything for her. If they are sent to one call after another for most of the shift with very little rest, they know that it is because the shift is a very busy one, not because they are getting an unfair load. Some of them might slag Fiona a bit if they went for a drink after work but it would be good-natured. They know she tries her best for them.

Fiona is at ease with the ambulance crews. More important, she is comfortable with the job. She has done most jobs in the center at one time or another, even stood in for the supervisor on occasion. She understands how all the equipment works, and so she knows which systems to use and which to ignore. Without a thought she knows to use the electronic map in the older parts of her area but to ignore it in the newer parts. The maps are just not updated often enough to be useful in areas where new houses and streets are being built. This can be frustrating, but Fiona is more frustrated by the money spent on the new system. She manages ambulance dispatch the way she sees fit. But this means that the expensive new system is of no help to her. But Fiona won't let that spoil the job for her.

Fiona's radio operator is busy, so she radios Mrs. Phillips's call to ambulance 12 herself.

"Good morning, emergency for you please. And it's Forty Seven Chequers Close in Castletown."

"Forty seven where, love?"

"Chequers Close Castletown." (Fiona is slower and more deliberate here.)

"Chequers Close Castletown."

"Yeah. It's a Mr. Phillips, and his wife's found him collapsed. She thinks he may have taken tablets and alcohol."

"Yeah."

"Okay, it's job number 92 at 0721."

"Okay, love."

"Okay, thank you."

"Right."

"Bye."

Ambulance 12 lights up on the map in front of Fiona. The ambulance moves away. Fiona expects this to be a clean, straightforward pickup. She looks up. No emergencies and four urgent still on her board. She must keep an ambulance in station 2 for any emergency in the area, so she decides to send one of the ambulances from station 3 to an urgent call that is just out of their area. She thinks the crew will understand.

In center 1, Tony calls the Midton Ambulance Station, at Midton Hospital, to dispatch an ambulance.

"Hello Midton, this is ambulance control. I have a 999 for a road traffic accident between Carrigside and Easton by Imphric railway gates."

"Where?"

"Imphric P H R I C, I M P H R I C."

"I don't know that."

"Hang on, Jim Walsh is here. He will give you directions."

"All right. Thanks a lot."

"Hello!" [Jim, emphatically]

"Hello Jim, how are you?"

"How are you, Mary girl? Who's on tonight? Is it Liz? Okay. Listen. Just after going over the bridge outside town there she'll be by Reynolds's pub and service station, the service station there on her left-hand side. About twenty yards above that there's a small road going up to the right."

"Right."

"She should take that road for about two miles, and then there's a right turn marked for Carrigside. Imphric railway gates are about a mile down. There's no railway there, but the locals still know it that way from when there was. Anyone will show her if she gets lost there. The road widens for about quarter of a mile, and the gates are on that wide stretch. Tony says there are a few cars involved, so she won't miss it."

"All right."

"Lovely. Get her to radio Tony when she's en route and he'll fill her in on the scene. Be good."

"Thank you very much."

"Good luck."

"Bye now, bye."

Jim leaves just after that call. Two minutes later, ambulance 9 calls for details. Tony and the crew of ambulance 9 agree that it would be best to have a fire brigade there. There is bound to be oil on the road even if the cars are fairly safe. Tony calls the fire brigade and the police and asks them to send units to the scene.

Being a Controller

All in all, Fiona likes her job. It has its difficulties, but then doesn't every job? She enjoys the basic challenge of solving problems, often under pressure. Fiona was always good at problem solving , and she can imagine pushing herself a little further when the time comes. Perhaps going for a supervisor job. One of the things Fiona really appreciates about her job is that no two days are the same. When she comes on shift, she has no idea what to expect. She feels energized by that variety. Every day and even every call presents a different challenge, depending on where ambulances are at the time, what the lists are like, where the call is coming from, and what the state of the patient is. She really enjoys her relationship with the ambulance crews. They trust her and are fair with her. She looks out for them but also feels comfortable pushing them a little when she has to. She gets satisfaction from managing her ambulances to ensure that all needs are met, and especially from getting ambulances to emergencies on time and possibly saving lives. She doesn't mind not being the one on the scene. That wouldn't be her thing at all. She knows that she is doing what she is good at.

Fiona is not sure about what management is trying to do to her job. The systems they introduce seem designed to take away the say she has in how she does her job. She gets around this by working out her own system. A big part of her satisfaction with the job is the sense that she is making the decisions. Another is the relationship she has with the crews. When she is dealing with a call, she has always had a sense of commitment to the patient and loyalty to the crew. The new systems interfere with some of that and seem to demand loyalty to management over crew. Fiona doesn't think this is necessary. She feels that it is possible to satisfy both, if only they would let her get on with it. So far she has worked around the new systems. But what if they introduce something else that ties her hands tighter? It wouldn't be the same job then.

Jane is different. Getting into ambulance control was a deliberate move by her. She was getting bored with being the telephonist in the hospital. The job was nothing but directing calls. When she spoke to friends who were call receivers in ambulance control, they told her about the satisfaction of being involved. You're not just passing on calls. You're involved in getting ambulances to people who need them. Jane really appreciates this. But, unlike Fiona, she wants to know what to expect in her work. She is very satisfied with knowing more or less what to expect every day. She can handle working under pressure when there are a lot of calls, but she would not like to have to make the kind of decisions Fiona makes every day. She prefers a challenge that is ordered and well within her scope.

Tony's pleasure is in seeing his calls through from beginning to end. He is the one who deals with the caller—trying to get enough information to see how serious the call is and to be sure of getting the ambulance to the right location, deciding whether a call is an emergency, hearing the caller's panic or his certainty about diagnosis. Calming the caller. Reassuring the caller that he will send an ambulance immediately. Building up a picture of the scene (for example, cars, lights on in a window, and somebody standing, waiting at a gate). Doing whatever is necessary to get the drivers what they need. Describing the scene to the ambulance crew. The caller and how in control he seems to be. The patient. What is wrong and what they might have to do? Getting them there. Joking with drivers but preparing them for what to expect. The feeling of making it happen. The satisfaction of helping. The pleasure of pulling all the pieces together.

Because he has done it for so long, and because he was on ambulances before that, Tony has a strong sense of what the job is about and how most calls will turn out. He has a strong intuition for bogus calls. He spots them about three quarters of the time. And he is good at dealing with drunks; he can often get one to go home without sending out an ambulance as a taxi. Tony knows that the callers call the shots. It is his job to respond to what they need. But he also knows that the best way to do that is for him to take charge. And although the callers always come first, he knows that the best way to satisfy them in the long run is to keep the crews happy. He can hear the older controllers telling him that the crews do most of this job and that all he has to do is to give them a fair chance and the job would get done. It's still true as far as Tony is concerned.

Some Important Themes

Like the two previous case studies, this one shows how several of the concepts identified in earlier chapters are central to understanding felt experience. The comparative element of this case study allows us to see how some concepts play more of a role in understanding some situations than others.

Sense Making and Work

This case study illustrates the importance of a rich understanding of the meaning of work for workers. We see in action a number of different kinds of sense making, all of which have been discussed in chapters 3–5.

The immediate, pre-reflective *sense* of a situation ran through the case study. For example, the red light creates the pervasive quality of emergency. Jane does not have to reflect on the meaning of that light; it is intrinsic to it. We also had reference to the sense of there being something wrong with a call (it just doesn't sound right) or something difficult about a call (the caller seems confused and anxious). We also saw—though perhaps less directly in this case study than in the others—workers *reflecting* on and *recounting* their experiences. An example is the good-natured teasing Fiona sometimes gets from her ambulance crew colleagues. We can imagine them revisiting calls and reconstructing their status. Was that one really an emergency? They could easily have waited an hour or two until we had cleared the real emergency calls. We can see classification being reshaped after the event and feeding into future decisions about the status of calls. In the unfinalizability of experience, reflecting and recounting become sense making.

Fiona's and Tony's experiences of ambulance control seem to embody a tension between the *extrinsic* and *intrinsic* meaningfulness of what they do and how they do it. In what might be a rare example, we had Tony during a very demanding spell enjoying ambulance control for its own sake. He can feel the clarity of communication and the creativity of coordination, the beauty of a perfect hour of controlling (directing, coaxing, improvising) enjoyed for its own sake. The tension between intrinsic and extrinsic meaningfulness of the caller is a more common experience for Tony than for Fiona. He likes people for their own sake, and he likes interacting with them and helping them (intrinsic). But he must also use them as a source of information about the scene of the emergency (extrinsic). Both Tony and Fiona are concerned with the members of the ambulance crew for their own sake. In the broader context (the systems view, perhaps), they are extrinsically meaningful as a means to the end of getting patients to hospital. However, in terms of local relationships, although Fiona and Tony are aware of the usefulness of the ambulance crew, they also value them as people who should be prepared for difficult situations and treated fairly.

We also get a sense in this case study of the struggle for meaningfulness that these controllers engage in and how the struggle and the meaningfulness differ from person to person. We get a sense of three people who frame or author their work experiences differently. Jane, who seems to have moved into ambulance control to have a stronger sense of involvement in something intrinsically meaningful than she had in her previous job, frames her experience in terms of the beginning and end of individual calls. And the technology that she uses in her work—the electronic form and the gazetteer—seems to support that framing. Fiona, faced with a technological change that threatens her autonomy and her relationship with ambulance crew, creatively overcomes the limitations of the technology to retain the autonomy and relationships that contribute so much to the meaningfulness of ambulance control for her. Fiona clearly needs more than that minimal engagement to satisfy her need for challenge. She takes on more varied work and work that entails more responsibility and she enjoys it. So much so that she would consider increasing that challenge in time. For her, the meaning is in the challenge and the relationships. She likes the sense she has of working with the ambulance crews. The trust and teamwork is important to her. She also enjoys the challenge of getting the most out of the resources available to her. Her contribution is in managing resources such that all her calls are dealt with satisfactorily and the emergency ones are dealt with in the speediest way possible. The meaning of ambulance control for Tony is in seeing each call through from beginning to end. He is engaged in the whole process of getting ambulances to patients—dealing with the callers, managing resources, dealing with ambulance crew—and without that whole engagement, it would be less meaningful for him. This may be related to his background as ambulance crew. He was used to dealing with patients and family, hospitals, and controllers. Anything less now would leave a gap in his felt experience of ambulance control.

Sensual Engagement

Because Tony takes each call from beginning to end, his sensual engagement is more sustained than the other two. He hears the panic or the certainty in the caller's voice. Of course, Jane does too, but she is not the person talking to the ambulance crew about the call and caller. Tony's engagement has always been sensual. As ambulance crew, he saw the relief and anguish in a caller's face, he heard the anxiety in a patient wondering if they were dying, he smelt the burning and the oil after a crash. As a controller he depends on the same sensibilities, listening for a note or register in the caller's voice. He makes his judgments on that kind of immediate sense of a situation.

Situated Creativity

In both ambulance-control centers, we can see situated creativity in action. Fiona, working around the constraints of a new technology that seems to take away some of her autonomy, creates a personal record of ambulance movements that allows her to maintain her working relationship with the drivers and to use her judgment in choosing which ambulance to dispatch. There is also a more basic sense in which she exercises creativity in carrying out her work. She is constantly reviewing and creating goals depending on the situation that was continually changing in front of her. Keeping one ambulance in station at station 4 could suddenly become important if there were a run of calls for station 4 and she would have to work out alternative ways of satisfying the needs of callers from the station 4 area until some ambulances return to base. This would involve drawing ambulances from other stations, perhaps even getting them to leave station and park up closer to the boundary with station four area in anticipation of further demand.

Tony, faced with the vagaries of a large rural area, uses whatever resources he can muster to get an ambulance to the scene of an emergency. They can be drivers who happen to be in the center with him, local landmarks, or even transient features such as the caller standing at a gate. His interactions with callers can also be very creative. For example, he sometimes gives a very anxious caller things to do at the scene even if they aren't really necessary, just to keep them active. He also calls them back when he has the time to do so to talk them through the situation.

These examples of situated creativity are not unrelated to the process of making work intrinsically meaningful. For example, for Tony, an intimate relationship with the caller and patient is central and so much of his effort goes into getting them through the emergency as well as possible. His engagement with the callers leads him to work for them in as creative a way as possible in dealing with their calls. Of course this is not just a sensory engagement. It is also emotional.

Emotional Engagement and Centers of Value

As we noted in reflecting on the first case study in chapter 6, our fore-grounding of the emotional-volitional nature of the act highlights aspects of the felt experience such as concern, fear, desire, and need as they emerge through continuous engagement between self and other as two centers of value. In the case study presented in this chapter, we see two broad sets of relationships that constitute the work of ambulance control. Although composed differently in the two centers, there is in both a relationship between controllers and callers and a relationship between controllers and drivers. While the relationship with drivers is direct and immediate in both centers, the relationship with callers differs from center to center.

Having been a member of an ambulance crew for many years, Tony has a strong commitment to the crews. As far as he is concerned, a major part of his job is in supporting them to deal with emergencies. Getting the best directions possible for them. Tony has a very strong sense of their impor-tance in the work that they do together. So does Fiona. She has gone to the trouble of developing an alternative personal record of ambulance move-ments, to ensure a fair distribution of work. She values them and their trust in her.

Although both are also concerned with looking after the caller, the emo-tional engagement with the caller is more immediate for Tony. He hears their voice and briefly gets to know them in a personal way. He hears their worry and anxiety and tries to calm them down. He has the intimate moment with them, when perhaps they are at their most vulnerable. He tries his best for them personally, the particular person he has come to know briefly but intimately. Jane's contact with the caller is kind but busi-nesslike, driven as it is by the demands of a gazetteer. And Fiona, although she is deeply concerned to get ambulances to emergencies efficiently, never even hears the caller's voice.

This difference is reflected somewhat in their respective senses of answer-ability. Fiona seems to be answerable to callers in a global way. If she manages her resources efficiently, they get a good service. Tony's answerability is more immediate and more particular. It comes from his personal engagement with a person who needs his help.

Intonation

We can also see this case study as illustrating some of Bakhtin's ideas of intonation and utterance—something like the dialogical space mentioned in the first case study on Internet shopping. In both centers, the controllers appear to have an ever-present responsivity to ambulance crew, even when they are not physically present. It is as if the controllers are in dialogue with ambulance crew when dealing with callers and managers. As we saw in the examples above, the controllers' requests for information are intoned with the voices of the ambulance crew. From Bakhtin's perspective on the dialogicality of experience, we see an utterance as always expressed from a point of view and that point of view as being produced by a voice entailing register, positioning, subject's perspective, conceptual horizon, worldview, and values. And so it seems that controllers speak from a point of view that includes the register, positioning, worldview, and values of ambulance drivers and their crew. The fact that some controllers have been members of an ambulance crew before doing their current job would go some way toward explaining a voice that intones for the ambulance crew also. But even where they do not have that particular shared history, they have a history of working together in their current roles. Fiona has spent time trying to understand the needs of ambulance crew in carrying out their work. She has spoken to them about it. She tries to imagine what it must be like for them.

As well as the voice of the author, the perspective, position, and worldview of the listener is crucial to understanding how Bakhtin sees dialogical meaning making happening. For example, the ambulance controller speaking to the caller voices into a dialogical context that includes the knowledge, interests and values of the caller. The register is clear, helpful, but possibly firm and directive. After all, they must elicit the most useful information about the location of the scene of the emergency to get the ambulance to the scene as quickly as possible. Whereas the controller knows what kind of information this is, the caller often does not. The register and tone is quite different when in dialogue with the ambulance crew. Referring back to our earlier discussion of the relationship between aesthetic and ethical experience, the controller completes the caller and the driver in dialogue with them and, in so doing, is answerable to them. As a consequence, different voicings are used in response to the different voices of the other.

Conclusion

In the last three chapters we have presented concrete, particular examples of people's felt experience with technology. The interaction with technology was immediate and direct in the Internet shopping case. In chapter 7, the focus was on the experience of procedures provided for interacting with technology. In the current chapter, technology was just one element in a work situation, where many of the other elements seemed more important in terms of the felt experience of work. The point of presenting each of the three cases was to illustrate the concepts we had described and discussed in chapters 3–5.

In the next and final chapter, we want to tie up some loose ends and to explore some implications of our approach for HCI. Although the case studies were intended to be illustrative, they also have delivered a few new insights and developments that we would like to relate to the position we were in at the end of chapter 5. We would also like to take a final opportunity to briefly reprise what we think is made visible by focusing on felt experience over and above what is made visible by the activity and practice theories discussed in chapter 2. In the process of doing this we will tackle some questions that have come up for us in writing this book about the quality and variety of experience. Finally we will go back to where we started and reflect on the implications of our approach for HCI design and use.

Designing for the full range of human experience may well be the theme for the next generation of discourse about software design.

—T. Winograd (1996, p. xix)

As the epigraph to chapter 1 suggests, our main aim in writing this book was to make lived experience with technology the primary reality in practice and comment on relations between people and technology, especially in Human-Computer Interaction and in Computer-Supported Cooperative Work. Although HCI has its roots in laboratory subjects such as psychology and computer science, it has in recent times been strongly influenced by concern for experience. We can see this in two broad areas. First, the academic voices of practice and activity theorists have taken HCI out of the laboratory and into the field, where greater attention has had to be paid to contexts of use. Second, we see in advertising and on company web sites the emergence of a commercial imperative to attend to user experience as computers and related information and communication technologies become categorized as consumer products. While both promote concern for the needs of users, their activities, relationships, and contexts of use, they seem to us to lack the kinds of sensibilities to the felt and personal that we associate with experience. Like Geertz (1986), we think there is a danger that the cultural analysis being developed in HCI and CSCW in the name of practice theory, activity theory, or user experience can be used in a meaningless manner, separate from people fearing, hoping, imagining, revolting, and consoling. Geertz's response to that danger—and ours—is that analyses of relations between people and technology "must engage some sort of felt life" if they are not "to float several feet above their human ground" (ibid., p. 374). Therefore, in attempting to turn consideration of technology toward experience, we have been keen to emphasize the felt, emotional quality of experience.

Our contribution toward developing sensibilities to felt life with technology has been made twice in this book. First, in chapters 3–5, we attended to clarifying the concepts. We drew on the work of Dewey and Bakhtin to review lived, felt experience as prosaic, open, and unfinalizable, situated in the creativity of action and the dialogicality of meaning making, engaged in the potential of each moment at the same time as being responsive to the personal stories of self and others, sensual, emergent, and answerable. Our aim was not so much to develop a theory of experience with technology as to suggest an approach to viewing technology as experience that is open to the sensual, emotional, volitional, and dialogically imaginative aspects of felt experience. Through discussion and exemplification we introduced a set of concepts that we have found useful in our own practice and comment. What our presentation of these concepts adds up to is a foundation for an aesthetic approach to seeing technology as experience.

Our aim in chapters 3–5 was not to present a unified theory. Rather, our aim was to demonstrate what could possibly be seen with an aesthetic-experiential lens on technology. This lens makes visible the potential for charm, enchantment, love, excitement, alienation, and irritation in our relations with technology. It also makes visible the quality of space-time in which we relate with technology and the sensory and sensuous character of the experience. Perhaps the most important aspect of experience that it makes visible is the potential for surprise, imagination, and creativity, which is immanent in the openness of each moment of experience. In demonstrating the potential of an aesthetic lens, we hope we have heightened sensibilities to the aesthetic and emotional in action and interaction.

Of course it is possible to criticize our approach in these chapters. We have put two writers in dialogue with each other who are not often even mentioned in the same philosophical or social-theoretical conversations. We recognize the differences between Dewey's and Bakhtin's approaches to experience. Dewey was oriented toward asserting a continuity between the natural and the phenomenological. Bakhtin, much more radically oriented toward the humanities and literature, prized deep exploration of the particular and the personal above the precision and generalization of the natural sciences. Yet we see sufficient common ground between them for a meaningful dialogue, and we value the differences between them as an enrichment of that dialogue. Neither Dewey nor Bakhtin had much time for systematic philosophy or theoreticism. Both were oriented toward the ordinary everyday and, in many ways, the practical. Both have been used to review education, politics, and to a lesser extent technology. In their attempts to overcome the traps of dualism, both emphasized the relational or dialogical. And to our ears both sound like advocates for imaginative, revisionary conceptualization rather than representation. Another criticism would be that we have been selective in our readings of Dewey and Bakhtin, to which we plead guilty. We have scavenged ideas from both to advance our understanding of lived, felt experience, without feeling the need to deal with every concept that they generated in their extensive, often changing, writings.

Having made our contribution conceptually in chapters 3–5, we made it again in chapters 6–8, but this time in a more intuitive, commonsense way. In those chapters, we tried to heighten sensibilities to the aesthetics of experience with technology by presenting case studies.

One of us told the story of his own experiences with Internet shopping. This story illustrates the dialogical character of even the very prosaic experience of shopping. The voices of other shoppers, neighbors, Virginwines, and his wife interpenetrate each other creating a dialogical space in which this shopping experience takes place. In this dialogical space, we saw judgments made on the basis of the shopper's desire to please his wife. His emotional responsivity to his wife's feelings and values permeated the decisions he made and the ways in which he made those decisions. As did his responsivity to the retailer, with whom he sometimes identified, and other buyers, with whom he seemed to feel he was sharing an experience. Finally, this case study shows the potential of each moment and the openness of experience. While we tend to construe this openness as positive, the case study also shows that when technology fails to meet our expectations openness becomes an obstacle to fulfillment.

In the second case study, we recounted the story that Captain Roy told us about his life as a commercial airline pilot. His was a story of a person continually constructing and reconstructing a self at the boundaries of many practices. Unlike some practice theory accounts of self in community though, Captain Roy's story made the felt life of working at boundaries and the moment-to-moment oughtness and ethical weight of becoming a pilot very apparent. We saw how the job of flying planes is a highly proceduralized one, and how the procedures, while seeming to be the final word on what to do in the event of an emergency, turn out to be anything but the final word. We saw how a multitude of value-laden voices in Captain Roy's experiences are instrumental in telling him what to do—the voices of the aircraft manufacturers, his employers, the simulator trainers, the voices of other people from other companies and other times in Captain Roy's life. Captain Roy's response to this dialogue was to create his own annotated reference handbook, and then a properly word-processed version. But this in turn brought its own dilemmas that had to be resolved. This case study not only showed us how users design technology in use, but it also gave us a clear view of the felt life of continually becoming an airline pilot.

In the final case study, we created a story of ambulance control from observations and interviews we made in some ambulance-control centers. Methodologically this case study illustrated the possibility of developing an account of felt, lived experience from a third-person perspective. Stylistically, it attempted to convey something of the heterogeneity of voices involved, even though the narrator is always outside. One of the key things it made visible is the richness of meanings of ambulance control created by the controllers themselves. The pre-reflective sense of a situation plays a strong part in their felt experience of ambulance control. We saw that the intrinsic meaningfulness of their work, the choreographed rhythms of control and the felt commitment to teamwork, gives shape to their moments and to their days. We also saw the sense and sensibility of continued engagement between controller and caller and the hot-blooded creativity of constructing and re-describing goals in the height of activity. Finally, we saw the concern that colleagues have for each other in their continuous engagement with each other as separate centers of value.

These case studies were not intended to prove or even to explain anything. Rather, they were intended as concrete, particular illustrations of the ways in which we have looked at people's relationships with technology with the sensibilities to lived, felt experience that we had been evoking in the earlier chapters. Whereas chapters 3–5 were intended to appeal intellectually, the case studies were intended to appeal intuitively. To use the language of the earlier chapters, they were intended to give readers a feel for what people's experiences with technology looks like when we try to get at the emotional, valuational, and dialogical character of it. By presenting these illustrative case studies, we have demonstrated both the value of looking out for the feltness of experience and the value of concrete stories of particular people and events as part of an approach to analyzing experience in HCI. We have shown that these stories can take a variety of forms and perspectives—event-driven, situational, biographical, autobiographical—and still express a sense of the felt life or event.

Having reviewed our main contribution and how we made it, it might be worth reflecting briefly at this stage on where this contribution has taken us in terms of ongoing attempts to embed discussions of technology in concern for people's ordinary everyday activities.

From Practice Theories to Felt Experience

In terms of the way in which we structured the book, our attempts to describe felt experience and to demonstrate its power as a lens on living with technology came from identifying a lacuna in the turn to practice. While we have for a number of years found this turn liberating in our own attempts to think about human-computer interaction, we have also been nagged by a touch of ambivalence. For our taste and interests there is something lacking in most of the approaches that have been characterized as constituting the turn to practice in HCI.

As we stated in chapter 2, the turn to practice in HCI has made a number of very useful contributions. It has rendered problematic a mindset that is happy with "in principle" statements or abstract models of interaction in which any empirical contribution is limited to laboratory experiment. In its place, the turn to practice is committed to understanding technology through empirical analysis of technology in use. Since the early 1990s, this has resulted in a steady flow of field studies of people working with technologies in air traffic control centers, print shops, airports, ambulance and train control centers, offices, hospitals, medical centers, banks, and homes. Many of these studies have enriched our understanding of the nuances of the coordination of work activities, social practices of accountability, and situated construction and use of resources. As a consequence, they have influenced design deliberation in these and related work settings. However—and here is the core of what we see as missing in these approaches—few of them have given us any sense of how individuals in any of these settings feel about their work and their colleagues, what their emotional response is to the situations in which they find themselves, and what the emotional and ethical weight of a moment or event in these settings is like. Moreover, despite the presence of a discourse on reflexivity in related social theory, many contributions from practice and activity theorists have a strong sense of the third person about them. It is into these gaps that we wanted to press our particular contribution and in doing so we have found ourselves clarifying our relationship with some of the social-practice contributions to HCI and CSCW.

Throughout the book we have emphasized what we now think of as the openness of our experiences with technology: for example, the engagement and unfinalizability of experience that we discussed in chapters 3–5, the fun and frustration of Internet shopping, and the committed creativity of piloting and ambulance control that we described in chapters 6–8. We have invested "technology as experience" with the weight of becoming in contrast to "the unbearable lightness of being" visited on the disengaged. This weight is emotional, valuational, and intellectual, and points to the aesthetic quality of experience too often underplayed in sociologically inspired accounts of experience. As such the weight of becoming is not a burden, it is not a weight that holds us back; rather, it is the weight of responsive relating that underpins the dialogical imagination. And this is where we locate the playfulness of experience. It is in the simultaneously aesthetic and ethical consummation of an other as a center of value separate from ourselves that we play with our own selves, making dialogical moments complex, deep, and open.

Phil Agre, in *Computation and Human Experience* (1997a), presents an analysis of practices of theorizing and conceptualizing in which he demonstrates how the metaphors we use when conceptualizing bring some phenomena to the center and put others at the margins. We see our own work as putting the playfulness, openness, and emotionality of experience at the center of our concerns. In doing so we identify with the sociologist Ian Craib (1998) when he wonders why, in contemporary social theory, it seems so hard to construe people as both social and individual, or (to use another metaphor) as having both an external and an internal life. Some social theorists seem to avoid the complexity and openness of a view of humanity as living on boundaries rather than being determined by one side or the other.

It may be that we are at our most imaginative, and definitely dialogical, when we live on boundaries. Referring back to Agre's treatment of metaphor above, one might say that centering the social and marginalizing the individual or vice versa is a very useful way of reducing complexity and openness. However, if we want to reflect on what it is like to live on boundaries, negotiating between the social and the individual, these simplifications may not be available, and we may have to place dialogue at the center or even avoid the hierarchical modes of thinking—scientific and philosophical for example—that make centering and marginalizing inevitable. One of Bakhtin's insights was that literary or prosaic thinking could entertain many aspects and dimensions of experience simultaneously. We noted earlier, in chapters 3 and 4, Bakhtin's commitment to the novel as a way of seeing. Particularly, we drew attention to his treatment of the novel of emergence as a way of seeing the fullness of time, which is hidden in many other ways of seeing. The novel of emergence makes visible people living into the future, always becoming, characterized by potential, creativity, freedom, and initiative. It provides a useful model of people making sense of their experience in terms of a life partly lived and partly yet to be lived. This is the kind of sense making that we see in people's interactions with technology.

Richer models for human-computer interaction are required if we are to take account of experience and people making sense of it. Perhaps Bakhtin's treatment of the novel and Dewey's treatment of art as models of aesthetic experience suggest that it is time for the development of a strong literary or art-related approach to HCI and CSCW. This would enable us to review the humanity for which we design, evaluate, and polemicize as simultaneously social and individual, as having rich external and internal life, and as always becoming.

Some social-theoretical approaches may also be of value in reframing HCI and CSCW. One of the main aims of these approaches is to understand becoming, yet they have largely been ignored in the study of relationships between people and technology. One such approach has been developed by Valerie Walkerdine and is based largely on a reading of Foucault. In a critique of Jean Lave's approach to cognition in practice, Walkerdine (1997) argues that Lave's formulation of practices as activities and people acting in a setting, specified by a dialectical relationship, carries the danger that neither person nor setting is adequately theorized. Instead of viewing situated cognition as people thinking in different contexts—a conceptualization in which she still finds the dualism that practice theories claim to overcome—she views it as subjects or persons produced differently in different practices. She argues that the production of the person within practices is lacking in

Lave's largely cognitivist account. The alternative she offers is a fusion of the material and discursive that looks closely at how signification within practices can be presented as relating to dimensions that are largely ignored in Lave, such as desire, longing, need, uncertainty, and confusion.

It might be interesting to consider for a minute why HCI and CSCW latched on to the anthropological cognitivism of Lave, the external consciousness of activity theory, and the observable technology of interaction and accountability highlighted by ethnomethodology, and still largely ignored those social theorists concerned with the production of the subject or person. Could it be that, social theoretic insertions and the rejection of information processing notwithstanding, HCI and CSCW still hankers after a rationalism that would be challenged by a turn to the person and then unavoidably to desire, value, and emotion? Making the person—and particularly the emotional-volitional character of the person that we recognize in desire, longing, and joy—central, would radically challenge the rationalist assumptions of studies of people and technology in ways that HCI and CSCW may not be ready to do. While we have not taken the Foucault-Walkerdine line in this book, we have tried to use Dewey and Bakhtin to bring the emotional, sensual, and valuational aspects of experience to the fore in ways that do not require a rejection of the intellectual. In this regard, Dewey has been a bridge for us from the practice theorists to felt experience and Bakhtin has suggested an altogether more literary approach that plays around with the variety of experiences that people engage in.

The Varieties of Experience

Shifting the focus of conceptualizing human-computer interaction from the representation of observable technologies of accountability, contextualized cognition, and external consciousness to the emotional-volitional play of observable and unobservable, cognition and emotion, internal and external puts the weight of each particular moment at the center and brings into focus the variety of experiences that people engage in. Shifting focus from one pre-constituted structure or another—mind or society—to the interplay that constitutes both enables us to see participation as well as non-participation, multiple identificatory possibilities, lags in participation, and conflictual moments of identification. In bringing the language of identity and difference to sociocultural analysis, authors such as Hodges,

Walkerdine, and Hicks highlight the possibility for agonized compromise, discomfort, joy, or ambivalence in becoming a member of any community. They point to the weight of the moment, the texture of the character, and the variety of experience that, in our analysis, Bakhtin also points to. For example, responsivity to an other as a separate center of value suggests an emotionally intoned sense of trust and commitment that we don't really see in Winograd and Flores's (1986) formal analysis of commitment. Bakhtin points us toward the variety of feelings that constitute any particular interpersonal commitment so that we orient toward the variety of commitments in our case studies rather than assuming that a formal description of commitment covers them all. The commitment of Captain Roy to safe flying, trainee pilots, and his peers. The commitment of ambulance controllers to drivers and callers in different ambulance-control centers. The commitment of a retailer to a purchaser. They all feel different and, in considering relations between people and technology, should be prized for the variety of experiences they point toward.

Bakhtin's unfinalizability and multi-voicedness and Dewey's attention to the pragmatics of change in experience suggests an experiential approach to self and identity that foregrounds, variety, change, ambivalence, and complexity. When Samuel Beckett's character Winnie asks "How is it that I have always been who I am yet no longer am who I was?" we sense a play between history and fiction, narrative and autobiography, the given and created that makes identity and self playful and played with. Instead of thinking of identity and self as given or conferred by a social context, we can think of them as participating in the variety of experience. Sherry Turkle has already commented extensively on the participation of self in felt life with contemporary technologies, where the computer, the Internet, a cyber-pet, or a computer game becomes a tool that facilitates playing around with our sense of self.

Putting self and identity into play in this way is at the heart of openness, unfinalizability, and the variety of experience. Whereas some of the social-theoretical approaches that have been used to reflect on relationships between people and technology, especially those that opt to put social processes at the center and to marginalize self and identity, emphasize the routine and the sameness in life, an orientation toward felt experience emphasizes the ways in which people deal with routines. For some people, a particular work routine can be experienced as alienating, for others it can be experienced as stimulating. Focusing on the routine itself misses out on the variety of feelings toward the routine and ways of dealing with it. If we sacrifice the uncertainties, the anxieties, the clarity, and the insight that we experience when dealing with the routines of life to a synthesis at the level of social practices, we close off our conceptualizing to variety, change, and complexity.

In practice, when those of us who are interested in commenting on relationships between people and technology close off to the variety of experience, we miss out on the fun, wonder, magic, and enchantments of technology. HCI has begun to realize this lack in recent years as we can see from the emergence of books and papers on affective technologies (Jordan 2000; Blythe et al. 2003). In one such collection, we have written impressionistically about the enchantments of technology, the sense of being caught up and carried away by a particular artifact or design, and the sense of possibility in every thing (McCarthy and Wright 2003). Reflexively, it seems to us that enchantment is one of the experiences missing from many analyses of people's relationships with technology, not just the enchantment of the person whose experience is described, but also the enchantment of the analyst or commentator. Many of us have lost the sense of the magic of technology that attracted us to this area of study in the first place. The sense of wonder at what an ordinary computer could do and how it did it. The sense of the magic of contacting people over distances and time zones using email. The sense of awe and anxiety at the precision of an industrial robot arm. The early sense of disbelief at the idea of shopping online that has quickly turned to routine. Our participation in academic and professional communities that have already determined what every thing is—for example, curricula and textbooks that define 'computer', or 'society', or 'self' such that our curiosity is lessened—diminishes our enchantment with technology. The experience of enchantment requires that we approach our subject open to the possibility of every thing becoming and to our own authorship of the thingness of things—computers, communities, and selves—in dialogical relationship with them. It requires a dialogical imagination that Bakhtin has described for us. For him, the world is an open place full of potentiality, freedom, newness, and surprise. In this world, the potential for enchantment rooted in the experience of novelty is everywhere. We conclude our work by imagining what such a perspective means for design.

Dialogicality and Design

In a pragmatically oriented work such as this, it feels right to try to draw the discussion to a close with one final reflection on the potential usefulness of the position we have been developing for design. In many of the foregoing chapters, we have attended to aspects of how our approach could be used to enrich experience. For example, in chapters 4 and 5, where we described the threads of experience and processes of making sense in and of experience, our orientation was toward using these ideas to review experiences such as going to a film and creating stories in POGO World. This reviewing can be understood in terms of richly seeing a context of use and evaluating people's experience with technology in an open world full of potentiality and surprise. The case studies in chapters 6–8 can be read as exemplifying this rich seeing in practice as they evoke the historicity and emergence of the prosaic experiences of shopping, piloting, and controlling ambulances. In each case, the context being described and the work system being evaluated is always becoming in the felt and lived experience of the particular people involved. Even if Captain Roy is an atypical character, that is beside the point. In a revisionary view of design, it is seeing his particular experience that opens up a new space of possibilities for design.

Openness to potential is a mark of exciting design. But we are not professional designers and we sometimes feel a bit out of our element when writing and talking about design. It feels like something special to us, something outside of our experience that depends on knowledge and skills to which we have limited access. It feels like something that requires distance and circumspection when we talk about it. In that respect, it feels a bit like art, to be admired from a distance. Of course, that is where we started our dialogue with Dewey. As we have already noted, Dewey's *Art as Experience* is a sustained attempt to restore the continuity between aesthetic and prosaic experience, which had been fractured by the reification of art into unapproachable art objects housed in museums. Perhaps one of the ways in which our approach to technology as experience might prove useful is in restoring the continuity between the aesthetic experiences of designing technology and living with it. This would make design more approachable by undoing the separation that we feel between professional design practice and the prosaic design that we do in our daily lives. Even though we are not all professional designers, we all experience design and designing in our daily lives as we make something of the always becoming world in which we live. We customize computer applications, create designed spaces in our houses, and personalize some of our possessions. And, as we have already seen in chapters 6–8, Captain Roy, the ambulance controllers, and the Virginwines shopper complete the designs with which they are presented. Restoring the continuity between professional and prosaic design, puts us in a similar position to Dewey when he challenged the establishment of art. It enables us to challenge the establishment of design.

When design is professionally established, it is reified and placed beyond us. But, when we restore the continuity between professional and prosaic design, we begin to see the playful experience of design. Design as putting some thing into play, into the world of experience that Gadamer characterizes as "being-in-play." Design as something like the dialogical characterization of activity evoked in the analogy with children at play deployed earlier in the book, where means and ends are simultaneously created and problem situations are re-described. This is the kind of approach to design we see in a number of the chapters in an edited collection on user enjoyment (Blythe et al. 2003). For example, Andersen, Jacobs, and Polazzi (2003) explore the sense of privation felt by people who are emotionally close yet geographically distant through the use of enchanting games that focus on the felt life of living apart. This provides them with a way of entering into dialogue with participants about the possibilities for emotional and sensual engagement over distance mediated by technology. In another chapter, Sengers (2003) describes an interactive installation, called the Influencing Machine, that was designed to allow people to play with the idea of machines having emotions. When people enter the Influencing Machine, they see images of children's drawings and hear a soundscape designed to evoke a sensual and emotional response. In the middle of the room is a mailbox, through which they can post cards or art reproductions from a set supplied with the installation. When something is posted, the mood of the images and soundscape changes. The idea is that people can think about what a card means to them emotionally and then post it to see what it means to the machine. People have been observed interacting with the machine for 20 minutes and debating with each other how a computer can be said to have emotion. Interacting with the Influencing Machine can be seen as quite dialogical as users explore their own ideas and feelings by comparing them with other users and with the emotions of a machine.

These two examples show how designers can put fairly straightforward artifacts into play in a way that also brings people's experience to the fore, and that challenges the reification of design.

One way to cut against the reification of design is to question the assumptions on which this reification is built. So, for example, instead of accepting the idea that design is a predominantly scientific or mathematical practice, we can try to imagine a strong literary or art-related approach to design. This can take the form of the appropriation of literary techniques by designers such as Dix (2003), who, in another chapter from the Blythe et al. collection, draws on deconstruction to reflect on how to design for experience. He shows how a piece of poetry can be analyzed in terms of resonances, dissonances, and paradoxes at a number of levels, and then applies the technique to deconstructing the experience of pulling a Christmas Cracker, with a view to designing a "virtual cracker" web site that orients toward the reconstructed cracker experience. Other more radical literary approaches offer a way of seeing potential and becoming in ordinary experience with technology, by focusing on the weighty particularity of felt moments full of possibility, fear, desire, and hope. This brings particular experiences and characters into play. We can see this approach being developed in methods such as Nielsen's (2002) character-based scenarios, which aim to provide a sense of a thinking feeling individual; Orr's (1996) stories of the successes and frustrations of photocopier technicians; and the accounts of people's own stories of their lives with technology given by Blythe et al. (2002).

The visual arts have also been recruited to produce new ways of seeing design. For example, Dunne (1999, p. 12) brings art sensibilities to bear on electronic product design when he comments that, although "industrial design is not art," "design research in the aesthetic and cultural realm should draw attention to the ways products limit our experiences." In following this critical agenda, Dunne uses the design of conceptual electronic products to provoke reflection on the designed environment we inhabit. Cultural probes also come out of an art and design tradition (Gaver, Dunne, and Pacenti 1999). This is a technique that asks people to use materials such as postcards, photographs, and a diary to describe the detailed texture of their lives, more specifically their beliefs, feelings, and values. In one project, cultural probes were used to involve elderly people living in purpose built accommodation to participate in designing technology for their own public spaces.

Literary and art-related approaches resonate with the kind of dialogical worldview that Bakhtin identified in the novel of emergence where characters change with their experience and where the world, in the fullness of its time and place, is changed by experience. These dialogical approaches treat each person interacting with technology as a source of creative potential, who comes to the interaction with a rich history of experience that engages with the technology in a dialogue about what the technology is and could be and what the person is and could be. If we reflect, for a minute, on Kuutti's (2001) characterization of the history of "the user" in HCI, which we outlined in chapter 1, we see that a dialogical approach to design requires a richer conceptualization of the user than any of those he described. Kuutti suggested that the user who started out as a cog in a machine, became a source of error, a social actor, and is now a consumer. Well, the user that we encounter in dialogical approaches to design may be all of these and much more. The users in the case studies in chapters 6–8 (the Internet shopper, Captain Roy, the ambulance controllers) can be compliant, social, and even at times mechanistic. But these users are also actively making sense of the situations they encounter, resisting some of their ramifications and accepting others, radically reshaping their experiences with technologies, chasing their own desires in the face of sometimes unhelpful technologies, making something of what they are given and making sense of themselves in the process. As well as being cogs, social actors, and consumers, these users are authors, characters, protagonists, and co-producers (Dunne 1999). These qualities of personhood are redolent of those highlighted in Bakhtin and Dewey's conceptualizations of aesthetic experience and must be accommodated in design for experience.

When we think of design as dialogical, concerned with the ways in which people interacting with technologies consummate themselves in the technologies and the technology in themselves, we point to the openness and unfinalizability of a world that, though already half-designed, is always becoming. This is a complex, changing world, marked by ambiguity. In such a world, design is always for potential, for what is already becoming. It is an act of reframing experience in a way that points beyond the reframing. This involves the designer giving to the user a surplus, which allows them to play into their potential. It does not involve giving them a poorly designed artifact, like some of those described in our case studies in chapters 6–8. Poorly designed technology takes the user away from what might be, to a constant struggle with the limitations of the technology as broken object. Design for aesthetic experience is concerned with zestful integration, not fitful disintegration.

When we gather together the variety of characters and experiences that we have described in this book, we point to the ordinariness of emergence in relations between people and technology. When we see their zestful integration, we are richly seeing technology as simultaneously prosaic and aesthetic experience, contributing to the liveliness of our experience, as might a saxophone stretched to its limits or a mindfully prepared meal.

Bakhtin argued that there can be no final word, and this book will not be the final word on technology as experience. Rather, we see it as an utterance in a dialogical space that is emerging around HCI. Dourish (2001), Shneiderman (2002), Norman (2004), and Blythe et al. (2003) are voices in this space redefining how we think about users, context, technology, and experience. We hope that the texture and register of our voice in this dialogue is edgy and open, like a provocative comment or question. It remains to be seen what will emerge.

References

Agre, P. E. 1997a. *Computation and Human Experience*. Cambridge University Press.

Agre, P. E. 1997b. Living math: Lave and Walkerdine on the meaning of everyday arithmetic. In D. Kirshner and J. Whitson, eds., *Situated Cognition*. Erlbaum.

Alexander, T. M. 1998. The art of life: Dewey's aesthetics. In L. Hickman, ed., *Reading Dewey*. Indiana University Press.

Anderson, R. J. 1994. Representation and requirements: The value of ethnography in system design. *Human-Computer Interaction* 9: 151–182.

Andersen, K., Jacobs, M., and Polazzi, L. 2003. Playing games in the emotional space. In M. Blythe et al., eds., *Funology*. Kluwer.

Austin, J. L. 1962. *How to Do Things with Words*. Harvard University Press.

Bakhtin, M. 1984. *Problems of Dostoevsky's Poetics*. University of Minnesota Press.

Bakhtin, M. 1990. *Art and Answerability: Early Philosophical Essays*. University of Texas Press.

Bakhtin, M. 1993. *Toward a Philosophy of the Act*. University of Texas Press.

Bakhurst, D. 1997. Activity, consciousness, and communication. In M. Cole et al., eds., *Mind, Culture, and Activity*. Cambridge University Press.

Bannon, L., and Bodker, S. 1991. Beyond the interface: Encountering artefacts in use. In J. Carroll, ed., *Designing Interaction*. Cambridge University Press.

Benson, C. 1993. *The Absorbed Self*. Harvester Wheatsheaf.

Berg, M. 1997. *Rationalizing Medical Work: Decision-Support Techniques and Medical Practices*. MIT Press.

Beyer, H., and Holtzblatt, K. 1997. *Contextual Design*. Morgan Kaufmann.

Bjerknes, G., Ehn, P., and Kyng, M. 1987. *Computers and Democracy: A Scandinavian Challenge*. Avebury.

Blomberg, J. L. 1995. Ethnography: Aligning field studies of work and system design. In A. Monk and N. Gilbert, eds., *Perspectives on HCI*. Academic Press.

Blythe, M., and Monk, A. 2002. Notes towards an ethnography of domestic technology. In *Symposium on Designing Interactive Systems*. ACM Press.

Blythe, M., Monk, A., Overbeeke, C., and Wright, P., eds. 2003. *Funology*. Kluwer.

Bodker, S. 1991. *Through the Interface: A Human Activity Approach to User Interface Design*. Erlbaum.

Bodker, S. 1998. Understanding representation in design. *Human-Computer Interaction* 13: 107–125.

Bodker, S., Ehn, P., Kammersgaard, J, Kyng, M. 1987. A Utopian experience. In G. Bjerknes et al., eds., *Computers and Democracy*. Avebury.

Boorstin, J. 1990. *Making Movies Work: Thinking Like a Filmmaker*. Salaman James Press.

Bowers, J. 1992. The politics of formalism. In M. Lea, ed., *Contexts of Computer Mediated Communication*. Harvester.

Bowker, G., and Star, S. L. 1999. *Sorting Things Out: Classification and Its Consequences*. MIT Press.

Brown, J. S., and Duguid P. 1991. Organizational learning and communities of practice. *Organization Science* 2, no. 1: 40–57.

Brown, J. S., and Duguid, P. 2000. *The Social Life of Information*. Harvard Business School Press.

Bruner, E. M. 1986. Introduction: Experience and its expressions. In E. M. Bruner and V. Turner, eds., *The Anthropology of Experience*. University of Illinois Press.

Bruner, E. M., and Turner, V., eds., 1986. *The Anthropology of Experience*. University of Illinois Press.

Bruner, J. 1990. *Acts of Meaning*. Harvard University Press.

Bruner, J. 1991. The narrative construction of reality. *Critical Inquiry* 18: 1–21.

Bruner, J. 1996. *Cultures of Education*. Harvard University Press.

Bullen, C., and Bennett, J. 1990. Learning from user experience with groupware. In Proceedings of CSCW '90, Los Angeles.

Button, G. 2000. The ethnographic tradition and design. *Design Studies* 21: 319–322.

Card, S., Moran, T., and Newell, A. 1983. *The Psychology of Human Computer Interaction*. Erlbaum.

Coyne, R. 1995. *Designing Information Technology in the Postmodern Age: From Method to Metaphor*. MIT Press.

Coyne, R. 1999. *Technoromanticism: Digital Narrative, Holism, and the Romance of the Real*. MIT Press.

Craib, I. 1998. *Experiencing Identity*. Sage.

DeCerteau, M. 1984. *The Practice of Everyday Life*. University of California Press.

Dewey, J. 1929a. *Experience and Nature*, second edition. Open Court.

Dewey, J. 1929b. *The Quest for Certainty*. Putnam.

Dewey, J. 1934. *Art as Experience*. Perigree.

Dewey, J. 1938. *Experience and Education*. Touchstone.

Dix, A. 2003. Deconstructing experience: Pulling crackers apart. In M. Blythe et al., eds., *Funology*. Kluwer.

Dourish, P. 2001. *Where the Action Is: The Foundations of Embodied Interaction*. MIT Press.

Dunne, A. 1999. *Hertzian Tales: Electronic Products, Aesthetic Experience and Critical Design*. London: Royal College of Art.

Emerson, C. 1993. American philosophers, Bakhtinian perspectives. Paper presented at the Transnational Institute Conference, Moscow.

Gadamer. H. 1976. *Truth and Method*. Sheed and Ward.

Garrett, J. J. 2002. *The Elements of User Experience: User-Centered Design for the Web*. New Riders.

Gaver, B., Dunne, T., and Pacenti, E. 1999. Design: Cultural probes. *Interactions*, January-February 1999: 21–29.

Geertz, C. 1973. *The Interpretation of Cultures*. Basic Books.

Geertz, C. 1986. Making experiences, authoring selves. In E. M. Bruner and V. Turner, eds., *The Anthropology of Experience*. University of Illinois Press.

Heath, C., and Luff, P. 1992. Collaboration and control: Crisis management and multi-media technology in London Underground line control rooms. *Computer Supported Cooperative Work* 1: 69–94.

Hicks, D. 1996. Learning as a prosaic act. *Mind, Culture, and Activity* 3, no. 2: 102–118.

Hicks, D. 2000. Self and other in Bakhtin's early philosophical essays: Prelude to a theory of prose consciousness. *Mind, Culture, and Activity* 7, no. 3: 227–242.

Hirschkop, K. 1986. Bakhtin, discourse and democracy. *New Left Review*, November-December: 92–113.

Hodges, D. 1998. Participation as dis-identification with/in a community of practice. *Mind, Culture, and Activity* 5, no. 4: 272–290.

Holquist, M. 1990. *Dialogism: Bakhtin and His World*. Routledge.

Jackson, P. W. 1998. *John Dewey and the Lessons of Art*. Yale University Press.

James, W. 1902. *The Varieties of Religious Experience: A Study in Human Nature*. Penguin.

Joas, H. 1993. *Pragmatism and Social Theory*. University of Chicago Press.

Joas, H. 1996. *The Creativity of Action*. Polity Press.

Jordan, P. 2000. *Designing Pleasurable Products: An Introduction to the New Human Factors*. Taylor and Francis.

Kasesniemi, E.-L., and Rautiainen, P. 2002. Mobile culture of children and teenagers in Finland. In J. Katz and M. Aakhus, eds., *Perpetual Contact*. Cambridge University Press.

Katz, J. E., and Aakhus, M., eds., 2002. *Perpetual Contact: Mobile Communication, Private Talk, Public Performance*. Cambridge University Press.

Klein, N. 2000. *No Logo*. Flamingo.

Kuutti, K. 2001. Hunting for the lost user: From sources of errors to active actors—and beyond. Paper presented at Cultural Usability Seminar, Media Lab, University of Art and Design, Helsinki, 2002.

Lave, J. 1988. *Cognition in Practice: Mind, Mathematics, and Culture in Everyday Life*. Cambridge University Press.

Lave, J. 1993. The practice of learning. In S. Chaiklin and J. Lave, eds., *Understanding Practice*. Cambridge University Press.

Lave, J., and Wenger, E. 1991. *Situated Learning: Legitimate Peripheral Participation*. Cambridge University Press.

Laurel, B. 1991. *Computers as Theatre*. Addison-Wesley.

Loriggio, F. 1990. Mind as dialogue: The Bakhtin circle and pragmatist psychology. *Critical Studies* 2, no. 1/2: 91–110.

MacIntyre, A. 1981. *After Virtue*. Duckworth.

Maturana, H., and Varela, F. 1980. *Autopoesis and Cognition: The Realisation of the Living*. Reidel.

McCarthy, J. C., and O'Connor, B. 1999. The context of information use in a hospital as simultaneous similarity-difference relations. *Cognition, Technology and Work* 1, no. 1: 25–36.

McCarthy, J., Wright, P., Healey, P., Dearden, A., and Harrison, M. D. 1997. Locating the scene: The particular and the general in contexts for ambulance control. In Group '97: Proceedings of the International ACM SIGGROUP Conference on Supporting Group Work.

McCarthy, J. C., Wright, P. C., Monk, A. F., and Watts, L. A. 1998. Concerns at work: Designing useful procedures. *Human Computer Interaction* 13, no. 4: 433–457.

McCarthy, J. C., and Wright, P. C. 2003. The enchantments of technology. In M. Blythe et al., eds., *Funology*. Kluwer.

Mead, G. H. 1934. *Mind, Self, and Society*. University of Chicago Press.

Menand, L. 2002. *The Metaphysical Club*. Flamingo.

Morson, G. S., and Emerson, C. 1990. *Mikhail Bakhtin: Creation of a Prosaics*. Stanford University Press.

Murray, J. 1997. *Hamlet on the Holodeck*. MIT Press.

Nardi, B. A., and O'Day, V. L. 1999. *Information Ecologies: Using Technology with a Heart*. MIT Press.

Nielsen, L. 2002. From user to character: An investigation into user descriptions in scenarios. In *Proceedings of DIS2002 Designing Interactive Systems*. ACM Press.

Norman, D. 1988. *The Psychology of Everyday Things*. Basic Books.

Norman, D. 2002. Emotion and design: Attractive things work better. *Interactions* 9, no. 4: 36–42.

Norman, D. 2004. *Emotional Design: Why We Love (or Hate) Everyday Things*. Basic Books.

Nussbaum, M. 2001. *Upheavals of Thought: The Intelligence of Emotions*. Cambridge University Press.

Orr, J. 1996. *Talking about Machines: An Ethnography of a Modern Job*. Cornell University Press.

Pacey, A. 1999. *Meaning in Technology*. MIT Press.

Preece, J., Rogers, Y., and Sharp, H. 2002. *Interaction Design: Beyond Human-Computer Interaction*. Wiley.

Prigogine, I., and Stengers, I. 1985. *Order out of Chaos: Man's Dialogue with Nature*. Flamingo.

Rabinow, P., and Sullivan, W. M. 1987. *Interpretive Social Science: A Second Look*. University of California Press.

Rheingold, H. 2000. *The Virtual Community: Homesteading on the Electronic Frontier*. MIT Press.

Ricoeur, P. 1971. The model of the text: Meaningful action considered as text. *Social Research* 38, no. 3: 529–562.

Rizzo, A., Marti, P., Decortis, F., Rutgers, J., and Thursfield, P. 2003. Building narrative experiences for children through real time media manipulation: POGO World. In M. Blythe et al., eds., *Funology*. Kluwer.

Rogoff, B., Matusov, E., and White, C. 1996. Models of teaching and learning: Participation in a community of learners. In D. Olson and N. Torrance, eds., *The Handbook of Education and Human Development*. Blackwell.

Schuler, D., and Namioka, A. 1993. *Participatory Design: Principles and Practice*. Erlbaum.

Searle, J. R. 1969. *Speech Acts*. Cambridge University Press.

Sengers, P. 2003. The engineering of experience. In M. Blythe et al., eds., *Funology*. Kluwer.

Shackel, B. 1990. Human factors and usability. In J. Preece and L. Keller, eds., *Human-Computer Interaction*. Prentice-Hall.

Shapiro, D. 1994. The limits of ethnography: Combining social sciences for CSCW. In Proceedings of CSCW '94, Chapel Hill.

Shneiderman, B. 2002. *Leonardo's Laptop*. MIT Press.

Shusterman, R. 2000. *Pragmatist Aesthetics: Living Beauty, Rethinking Art.*, second edition. Rowman and Littlefield.

Silverman, H. 2000. Postmodern turns. Paper presented at Phenomenology and Culture, British Society for Phenomenology Conference, University College Cork, Ireland.

Star, S. L 1995. *The Cultures of Computing*. Blackwell.

Star, S. L., and Griesemer, J. R. 1989. Institutional ecology, translations and boundary objects: Amateurs and professionals in Berkeley's Museum of Vertebrate Zoology, 1907–1939. *Social Studies of Science* 19: 387–420.

Star, S. L., and Ruhleder, K. 1996. Steps towards an ecology of infrastructure: Design and access for large information spaces. *Information Systems Research* 7: 111–134.

Star, S. L., and Strauss, A. 1999. Layers of silence, arenas of voice: The ecology of visible and invisible work. *Computer Supported Cooperative Work* 8: 9–30.

Stuhr, J. J. 1998. Dewey's social and political philosophy. In L. Hickman, ed., *Reading Dewey*. Indiana University Press.

Suchman, L. A. 1987. *Plans and Situated Actions: The Problem of Human Computer Interaction*. Cambridge University Press.

Suchman, L. A. 1993. Do categories have politics? The language/action perspective reconsidered. In G. de Michelis et al., eds., *Proceedings of the Third European Conference on Computer-Supported Cooperative Work*. Kluwer.

Suchman L. A. 1995. Making work visible. *Communications of the ACM* 38: 56–68.

Taylor, A. S., and Harper, R. 2002. Age-old practices in the New World: A study of gift-giving between teenage mobile phone users. In *Proceedings of CHI 2002*. ACM Press.

Tulviste, P. 1999. Activity as an explanatory principle in cultural psychology. In S. Chaiklin et al., eds., *Activity Theory and Social Practice*. Aarhus University Press.

Turkle, S. 1995. *Life on the Screen: Identity in the Age of the Internet*. Phoenix.

Turner, V. 1986. Dewey, Dilthey, and drama: An essay in the anthropology of experience. In E. Bruner and V. Turner, eds., *The Anthropology of Experience*. University of Illinois Press.

Walkerdine, V. 1990. *Schoolgirl Fictions*. Verso.

Walkerdine, V. 1997. Re-defining the subject in situated cognition theory. In D. Kirshner and J. Whitson, eds., *Situated Cognition*. Erlbaum.

Wenger, E. 1998. *Communities of Practice*. Cambridge University Press.

Wetherell, M. 1998. Positioning and interpretative repertoires: Conversation analysis and post-structuralism in dialogue. *Discourse and Society* 9: 431–456.

Winograd, T. 1996. *Bringing Design to Software*. Addison-Wesley.

Winograd, T., and Flores, F. 1986. *Understanding Computers and Cognition: A New Foundation for Design*. Ablex.

Wittgenstein, L. 1953. *Philosophical Investigations*. Blackwell.

Wright, P. C., and McCarthy, J. C. 2003. An analysis of procedure following as concerned work. In E. Hollnagel, ed., *A Handbook of Cognitive Task Design*. Erlbaum.

Wright, P. C., McCarthy, J. C., and Meekison, L. 2003. Making sense of experience. In M. Blythe et al., eds., *Funology*. Kluwer.

Wright, P. C., Pocock, S., and Fields, R. E. 1998. The prescription and practice of work on the flight deck. In *ECCE9, Ninth European Conference on Cognitive Ergonomics*. EACE.

Index